JOHN SKELTON

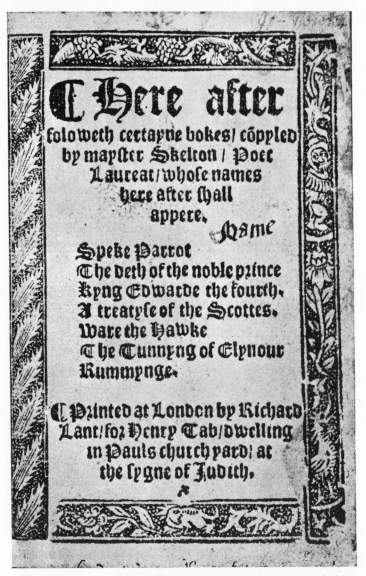

John Skelton's *Certain Books* (c. 1545), reproduced by permission
from the copy in the Huntington Library, California.
The 'shame' is a manuscript addition by some disapproving critic.

JOHN SKELTON

POET LAUREATE

BY

IAN A. GORDON

M.A., PH.D. (EDINBURGH)

1970

OCTAGON BOOKS

New York

128827

First published 1943

Reprinted 1970

*by permission of Melbourne University Press by
arrangement with Cambridge University Press*

OCTAGON BOOKS

A DIVISION OF FARRAR, STRAUS & GIROUX, INC.

19 Union Square West

New York, N. Y. 10003

AM

Reproduced from a copy in the Yale University Library

LIBRARY OF CONGRESS CATALOG CARD NUMBER: 70-96157

Printed in U.S.A. by
TAYLOR PUBLISHING COMPANY
DALLAS, TEXAS

ACKNOWLEDGMENTS

THE BULK OF THE WORK FOR THIS STUDY WAS DONE DURING MY tenure of the Pitt Scholarship in Classical and English Literature, the Dickson Travelling Scholarship, and the Scott Travelling Scholarship of the University of Edinburgh, to which I am also indebted for a grant from the Moray Fund for the purchase of books and photostats. I acknowledge with gratitude the assistance of the officials of the University Libraries of Edinburgh and Glasgow, the Bodleian, the British Museum, Somerset House, the Public Record Office, the Dean's Office of Norwich Cathedral; and particularly the criticisms, the suggestions and the ready help of Mr. William Beattie, Keeper of Manuscripts in the National Library of Scotland, Mr. Lawrence Tanner, Keeper of the Muniments in Westminster Abbey, Dr. George Kitchin of the University of Edinburgh, Professor Bruce Dickins of the University of Leeds, and Professor A. W. Reed of the University of London; above all the encouragement I received both as undergraduate and as member of his staff from Sir Herbert J. C. Grierson. This volume would have been published some years ago had not my translation in 1937 to a chair in the Antipodes created unexpected difficulties in the completion of a book on the sixteenth century in a country which itself began in the nineteenth century and is developing proper libraries only now in the twentieth. In the interval other scholars have, happily, been working on Skelton. I have, I hope, scrupulously acknowledged my indebtedness for any material which was new to me (especially to Dr. William Nelson of New York City, with whom I had some stimulating meetings on a recent visit to the United States). This volume, however, is essentially an independent survey of the original sources, both manuscript and printed, for a critical reassessment of John Skelton.

Victoria University College,
Wellington, New Zealand.   August, 1941.

CONTENTS

Chapter I

THE AGE OF TRANSITION

IN THE YEAR 1566-7—TEN YEARS AFTER THE PUBLICATION OF *Tottel's Miscellany*—two books were entered on the Stationers' Register that represent a triumph and a defeat. They were both published shortly afterwards, the *Pithy, pleasaunt and profitable workes of maister Skelton, Poete Laureate* in 1568, and the *Merie Tales Newly Imprinted and made by Master Skelton Poet Laureat* in 1567, the one containing his poetry, the other the mass of legend that had accumulated around his name after his death in 1529. Since these two volumes appeared, so little has been discovered about the life of this 'Poete Laureate' that subsequent criticism has repeated the *Merie Tales* more frequently than it has examined his verse, and the whole conception of the poetry of Skelton has been coloured by the character of buffoon and playboy which he bears in these apocryphal anecdotes. There are few things so astonishing in the history of English literature as the eclipse of John Skelton. In his lifetime a poet popular with court and with commons, the most original and the greatest of his day, he died without leaving any succession. Few of his poems were printed till the fifties and sixties of the sixteenth century, but by that time his reputation had already declined, and the decline has continued unchecked till a few years ago, when a group of contemporary poets found in him one of their poetic ancestors.

The eclipse of his poetry has been not unnaturally accompanied by a corresponding neglect both of his life and work by scholars. The only biography by a contemporary is that in Bale's *Catalogus* of 1557, and though Skelton subsequently appeared in innumerable critical works and histories of English poetry from Webbe's and Puttenham's to Warton's, and in the majority of the historic encyclopaedias of poetry and biography from those of Pits and Tanner and Antony à Wood to Fuller's *Worthies* and Cibber's *Lives of the Poets,* none of these studies have added one authenticated fact to his life, while they have accepted an increasing amount of untested fiction from the *Merie Tales*. The first critical biography of Skelton was that prefaced to Alexander Dyce's monumental edition of his poetry in 1843. Dyce relegated the *Merie Tales* to an appendix and collected all the contemporary references to Skelton that he could discover in manuscript or in printed book—a collection that must form the basis for any subsequent study of the poet.

In more recent years Skelton has been the subject of studies by German, English and American scholars,[1] but even to-day there is much in his poems that demands further study. Their very subject is still occasionally under dispute; there has never been a complete chronology of his poems; fresh biographical material has been discovered since Dyce's day—some of it printed for the first time in this study; his relationship with the movements of his day— Humanism, Reformation and Renaissance—has been only partially investigated; unfounded traditions of his 'merie' conduct in his parish and elsewhere must vanish before the concrete evidence of cathedral records; the legend of the renegade priest must be discounted by a careful study of his profoundly serious religious poetry; the tale of his flight from Wolsey to the sanctuary of Westminster must be modified in the light of new evidence from the Abbey Muniments; and above all a place must be found for the poet in the history of English literature. What part had the Middle Ages in his make-up and how far is he a child of the Renaissance? These and many similar questions must be answered before the true importance of the poet will emerge from the disreputable legends that have surrounded the 'beastly Skelton' of Pope and critics even less acute.

The age of Skelton was an age of transition, when the modern world was coming into being and the Middle Ages had not yet crumbled into complete decay. New creeds were fermenting in Europe and new modes of thought were spreading northwards from the Arno and westwards from Constantinople. Some of these changes were tardy in coming to England, but their ultimate arrival was inevitable. In the century and a half between the

1. The most important are the monographs of Brie, Koelbing, Ramsay and Thümmel and Berdan's *Early Tudor Poetry;* more recently the work of William Nelson, L. J. Lloyd, H. L. R. Edwards and F. M. Salter. See Bibliography.

death of Chaucer and the publication of *Tottel's Miscellany*, English civilization underwent a radical transformation, and English poetry broke for ever with the formulae of the Middle Ages. The year 1500 may be regarded as the turning point, the end of the old culture and the beginning of the new. During the sixteenth century the major problems found a gradual solution and the Renaissance replaced the synthesis of the Middle Ages.

Three crucial problems distinguished the two modes of thought, the social, the intellectual and the religious; and on the response of the poet or scholar of the early sixteenth century to these three issues depends his final position in the history of English thought and English poetry. The scholars and poets of the reigns of Henry VII and Henry VIII found their natural place either as survivors of the waning Middle Ages, content to form into new arrangements their time-worn material, or as forerunners of the Renaissance who rejoiced in the innovations of the approaching revolution. The poets of this age must be considered not simply as poets but as representatives of the thought and the fashions of their time. It is the object of this book not merely to assess Skelton as a poet, but also to place him against this shifting background and discover how far he accepts or rejects the warring principles that were presented to the poet of his day.

The Wars of the Roses had settled England under a virtually unlimited monarchy, and the Tudor kings ruled without the mediaeval check of the nobles. During the fifteenth century the silent but persistent spread of the wool trade had raised a new wealthy commercial class whose every instinct was anti-feudal. With the breakdown of the feudal system, the poet of the early Renaissance had to choose between two audiences, a stately, conservative and educated nobility, who clung to their traditional literature as an anchor for a shifting age; the other a largely uneducated but dynamic body for whom the touch of experience and actuality was the greatest proof of an author's merit. One audience looked for traditional pattern and outer form, the other was concerned solely with content and directness of utterance. In the attempt to satisfy something of both demands is to be found the secret of Skelton's extraordinary range from the 'pullisshyd eloquence' of mediaeval aureate diction to the rude vernacular 'style direct' of the Renaissance bourgeois.

The reorientation of society was accompanied by a contraction of loyalties and a widening of horizons. The sense of community that pervaded mediaeval Europe had produced men whose scholarship and thought knew no national boundaries. Renaissance Europe abandoned the grandiose conception of a united continent and became fiercely national in its aspirations. Vincent of Beauvais and Abelard are European, but Colet is as undeniably English as Bembo is Italian and Ulrich von Hutten German. Yet in spite of the rise of national frontiers, European thought as a coherent whole was revolutionized at the Renaissance, and for Italian and German and English scholars the intellectual boundaries of the Middle Ages were as widely extended as the boundaries of the known world by the new voyages of discovery.

The intellectual issue of the age lay between the forces of Scholasticism and of Humanism. On the one side was the philosophy and logic of St. Thomas Aquinas and the schoolmen, a magnificently inflexible framework of steel, round which had grown up mediaeval civilization, resting ultimately on the major premises of the church. On the other side were the new humanists, weary of the domination of the category, the formula, the dogma and the authority, eager to extend the speculation of man from the exclusively religious and moral to the more 'humane' field of belles-lettres. To St. Thomas Aquinas the central object of all study was *sacra doctrina* and God was its *subjectum*. Scholastic method became the deadliest enemy of speculative philosophy and by the end of the fifteenth century its academic practitioners had lost the crystal-clear perception of Catholic fundamentals of Aquinas or Dante, and late mediaeval philosophy demanded mental gymnastics, logical virtuosity, syllogistic argument of the non-essential, and the interminable debate on set topics out of contact with human experience and the fundamentals of religion. One of the greatest satires of the early sixteenth century fastened on the obscurantism of scholastic teachers, the 'obscure men' who barred the way to intellectual progress. Humanism swept triumphantly through Europe, breaking the iron shackles of rigid creeds, enlightening the philosopher and poet, leading the mind from arid theological discussion to the re-discovered beauty of classical literature, to the study of the newly accessible Greek language, later to Hebrew and the original texts of the scriptures.

Mediaeval philosophy had been rooted in mediaeval religion. The new age witnessed a divorce of religion and speculation. When dogma could be questioned the individual spirit had freer play, and Humanism led on inevitably to the third great issue of the day, the issue of religion. Over half of Europe Catholicism, with its central tenet of salvation, super-rational and super-human, gave way before the demand for an individual reading of scripture that was the fundamental novelty of the Reformation. Neither in Germany nor in England was the Reformation entirely a religious movement. Partly it was an intellectual rebellion against the Scholasticism implicit in the mediaeval faith, partly a moral revolt against corruption in the church, and partly a purely economic and political rebellion against Rome. But the demand for emancipation of thought was the essential doctrine of the Reformation common to European countries that otherwise differed in their interpretation of the new movement.

The forces that uprooted mediaeval society, philosophy and religion finally killed the Middle Ages. They had been dying for a century. Nothing illustrates their decay so clearly as the history of English poetry in the fifteenth century. The serene confidence of Chaucer found no echo in the works of his successors, and Lydgate and Occleve are 'Chaucerians' only in their veneration for his works. He was their master and their model in the craftsmanship of poetry. With their death the tradition of mediaeval poetry finally hardened into an uncompromising convention, and to the later fifteenth century Chaucer, Gower and Lydgate were almost a composite poet from whose originals major deviation was an act of heresy to poetic faith. The greater minds of the earlier Middle Ages had possessed superlative brilliance and clarity. The *De Vulgari Eloquio,* the *Summa Theologiae,* and the *Canterbury Tales,* each in its own manner, revealed the minds of men who could look on life with clear eyes and steady appraisal, but the later Middle Ages lacked their clarity of vision. Fifteenth century England looked back on its poetic heritage with clouded minds and blunted perceptions, seeing only its external forms. An allegory was an allegory whether written with the delicate incisiveness of Chaucer, or the sprawling ineptitude of Lydgate. No distinction was felt between Chaucer's easy narrative movement and the broken-backed progression of his followers. Chaucer-Lydgate-Gower became a vague undifferentiated ancestor of later fifteenth century verse. One of the most significant passages in Skelton is that in *Phillip Sparow,* where in a dozen lines he individualizes each of the three poets and shows that he realizes the consummate superiority of Chaucer.

The poetry of the age of Skelton suffered from the imprint of the stereotype, and this is particularly true of the reign of Henry VII. Had the history of printing in England followed the lead of Caxton, it is doubtful whether his introduction of the art would have been accepted by later ages as one of the elements that accelerated the Renaissance. Caxton was as conservative as the royal and noble customers for whom he produced saint's legend and chivalric romance. The aristocratic audience at the close of the fifteenth century demanded the forms it knew, the allegory, the lament, the Latin complimentary verse, the courtly lyric, the fabliau, the saint's legend. Rime royal was as standardized as the couplet in the age of Queen Anne.

While the official poets followed the pattern, the fifteenth century was producing a vast anonymous body of poetry in the lyric, the ballad, and the carol, few of which found their way into print in their own age. The popular audience which rejoiced in these often lovely and unsophisticated forms was towards the end of the fifteenth century served once again by poets who have left at least a name. The new bourgeoisie began to grow vocal through the medium of such men as Copland and Skelton himself. These poets could abandon the conventions of aristocratic verse, and in poems like the *Hye Way to the Spyttel Hous* and *Elynour Rummyng* they frankly accepted the ribald attitude of the new generation. The contrast between such verses and the imitations of the conventions is violent. A stiff and ineffective dignity is replaced by an impudent but very effective vitality of treatment and characterization. Outspoken criticism of the upper class and direct attack on their artificialities are both characteristics of the new verse.

The reigns of Henry VII and Henry VIII were coincident with an outburst of song in which both poets and musicians took part. An English school of music had grown up, headed by John Dunstable in the time of Henry VI and when Henry VIII came to the throne, the pageantry of his receptions and dramatic evenings was enlivened by the music of his composers. A fine volume in the British Museum contains the words and music of many of these songs, written by a variety of hands—Cornysshe, Gilbert Banaster, Richard Davey, Turges, Sheringham and others, and the title of the volume, the *Fayrfax Book,* commemorates one of the most important of the Tudor composers. Skelton wrote the words for several of the songs in this volume, and took an active part in this newest development of English verse. Henry came to the throne an eager and brilliant supporter of many of the newer modes, and one or two of his songs show how far he was able to compete with his subjects. Under such encouragement, early Tudor song developed a certain pre-Elizabethan maturity which finds expression, among other places, in the lyrical poetry of Skelton.

Skelton's earliest poem belongs to the year 1483 and his latest to 1527. He began his poetic career in the stillness that followed the death of Occleve, a calm scarcely broken by the composition of such a negligible poem as George Ripley's *Compend of Alchemy.* His major contemporaries in the reigns of Henry VII and Henry VIII were Stephen Hawes and Alexander Barclay. When he died, Wyatt was a young man of twenty-six and Surrey a boy of eleven. The career of Skelton covers the critical years of the transition, and in many ways his poetry is an epitome of its progress. He is often old-fashioned and in his early poetry conventional, but when he is seen alongside his contemporaries, his verse stands out in sharp contrast from their standardized productions.

Stephen Hawes, courtier to Henry, father and son, wrote complimentary verses like *A Joyful Meditation* on the accession of Henry VIII, and versified sermons like *The Conversion of Swearers,* but he is happiest as one of the latest apostles of the allegory.

His *Example of Virtue* of 1503-4 is a moral allegory, and *The Pastime of Pleasure* of 1505-6 is an allegory of scholastic education. He personified the seven studies of mediaeval scholarship—the trivium and the quadrivium—and Grand Amour's quest for the love of La Bel Pucell is a parable of the pursuit of learning. Hawes was no poet. The stereotype of the allegory weighed heavily upon him, and though *The Pastime of Pleasure* is one of Elizabeth Browning's 'four columnar marbles' of *The Faerie Queene,* it is an inert mass of re-handled dream-convention, towers and palaces, the parliament of Venus and the siege of a lady's heart. Hawes never ventures a step beyond what his courtly audience would readily recognize. Fortune and Mars discuss free-will and pre-destination in the language of Troilus and Boethius; the Seven Deadly Sins, the Wheel of Fortune, the Jean de Meung discussion on creation from the second part of the *Roman de la Rose,* the armour of St. Paul, and the lament on the shortness of life, all slip appropriately into their places. The only real change is in the qualities allegorized. Danger and Franchise and Déduit have become Lady Grammar and Lady Fame and Geometry and Astronomy. Seldom does the *Pastime* break into real poetry. The often quoted

> For though the day be never so long
> At last the belles ringeth to evensong

is but a momentary clearing in the undergrowth of his allegory.

Alexander Barclay was of a different mould. His career began in the priesthood and finished in a Benedictine monastery, and the most persistent feature of his work is moral didactic. Though the cast of his mind is essentially mediaeval, his work is not so intolerably derivative as that of Hawes, and this in spite of his translations from such laborious didactics as Gringoire's *Chasteau de Labeur* and Sebastian Brandt's *Narrenschiff.* *The Ship of Fools* of 1509 and the *Eclogues* of 1513-14 established his reputation so strongly that Sir Nicholas Vaux asked Wolsey to send him out to the Field of the Cloth of Gold 'to devise histories and convenient raisons' with which to decorate the banqueting hall. Barclay's literary ancestors are not the writers of allegory. *The Ship of Fools,* with its absence of forward movement, its procession of characters in a straight line, is closer to the mediaeval 'tragedies' or to the wall-painting that inspired the *Danse Macabre*. His *Eclogues* come from Mantuan and from Aeneas Silvius, pioneers of the new movement back to the classics. Though Barclay uses a form new in English, he is too deeply immersed in didactic and mediaeval morality to grasp the possibilities of his discoveries. His conservative and orthodox tranquillity was profoundly disturbed by the more genuine novelties of John Skelton, and some of the few personal passages in his verse are attacks on the poet laureate.

In a world like this Skelton grew up to poetic maturity, a shifting, restless place alive with the sense of expectation. Alone of the poets of his day Skelton looked forward. While his contemporaries wrote in the accepted manner, he was producing a body of poetry, original in form and original in outlook, the one poet of his day who was really conscious of the new forces at work, although his recognition of their agency did not always result in surrender to them. It is in his awareness and his vitality that the interest of Skelton lies. The verse of his contemporaries is dead. Skelton's has a restless bustling energy that can vitalize even the formulae of the allegory.

One would not normally expect the reputation of such an original poet to decline so rapidly. The solution of the enigma lies in the originality itself. Skelton fell between the two periods, the receding Middle Ages and the advancing Renaissance, without being a part of either. He was too original and unconventional for the guardians of the old tradition, too conservative and mediaeval for the younger poets. He could be regarded neither with the honour due to a prophet nor with the respect due to an antiquity. He does not fit too comfortably into a history of English literature divided into schools and periods, and he has been gradually shuffled into an obscure position far below his real merits. 'To this day,' says Professor Saintsbury of John Skelton, 'it is difficult to see why this fit of stuttering should have come upon English.' Such a critical judgment ignores entirely Skelton's deliberate use of a novel and appropriate versification. It is the aim of the following pages to examine afresh the hitherto rather lightly accepted conception of this versatile and stimulating poet, in whom can be discerned the first movements of the approaching Renaissance.

B

CHAPTER II

THE CAREER OF JOHN SKELTON

THE MATERIALS AVAILABLE FOR A BIOGRAPHY OF JOHN SKELTON are scanty, and till recently were even scantier. Only here and there does he emerge from the contemporary records with a payment in his name, a dedication, a banquet on his behalf at London, a graceful compliment from a fellow scholar, an equally ungraceful and indignant sneer from a scholar less friendly, bald references to his death or to his will or to his tenement at Westminster, or his hand set to the last testament of others in the parish where he spent so many years. For brief but illuminating moments his life crosses the career of Wolsey, of King Henry VIII, of Erasmus; and because of the greater glory of such figures, these moments are on record or can be fairly easily authenticated. His contacts with lesser figures—with Barclay, the author of the English *Ship of Fools*; with William Lily, the schoolmaster of St. Paul's; with Christopher Garnesche, gentleman-usher at the court of Henry VIII and on paper at least one of Skelton's most despised rivals; with the friendly Bradshaw, the author of *The Life of St. Werburge;* with Robert Whittington, laureate of Oxford University, who wrote a set of complimentary Latin verses on this *Anglorum vatum gloria*—such and similar contacts can be established; to give them a time and place is a more difficult affair.

But by setting out the known record of his life, by cautiously examining the traditions of it, by establishing the chronological order of his poems, and by then placing all three lines side by side, an ordered career begins to emerge from the obscurity and indecision of casual references; and this in turn forms a criterion for subsequent dating of the more uncertain of his works and the less illuminated passages of his life. The character of John Skelton, student, tutor, laureated scholar, parish priest, translator of the classics, satirist, dramatist, fugitive, throughout all poet, stands out gradually from chance indications in allusions, records, and the man's own work.

His origin, in spite of the most patient research into State Papers, Parish Registers, Patent Rolls and other contemporary records, is still a mystery. There are many Skeltons on these pages, Skeltons in London, Skeltons in Northumberland (including Sir John Skelton[1] of Armathwaite), a tempting but misleading Sir John Skelton, Esquire for the Body, of Shelton and Snoryng Magna in Norfolk,[2] a John Shelton who incurred in 1526 the displeasure of Bishop Nicke of Norwich[3], but who turns out on examination to be a Benedictine monk of the priory attached to the Cathedral, a John Skelton who was appointed overseer by Sir Robert Southwell in 1511,[4] John Skelton, a vicar of Dultyng[5]—but none of these is the man we seek, though some of them have been assumed to be the poet by later writers.

To illustrate the difficulties that await the researcher, an extraordinary example of confusion of names may be quoted from the Norwich Cathedral *Institution Books*. In the parish of *Shelton* in June 1518 a new incumbent was instituted. The new rector was Dns. Iohannes *Skelton* presbuter.[6] Contrary to expectations he is not the poet laureate, for in April 1523 the next rector is instituted on the death of the said Iohannes Skelton.[7] The poet was alive till 1529. From Tanner's MS. list of incumbents,[8] the institution of Iohannes Skelton is confirmed, but further confusion is added by Tanner's note that the successor to Iohannes Skelton received the living on the presentation of John Shelton—presumably Sir John. Amid the confusion of John Skeltons and Sheltons one must walk warily indeed. When the search is extended to Skeltons who are not also Johns, the problem defies solution. Dyce related the poet to a certain Joanna Skelton,[9] Brie to a Cecelia Skelton, who appears in the Patent Rolls;[10] but there is no evidence of relationship beyond the unacceptable one of mere similarity of

1. cf. *Letters and Papers of the Reign of Henry VIII*, ed. J. S. Brewer, London, 1867, i 296 *et passim*.
2. cf. *Letters and Papers* i, 3946, 4715 *et passim*.
3. A. Jessop: *Visitations of the Diocese of Norwich*, pp. 198, 200 ff.
4. *Letters and Papers* i, 1742.
5. Wood, *Athenæ Oxonienses*, ed. Bliss, i, 47. This John Skelton appears later in *Valor Ecclesiasticus* as Rector of Westquamtoked in the diocese of Bath and Wells. He was a Bachelor of Canon Law at Oxford in 1518 and a Bachelor of Degrees 1525.
6. Norwich Cathedral *Institution Book* xvi, f. 45. Unpublished.
7. *Institution Book* xiv, f. 179b. Unpublished.
8. Two vols. in Norwich Cathedral. Unpublished.
9. Dyce i, v.
10. Brie, *Skelton Studien*. (*Englische Studien*, 1907).

names. A very rapid inspection of the *Early Chancery Proceedings*
for the period 1485-1530 will produce some twenty Skeltons all
distinct and separable, and the evidence of Dyce and Brie must be
rejected.[11]   There are too many Skeltons on record in the early
sixteenth century for one to assume without further evidence that
any one of them is related to the poet.

The most recent and most comprehensive survey of Skelton's
genealogy rejects the Norfolk Skeltons, suggests that the
Armathwaite Skeltons had a branch in London, and finds a possible
relative for the poet in Edward Skelton, serjeant-at-arms to Henry vi
in 1452, and a faithful supporter of the crown till his death in
1510.[12]   But of this there is no proof beyond a reasonable likelihood,
and while several false claimants to relationship have been finally
rejected, the problem of finding a family for John Skelton is still
unsolved, and, short of a lucky find, probably insoluble.

The closest contact discoverable with the numerous other bearers
of the same name is to be found in a group of records referring
to Westminster, with which Skelton was always closely associated.
In 1481 a lease was granted to one William Skelton, barber, of
Westminster, of certain tenements within the sanctuary of the
Abbey,[13] and William Skelton retained this tenancy for some years,
but apparently abandoned it towards the end of the century. This
is clear from two references, which provide limiting dates for his
departure. He was still in occupation in 1487. In that year the
Abbey granted to Richard Stone, gentleman, of Westminster,
divers cottages within the sanctuary, and they are described as
abutting on the tenements late let to William Skelton.[14] The lower
date is supplied by a grant in the Patent Rolls, where a tenement
is granted by the king in 1503 to one John Williams, Yeoman of
the Guard, with the following significant description:

. . . que quidem tenementa abbuttant ex vna parte super quodam
tenemento spectan. ecclie. parochiali ibidem et ex altera parte super
tenemento quondam spectan. cuidam Skelton.[15]

11. Public Record Office *Publications*, lists and indexes xx, xxix, xxxviii. *Early Chancery
Proceedings* (1485-1530).
12. H. L. R. Edwards: *John Skelton. A genealogical study* (*R.E.S.*, October, 1935).
cf. also R. L. Dunbabin, *M.L.R.*, vol. 12, 129 ff.
13. Westminster Abbey *Muniments*, 17854.   Unpublished.
14. Westminster Abbey *Register Book* 1, f. 20b.   Unpublished.
15. Public Record Office *Patent Rolls*, 16 December 1503.   (P.R.O., 593, 9.32.)   The
grant is calendared in a rough translation in the printed calendar of Patent Rolls, but the
all-important word '*quondam*' is omitted.

Between 1487, then, and 1503, William Skelton had left Westminster; but during the course of the next twenty years the poet
laureate lived for several periods of his life in a tenement also
within the sanctuary. The contact is teasingly close—closer than
any so far suggested—but one can do no more than hint at a
relationship between Skelton the poet laureate and Skelton the
barber of Westminster.

If the parentage of Skelton is still unknown, the date of his
birth is equally uncertain. The conventional date is 1460, deduced
from a reference in a manuscript collection of the Reverend
William Cole:

For I find one Scheklton M.A. in the year 1484, at which time
allowing him to be 24 years of age, he must be at his death A.D.
1529, 68 or 69 years old, which 'tis probable he might be . . .[16]

It would indeed be very probable—if Scheklton were actually
Skelton and not (as it is more likely to be), Shackleton.[17]   But
even if one disallows this attempt to relate Skelton with Cambridge
in 1484, his poem *Of the Death of the Noble Prince, Kynge Edward
the Fourth* proves him active in the year of that king's death, 1483.
If Skelton was adult in this year one cannot be far wrong in placing
his birth-year fairly close to the conventional 1460.

One more group of references and we are into the daylight of
tangible chronology. In the Receipts of the Treasury for the
year 12 Edward IV (1472), there are two references to a hard-
working clerk, John Skelton. The first is simply a record of a
payment made to him under the title of a *subclericus*:

Tribus subclericis videlicet Roberto Lane, Nicholao Newbold et
Johanni Skelton videlicet praedicto Roberto l.s. et praedictis
Nicholao et Johanni cuilibet eorum xls.[18]

The second reference is a record of payments made to several
clerks, among them the Nicholas Newbold and John Skelton
mentioned in the other entry, and they are specially commended as
'continue morantibus London' and *'assidue laborantibus circa
scripturas domini,'* and a gift (*'de dono Regis'*) is made to each

16. B.M. Add. 5880 (Unpublished). *Alphabetical Collections for an Athene Cantab.* Rev.
W. Cole. *sub.* Skelton.
17. cf. R. L. Dunbabin, *M.L.R.*, vol. 12. cf. A. Thümmel, *Studien uber John Skelton*,
pp. 26 ff.
18. Public Record Office. *Receipts of the Treasury*, 12 Edward IV. (P.R.O. E. 36/36/129,
f. 64.)

of them of forty shillings.[19] Yet there is no reference to a John Skelton in the official list of admissions to the office. Was this our Skelton clerking in his early manhood? Edwards[20] suggests that he may have obtained the post by the favour of the aforesaid Edward Skelton. One can only regret the absence of evidence. Skelton's career as a student must have been a long one, and not much time could have been left for the tenure of even a minor position in the Treasury. In any case, after these two entries— for the 23rd of February and the 9th of the previous December— the name appears to vanish from the Receipts and henceforth the fortunes of John Skelton are the fortunes of John Skelton, *poeta laureatus*.

One emerges from those inconclusive surmises to recount the known and discoverable facts about Skelton. The earliest life of the poet is that of John Bale, who published his *Summary of British Authors* in 1548, and his great *Scriptorum Illustrium maioris Britanniae Catalogus* in 1557, which gives the only contemporary life of the poet. Bale collected his material from men who had actually known Skelton, and such an account cannot be lightly neglected. The text is here reprinted in full from the Basel edition of 1557:

Ioannes Skeltonus.

Ioannes Skeltonus, poeta laureatus, ac theologie professor, parochus de Dyssa in Nordouologiae comitatu, clarus ac facundus in utroque scribendi genere, prosa atque metro, habebatur. facetiis in quotidiana inuentione plurimum deditus fuit : non tamen omisit sub persona ridentis, ut in Horatio Flacco, veritatem fateri. Tam apte, amoene, ac salse, mordaciter tamen, quorundam facta inamoena carpere nouit, ut alter videretur Lucianus aut Democritus, ut ex opusculis liquet. Sed neque in scripturis sacris absque omni iudicio erat, quamuis illud egregie dissimulauit. In clero non ferenda mala videbat, et magna et multa : quae nonnunquam uiuis perstrinxit coloribus, ac scommatibus non obscoenis. Cum quibusdam blateronibus fraterculis, praecipue Dominicanis, bellum gerebat continuum. Sub pseudopontifice Nordouicensi, Ricardo Nixo, mulierem illam, quam sibi secreto ob Antichristi metum desponsauerat, sub concubinae titulo custodiebat. In ultimo tamen vitae articulo super ea re interrogatus, respondit, se nusquam

19. ibid., f. 63, 63b.
20. Edwards. *R.E.S.* loc. cit.

illam in conscientia coram Deo, nisi pro uxore legitima tenuisse. Ob literas quasdam in Cardinalem Vuolsium invectiuas, ad Vuestmonasteriense tandem asylum confugere, pro vita servanda coactus fuit: ubi nihilominus sub abbate Islepo fauorem inuenit. De illo Erasmus in quadam epistola, ad Henricum octauum regem, sic scribit: Skeltonum, Brytannicarum literarum lumen ac decus, qui tua studia possit non solum accendere, sed etiam consummare; hunc domi habes etc. Iste vero edidit partem Anglice, partem Latine.

(Here follows a list of Skelton's works.)[21]
Vuestmonasterii tandem, captiuitatis suae tempore, mortuus est: et in D. Margarite sacello sepultus, cum hac inscriptione alebastrica: Ioannes Skeltonus, vates Pierius, hic situs est. Animam egit 21 die Iunii, anno Domini 1529, relictis liberis. De morte Cardinalis uaticium edidit: et eius heritatem euentus declarauit.

So far Bale on Skelton—he is a satirist of the clergy, who quarrelled with the Dominicans, a priest (with an unofficial wife) who was praised by Erasmus and yet had to flee to sanctuary because of his attacks on Wolsey, a writer clearly prolific. Round this nucleus we must build our character of Skelton.

Skelton's education followed the traditional lines of university learning before the Renaissance influence invaded Oxford and Cambridge. The trivium and quadrivium of mediaeval scholarship and the translation of the Latin classics occupied the earlier years of study. Greek was still unknown in the Universities and the non-humanist theological bias of his early reading is everywhere apparent in his later works. Oxford at first claimed him, and by 1490 Skelton had a formidable list of accomplishments to his name. He had by then been created *poeta laureatus* of the University of Oxford,[22] so gaining a degree that involved the prolonged study of grammar and rhetoric, but, in spite of the title of *poeta,* no special proficiency in poetry. He had travelled abroad[23] and obtained some distinction at a foreign university— probably (from a dedication to him by Robert Whittington *clarissimi Scheltonis Louaniensis*)[24] at Louvain.

He had already tried to justify the *poeta* title of his academic

21. Reprinted in Appendix C.
22. cf. the Cambridge reference of 1493 quoted below.
23. ibid.
24. Robert Whittington: *Opuscula* (Wynkyn de Worde 1519), cf. Dyce I, xvi.

degree.   When Edward ɪv died in 1483, Skelton wrote a
lament in the mediaeval manner of *The Fall of Princes*; and
on the death of the Earl of Northumberland in 1489 a heroic
poem followed, calling on Mars and Clio and Atropos and similar
classical deities and again in the mediaeval manner chiding 'fykkel
Fortune' and her double dice; this achievement he capped with a
few lines of Latin verse, *Ad dominum properato meum, mea
pagina, Percy.*   During this period he was studying the classics
assiduously, and he produced translations of Cicero's Letters *Ad
Familiares* and of Diodorus Siculus.[25]

The result of such learning and such court paid to the nobility
was unusual, and extremely gratifying to the young scholar.
Henry vɪɪ invited him to become the tutor to the young princes
and it appeared as if the fortune of John Skelton were already
secure.   The year of the Percy poems saw the production of the
first of his court poems—the lost *Prince Arthuris Creacyoun,*
which refers to the creation of Prince Arthur Knight of the Bath
in 1489 (or, possibly, to his creation Knight of the Garter in
1491).[26]

By 1490, then, Skelton was an established figure in the worlds
of scholarship and of the court.   In that year Caxton published
his *Boke of the Eneydos compyled by Vyrgyle* with an effusive
compliment to Skelton in the prologue:

But I praye mayster John Skelton, late created poete laureate in
the unyversite of oxenforde to ouersee and correcte this sayd
booke.   And taddresse and expowne where as shall be founde
faulte to theym that shall requyre it.   For hym I knowe for
suffycyent to expowne and englysshe euery dyffyculte that is
therein/   For he hath late translated the epistlys of Tulle/ and
the boke of dyodorus syculus. and diuerse other werkes oute of
latyn into englysshe not in rude and olde langage. but in polys-
shed and ornate termes craftely. as he that hath redde vyrgyle/
ouyde. tullye. and all the other noble poetes and oratours/ to me
vnknown: And also he hath redde the ɪx muses and vnderstande
theyr musicalle scyences. and to whom of theym eche scyence is
appropred. I suppose that he hath dronken of Elycons well . . .[27]

25. cf. Caxton's Prologue quoted below. Of his Cicero nothing further is known. The
ᴍs. of Diodorus (no. 357 of the ᴍss. of Corpus Christi, Cambridge) is unpublished, but
an edition is contemplated by the E.E.T.S. under the editorship of F. M. Salter and H. L. R.
Edwards.

26. cf. F. M. Salter: Skelton's *Speculum Principis* (*Speculum,* Jan. 1934).

27. *The Prologues and Epilogues of William Caxton.*   Ed. W. J. B. Crotch, E.E.T.S.,,
p. 109.

The prologue goes on to invite Skelton to correct any faults in the printed translation. Here is praise indeed. It is even possible that Caxton is thinking of the royal pupil to whom Skelton may expound this very book and teach English equally polished and ornate.[28]

Meanwhile his academic honours kept pace with his social distinctions. The University of Cambridge followed Oxford in admitting him a laureate in 1493:

Conceditur Johanni Skelton Poete in partis transmarinis atque Oxonie laurea ornato, ut aput nos eadem decoraretur.[29]

Two years later, 1495-96, when the University of Cambridge sent several of its officers to London to settle some controversy between the University and the citizens—'tempore controuersie inter vniuersitatem et oppidanos uille'[30]—Skelton seems to have taken some small part in the negotiations. He was twice entertained at the expense of the University. Master John Syclyng notes down the cost with his other outlays:

Item die Mercurii pro Jantaculo et cena cum Magistro Skelton quia fuit cum episcopo Sarum.   vd.[31]

Lest we imagine that *quia fuit* means that Skelton had his dinner only because he was with the Bishop, there is a later entry for the same year where the entertainment (in a Fleet Street tavern) is his alone:

Item die saboti pro Jantaculo cum Magistro Skelton apud Symsons.   iiijd.[32]

Graduate of three universities, tutor to the future king, travelling in company with bishops and dining with university officials, Skelton had become a figure of some consequence in the circles of London and the university towns.

Life at court went on as life at court always will. Skelton was not without enemies and detractors. It was the penalty of a prince's favour. So far he had written verse of the traditional mediaeval type and complimentary Latin verses. The line of compliments was continued when the elevation of Prince Henry as Duke of York evoked the graceful Latin hyperboles of *Ad tanti*

28. cf. F. M. Salter, loc. cit.
29. *Grace Book B. of the University of Cambridge.* Ed. M. Bateson. I, 54.
30. ibid., I, 83.
31. ibid., sub. 1495-6. I, 92.
32. ibid., I, 92. cf. 'apud Symsons in fletstreet' (I, 89).

principis maiestatem in sua puericia, quando erat insignitus Dux Eboraci.[33] This poem illustrates a loyalty to Henry that never wavered throughout the life of Skelton.

His relations with others at court were not so happy, and his initial efforts at self-defence and attack found a ready outlet in the satire that was to become characteristic of his life-work. *Agaynste a Comely Coystrowne,* written in 1495-6[34] against a court musician, and the companion Latin verses *Contra alium cantitantem . . . . qui impugnabat Skeltonida Pierium . . . .* indicate a dissatisfaction with court life that was perhaps natural in a man of Skelton's scholarly antecedents. It is to this period that one must assign his *Bowge of Courte,* which retains the prevalent allegory of the Middle Ages combined with a satire on court life that reflects personal experience of its less attractive side. Certainly, after a few years of court life, Skelton prepared a line of escape—or did he merely claim the reward of a churchman at court? *The Bowge of Courte* belongs to the year 1498.[35] This very year he entered into holy orders and was ordained subdeacon, deacon and priest in rapid succession. Under the date 31st March 1498, the entry appears for his subdeaconship:

In ecclesia conuentuali domus siue hospitalis sancti Thome martiris de Acon ciuitatis London. per Thomam Rothlucensem episcopum vltimo die mensis Marcis.

M. Johannes Skelton London Dioc. ad titulum Mon. beate Marie de Graciis iuxta turrim London.[36]

Similar entries appear for his ordination as deacon (in St. Paul's on April 14th), and as priest (in the Church of the Conventual Hospital of the Blessed Mary of Elsyng on June 9th), with the one difference that in these later entries the poet figures as Johannes Skelton poeta laureatus.[37] For whatever reason, Skelton had decided that his life-work was to be that of a priest and not of a courtier.

His association with the court remained unbroken. In November of the same year the King made an offering at a mass of the new priest:

33. Text printed by F. M. Salter: *Speculum,* Jan. 1934.
34. For this dating and an analysis cf. chapter VIII.
35. cf. chapter III.
36. Register *Hill,* 1489-1505 for the Diocese of London. cf. Dyce I, xxi.
37. ibid.

Item for offring at master Skeltons masse   xx s.[38]

When he became rector, a few years later, of the parish of Diss in Norfolk he continued to write court-poetry, both complimentary and satirical, and probably never ceased to visit the court till the fear of Wolsey drove him for a short period to sanctuary some twenty-five years later.   In 1499 Erasmus paid his second visit to England as the friend and protégé of Lord Mountjoy, and wrote his well-known tribute to the young Prince Henry in his Ode *De Laudibus Britanniae,* in the dedication of which he turns aside to praise the prince's tutor:

. . . et domi haberes Skelton, unum Britannicarum literarum lumen ac decus, qui studia tua possit, non solum accendere, sed etiam consummare.[39]

To crown such a tribute to Skelton's position and learning, the Dutch scholar composed in his honour an epigram of ecstatic and exaggerated compliments, where Skelton becomes the equal of Orpheus and the combined Homer and Virgil of Britain: the poet is addressed as

Aeterna vates, Skelton, dignissime lauro;

Calliope has inspired him and his song is sweeter than that of the swan.   When Skelton plays on his lyre he can tame wild beasts and move oak trees.   Rivers bend back in their courses and rocks can be moved.   At last English poetry can vie with the poetry of Greece and Rome:

Graecia Maeonio quantum debebat Homero,
Mantua Virgilio,
Tantum Skeltoni iam se debere fatetur
Terra Britanna suo:
Primus in hanc Latio deduxit ab orbe Camenas;
Primus hic edocuit
Exculte pureque loqui: te principe, Skelton,
Anglia nil metuat
Vel cum Romanis versu certare poetis.
Vive valeque diu![40]

Humanist adulation could hardly go further.

The attentions of the next few years, while scarcely as effusive

---

38. P.R.O. ms. E. 101-414-16. cf. Nelson, *John Skelton, Laureate,* 71.
39. B. M. Egerton 1651 f.l. (A small paper ms. volume of Erasmus epigrams.)
40. Printed from B.M. ms. Egerton 1651 (f. 6b) where it is grouped with other Epigrams of Erasmus. The poem had been formerly ascribed by Dyce (II, 485) to Pico della Mirandola. Egerton 1651 was first printed in Preserved Smith, *Erasmus,* 1923 (pp. 453-4).

as the praise of Erasmus, were equally acceptable. Skelton figures once more in the Cambridge accounts where another entertainment is recorded by Master Syclyng for the year 1500-1 :

Item eodem die pro cena nostra et Magistri Skelton   vj d.[41]

and again

Item in camera pro focali et potu cum Magistro Skelton   ij d.[42]

The King's favour was still his and he had every intention of retaining it. His next two works were designed for patrons' eyes. For the Countess of Richmond and Derby, the King's mother, he translated Guillaume de Guilleville's *Pèlerinage de la Vie Humaine* but no copies of this translation have survived:

> Of my ladys grace at the contemplacyoun,
> Owt of Frenshe into Englysshe prose
> Of Mannes Lyfe the Peregrynacioun
> He did translate, enterprete, and disclose.[43]

It sounds like a piece of work suited to a graduate of Louvain.

In the progress of his two charges he showed a real interest, and he composed for their princely education a manual of moral maxims. Such manuals for princes were common enough at Renaissance courts where there were humanist scholars in charge of the heir's education, but Skelton's *Speculum Principis*[44] (or *Methodos Skeltonis* as it has sometimes been called) had little of the spirit of the Renaissance and a great deal of mediaeval moralizing on the Seven Deadly Sins and other similar dangers to be avoided by the young princes. Written in 1501 'apud Eltham 28 Augusti' Skelton's maxims were impeccably virtuous and conservative. He appears to have been taking no chances of losing royal favour or of misleading his charges, and the *Speculum Principis* bears no comparison with Elyot's *Gouvernour* or any of the similar Italian treatises on princely courtesy and education. In the following year Prince Arthur died (2 April 1502) and Skelton was left to tutor Prince Henry only. In his later life all Skelton's memories of his court-period are associated with Henry, and he preserved a complete silence on the subject of

41. *Grace Book B*, I, 148.
42. ibid., I, 149.
43. *Garlande of Laurell* ll. 1219 ff.
44. A contemporary copy is preserved in B.M. MSS. Add. 26, 787. Text printed by F. M. Salter, *Speculum*, 1934.

Arthur.   A payment is recorded in the month of Arthur's death, which is almost certainly a payment to Skelton:

Item to the duc of Yorks scolemaster   xl s.[45]

To round off this period of progress, Cambridge again records an honour to the poet, the terms of which imply previous advancement both in Oxford and at the court:

An. 1504-5. Conceditur Johanni Skelton, Poetae Laureat. quod possit stare eodem gradu hic, quo stetit Oxoniis, et quod possit uti habitu sibi concesso a Principe.[46]

By 1504-5, then, Skelton had advanced from the poet laureate degree to a further degree (probably the Master of Arts, since he has several times now appeared as M. or Mayster—e.g. in the Cambridge accounts) and had been granted a 'habitus' or official uniform in virtue of his office in court—a habit with which his vanity was particularly gratified and which he proudly refers to as the King's colours, 'wyght and grene.'[47]

The poet is now approaching the close of what might well be called his first London period. From now on his name figures in the records of the parish of Diss and his connection with the court is for some years broken.

An even profounder change came over his writings. So far he had written only in the current manners, the Latin compliment, the allegorical dream convention of *The Bowge of Courte,* the heavy mediaeval lament of the Northumberland and Edward iv verses, translations from Latin and French—all of them standard types in the fifteenth century. With the change from London to the country parish came a revolution in his thought and poetry. The satirist who had been latent in *The Bowge of Courte* and *Agaynste a Comely Coystrowne* burst into vigorous life with an ever-increasing volume of breathless and often, to his colleagues and associates, scandalous verse. Skelton shed the paternal moralities and scholarly diffidence of the *Speculum Principis* and the vague mistiness of allegory for a more trenchant style of satire that gained direction and edge as his interest turned more and more to the topics of the day and the problems that

45. P.R.O. ms. E. 101-145-3 (for 29 April 1502). cf. Nelson 74. He suggests it may be the 'final payment' in the reorganization of Henry's household.
46. cf. Dyce, i, xiii.
47. cf. Skelton's *Poems Agaynst Garnesche* (3) and *Calliope.*

underlay them. That he was bitterly criticised for the change is
undeniable. He suffered the fate of all innovators in his
generation's lack of understanding and in the hostile criticism of
his fellow-scholars. But in the succeeding generation, which
usually swings the pendulum to the opposite side, he had the
misfortune to miss the innovator's tardy recognition. In the
interval the Italian Renaissance had swept English poetry off its
feet, and the novelties and originality of John Skelton were lost
in the sweeping changes that overtook the whole life of England,
and in the organic transformation that revolutionized English
poetry.

There is a mysterious reference (quoted by Dyce) to a Jo.
Skelton who was committed to prison in 1502:

10 Junii apud Westminster Jo. Skelton commissus carceribus
Janitoris Domini Regis.[48]

This, if it refers to our John Skelton, would certainly indicate
that his unpopularity was not wholly literary, and that he fell out
of favour with the King for some misdemeanour. A little more
light has recently been shed by the discovery of a fuller statement
of the case. John Skelton with the Prior of St. Bartholomew's
and others were held by Lady Margaret's husband, Reginald Bray,
for some unspecified obligation:

virtute obligacionis in qua prior sancti bartholomei et alii
tenentur.[49]

Skelton was committed to prison not as a criminal but as surety
for an unfulfilled 'obligation,' no doubt a loan or some similar trans-
action. How long the imprisonment lasted can only be conjectured.
His imprisonment at this time, unimportant as it was, may be the
reason for the appearance of Skelton (this time undoubtedly the
poet) in the Pardon Roll of 1509-10, where among a long list of
persons pardoned (their offences are not stated) appears for
October 21st the following comprehensive entry:

Johannes Skelton nuper de London clericus alias dictus Johannes
Skelton nuper de London clericus poeta laureatus alias dictus
Johannes Skelton nuper de Disse in Com. Norff. clericus alias
dictus Johannes Skelton nuper de Disse in Com. Norff. clericus
ac poeta laureatus alias dictus Johannes Skelton nuper de Disse

48. Dyce i, xxvi.
49. P.R.O. *Act Book of the Court of Requests.* Req. 1-3, fol. 2. Nelson prints the full
text p. 242.

in Com. Norff. clericus poeta laureatus ac rector ecclie. parochialis
de Dysse in Com. Norff. seu quorumque etc. Teste Rege apud
Westm. xxj die Octobr.

Per ipsum Regem.[50]

Pardon for what? For the 'offence' of June 1502, for which
he was committed to prison, or for some (perhaps very minor)
fault between the date of his leaving court and the year 1509?
It is significant that Henry vii died on 21 April 1509—the pardon
belongs to the first few months of the reign of Skelton's old pupil.
Whatever the misdemeanour and whenever it was committed, it
seems certain that Henry viii took fairly rapid steps to
re-establish his former tutor in royal grace. Probably even the
1502 imprisonment had not been regarded by the elder Henry as
a serious matter for very long. The Cambridge degree of 1504-5
already quoted indicates a warm support of Skelton both as scholar
and as a court figure that would have been impossible towards
anyone genuinely out of favour.

Skelton, however, left court. Years afterwards, as an honoured
poet, he remembered with gratitude that his 'Occupacyon' with
poetry had sweetened the disappointments of his departure. In
The Garlande of Laurell of 1523 Occupacyon reminds him of the
aid she had given him:

> Whan broken was your mast
> Of worldly trust, then did I you rescu,
> Your storm dryuen shyppe I repared new!

The next few years saw him mainly in his benefice of Diss. In
1504 we find him witnessing the will of one Margery Cooper, who
was buried in the parish church and who left the sum of 6s. 8d.
to the high altar. Her will is:

... witnessed by master John Skelton, laureat, parson of Disse,
and Sir John Clarke, sowle priest of the same town[51]

and was proved on 6 March 1504. 'Old' John Clarke, possibly
the father of the soul priest,[52] died two years later, in 1506,
leaving money for a pilgrim to go to Rome and pray for the souls
of John and his family, but Skelton, undeterred by such piety,

50. Public Record Office. *Pardon Roll* 1509-10. (P.R.O. c67/57/2, mem. 31.)
51. Rev. F. Blomefield. *Topographical History of Norfolk*. Vol. i, p. 18. (London, 1805.)
One is dependent on Blomefield's notes here, as the church records of Diss are no longer extant.
52. cf. Nelson 103, note 4.

wrote an uncomplimentary *Epitaphe* on the 'two knaves sometime of Dis'—*A Deuoute Trentale for Old John Clarke, Sometyme the Holy Patriarke of Dis* (1506) and on a companion rogue, *Adam Uddersall* (1507). The satirist had come into his own again. Yet in the same year (1507), when the town of Norwich was destroyed by fire, he returned to Latin Elegiacs to commemorate the *Lamentatio Urbis Norvicen.*

The tradition of Skelton's life is not free from the accusation of clerical misdemeanours. Bale relates that, '*sub pseudopontifice Nordouicensi, Ricardo Nixo,*' he was secretly married, but for fear of a public scandal kept his wife under the title of concubine— a relationship more tolerable than marriage in the eyes of the mediaeval church. On his death-bed he confessed that he regarded her in the eyes of God as his legal wife. From this note in Bale a tradition has grown up that for this misdemeanour Skelton was suspended from his benefice for a period by Richard Nicke, the Bishop of Norwich. The story is repeated and developed with growing circumstantial detail in Pits,[53] in Fuller,[54] and in Anthony à Wood.[55] But of contemporary evidence for this dismissal there appears to be not one scrap.

At some period of his life Skelton certainly fell out with Bishop Nicke. In *A C Mery Tales* printed by John Rastell in 1526 the story is told of Skelton's reconciliation with the Bishop:

It fortuned that ther was a gret varyaunce between the bysshop of Norwich and one mayster Skelton a poyet lauriat. In so moch that the bysshope commaunded that he sholde nat come in at hys gatys. This master Skelton dyd absent hym selfe for a longe season but at the last he thought to do his duty and studyed wayes how he myght obtayn the byshopys fauour and determynyd him selfe that he wold com to him with some present and humble himselfe to the byshop . . . .[56]

After various adventures Skelton ingratiates himself with the Bishop. This tale was printed in the lifetime of the poet, and although the actual 'tale' may be of doubtful authority, the incident supplies strong evidence for Skelton's 'varyaunce' with the Bishop.

On the other hand, a virtual denial of the tradition of his

53. J. Pits. *De Illustribus Angliae Scriptoribus.* Paris, 1619.
54. Fuller's *Worthies.*
55. A. à Wood. *Athenae Oxonienses.*
56. *A C mery talys.* Ed. W. C. Hazlitt. London, 1887.

suspension from the benefice has now come to light among the manuscripts of Norwich Cathedral. In the *Institution Book* for the years 1507-11, during which time Richard Nicke was Bishop, there is the record of a case that came before the ecclesiastical court. In 1511 William Dale, the rector of Redegrave, and Thomas Revet, of the same place, appeared before the court. The case occupies several entries, till on the 11th of November two arbiters are appointed:

Magister Simonus Dryver decretorum doctor, atque Magister Iohannes Skelton Rector de Disse.

The entry goes on to state that if agreement is not reached within eight days, the case is to be brought before the Bishop on the Monday after the feast of St. Edmund's.[57] Further proof of his orthodox behaviour in the parish of Diss may be found in a still earlier case in the Norwich Cathedral records, where on 3 December 1509 Thos. Pykerell is mentioned as having to answer for his offences against the Church:

ad promocionem Johannis Skelton rectoris ibidem eidem obijciendi.[58]

These records confirm the belief that springs from a careful reading of his poetry, that his relations with the church authorities were those of a normal parish priest. It is very doubtful if the traditional Skelton of the later (and less authentic) *Mery Tales* would have received this minor but official appointment from Bishop Nicke. The real Skelton was clearly regarded in 1511 by the Bishop as a responsible clergyman and a fit judge for a dispute. His 'varyaunce' with the Bishop must have occurred after that date and was possibly due to some private dispute. From 1511 Skelton was in close contact with court circles and it could scarcely have been in the character of a suspended clergyman.

A recent writer[59] has revived the legend by suggesting that a Dominus Johannes Shelton who was accused at the 1526 visitation of Bishop Nicke to the Cathedral of Norwich of *gravia crimina et nephanda peccata* is the poet laureate. The story at first sight looks plausible, but a closer examination of the records reveals

57. Norwich Cathedral *Institution Book*, xiv, f. 11.
58. Norwich Cathedral *Act Book of the Consistory Court*. The case reappears on 14 January and 4 February 1510. cf. Nelson 243.
59. J. M. Berdan, *P.M.L.A.* 29 (N.S.), 22, xxi.

C

that this Dominus Johannes Shelton was *not* Skelton the poet.
Dominus Johannes Shelton was a Benedictine monk at the Priory
attached to the Cathedral of Norwich. He appears in the
Visitation records for 1520 as:

Dompnus Johannes Shelton camerarius et eleemosinarius.

This is a different person from the rector of Diss. Similar
references to Shelton the monk appear throughout the Visitation
records, including that of his accusation before Bishop Nicke,
where his *nephanda peccata* are stated to have brought his office
of *camerarius* into disrepute:

Et sua culpa multum deterioratur officium camerarii cui olim
praefuit.[60]

Johannes Shelton, *camerarius et eleemosinarius,* is merely
another of the Sheltons and Skeltons who obscure the history of
the poet's life.

The silence of Bale, the story of the 'varyaunce' with the Bishop,
and the entries from the Norwich records are the only
contemporary pieces of evidence. They point to a dispute with
Bishop Nicke, but they contain no hint of Skelton's suspension
from his benefice. The tradition was a legend that grew up after
the death of the poet. Skelton probably had no real quarrel with
the authorities of the Church till he crossed swords with Cardinal
Wolsey.

It has been noted how the change from the court to Diss was
accompanied by new developments in his poetry. In 1508 came
the first-fruits of the new maturity. His *Phillip Sparow,* a lament
for a dead sparrow that was a mockery of the solemn Offices
for the Dead, created a sensation. Skelton broke for good with
his earlier poetry. The new verse was rude, unpolished and
vigorous, written in a scrambling series of runaway short lines
that offended the mediaeval courtly tastes of the contemporary
critics and poets; while the Goliardic satire of church services by
a priest in orders scandalized the conservative clergy. From now
on Skelton acquired an unpopularity that has had its echo up to
the present day. The respected priest, courtier and royal schoolmaster broke out into the most disrespectful of verses and
continued on his outspoken way for almost a couple of decades,

60. A. Jessop, *Visitations of the Diocese of Norwich,* pp. 198, 200, 201, 204.

undeterred by criticism or disparagement, writing with the fervour of a man who had at last found a mission in life. It was as if the headmaster of Eton turned to Communist pamphleteering. Skelton's former enemies had their hatreds confirmed, and new enemies rose to the attack, sneering at his new style of verse and his vanity and his ambiguous title of poet laureate. Barclay in his *Ship of Fools* (1509) repeated the current disdain from the secure position of a poet who had never betrayed the mediaeval conventions:

> I write no jeste ne tale of Robin Hood,
> Nor sowe no sparkles ne sede of viciousness;
> Wise men loue vertue, wilde people wantonness;
> It longeth not to my. science nor cunning,
> For Philip the Sparow the Dirige to singe.[61]

Skelton was unaffected. Beneath the rugged vigour of the new satire lay a passionate conservatism that his generation never once suspected. Goliard priest he might be—it was in an old enough tradition—but renegade never. When his church at Diss was desecrated by a neighbour priest who had the effrontery to fly his hawk up to the very altar, the full battery of the new verse was turned with devastating effect against the offender in *Ware the Hauke* (c. 1509), which so became the first of a long line of satires on the abuses of the clergy.

The accession of Henry VIII in 1509 turned Skelton's mind for a time from satire back to compliment. The new king was either insensible to, or, more probably, careless of, the court's disapproval of Skelton's latest ventures, and it is clear from the tone and style of the poems of the next dozen years that Skelton wrote not only with the King's approval, but even at his bidding. One of the King's earliest actions was to grant him the pardon already quoted. In that pardon Skelton is mentioned not only as *nuper de London* (after all, he had been some years in his parish) but, more significantly, as *nuper de Disse*. The implication is that he had already moved from regular residence in Diss by the end of 1509. From this year onwards his connection with the court grew again more intimate. His rivals and detractors looked on jealously and grumbled at his success, but Skelton played the new role of churchman-courtier in accents so fearless

61. *Ship of Fools*. Ed. Jamieson. Vol. ii. (Conclusion.)

and outspoken that he must have felt very sure of his backing by the King.

His connection with Diss was not, however, broken. There was no necessity for a priest to live in his parish continuously. 'Among the evidences of Thomas Coggeshill,' says Blomefield of a 1511 entry, 'I find the house in the tenure of Master Skelton, Laureat.'[62] Skelton's appointment as an arbiter at Norwich in a case dated November, 1511, has already been noted, and from these two references it is clear that he spent at least part of that year in his parish. He held his benefice till his death. There is no record of a further appointment in Diss till the next rector, Thomas Clerk, was instituted in 1529 *'Per mortem naturalem magistri Johannes Skeltonne ultimi Rectoris.'*[63] But from now on Skelton's life was not confined to his parish. He travelled over England, living at the court and spending periods at the country houses of families as noble as the Howards.

Skelton soon re-established contact with London. Among the records of Westminster Abbey a new and illuminating reference has come to light. In the book of the expenses of the household kept for William Mane, the Prior, there appears an entry for 5 July 1511 giving the expenses of the day's dinner of plaice, soles, saltfish, and 'congger snekes'; in the margin appears the note:

This day there dyned with your maistership the soffrecan and Skeltun the poet with vthers.[64]

The poet was probably reviving an acquaintance with colleagues whom he had seldom seen in the previous ten years. Once more Skelton was in the centre of affairs.

Not long after the accession, Henry granted Skelton a new honour. Skelton was partial to titles; the new title of Orator Regius, which he now begins to append to his poems, was as pleasing as his academic degrees and a decisive weapon against those who derided his proud use of his earlier title of poet laureate. There is no sign of a record of the grant of this new title; but in a group of poems[65] dated from c. 1512 to 1527, and all

62. Blomefield, loc. cit.
63. Norwich Cathedral *Institution Book*, XVII, f. 9b.
64. Westminster Abbey *Muniments*, 33325, f. 17b.
65. (1) *Henry VII Epitaph* (1512); (2) *Eulogy on his Times* (1512); (3) *Chorus de Dis contra Scottos* (1513); (4) *Against the Scottes* (1513); (5) *Chorus de Dis contra Gallos* (1513); (6) *Against Venemous Tongues* (c. 1515); (7) *Elegy on the Countess of Derby* (1516); (8) *Calliope* (late court period); (9) *Speke Parrot* (1521); (10) Dedication to the *Replycacion* (1527).

associated with the court, the poet is 'Orator Regius' as well as poet laureate. Once more he was in royal favour.

Following his usual custom, he celebrated the new reign both in English and in Latin. *The Rose both White and Rede* (1509) in a few stanzas of English verse expressed the patriotism that in more grandiose Latin was exhibited in the hexameters of *Ad serenissimam iam nunc suam maiestatem regiam Skeltonidis Laureati non ignobile palinodium,* in which Henry becomes in turn Alexis, Hector, Scipio, Marcellus, and similar classical heroes, and in which Skelton promises him the service of his poetry:

> . . . . illi mea carmina servo.[66]

How soon afterwards Henry accepted these services of his old tutor is uncertain. There are evidences of an interval in which Skelton was doubtful of his reception at court. The *Palinodium* concludes with the appeal:

> Tribuat michi Iuppiter Feretrius ne teram tempus apud Eurotam.

—an appeal to Jupiter to rescue him from Eurotas. Can Jupiter be Henry and Eurotas Diss? The experiment of retreat to a country parish had not been a complete success for an old courtier. The volume which contains the *Speculum* and the *Palinodium* is a contemporary one, bound in leather boards embossed with the royal arms—probably the very copy that Skelton presented to Henry[67]—and it concludes with a protest by Skelton against his exile:

> Tacitus secum in soliloquio ceu vir totus obliuioni datus.[68]

Skelton laments his fate and pleads for the royal generosity, which must have been forthcoming fairly soon, perhaps as a result of the presentation of this volume, to which Skelton had added an inscribed copy of the *Chronique de Rains* with dedicatory verses.[69]

The result of the renewed contact with court and Westminster circles is seen in his *Henrici Septimi Epitaphium* (1512), dedicated to his friend John Islip, the Abbot of Westminster, and the *Eulogium pro suorum temporum conditione* (c. 1512).

66. Text in *Speculum*, loc. cit., p. 37.
67. B.M.   Add. 26,787.
68. ibid., f. 29b.
69. M. R. James, *A Descriptive Catalogue of the Manuscripts in the Library of Corpus Christi College, Cambridge.* (Cam., 1912.) James suggests that the dedication is autograph.

England was now at war with France and on the eve of a war
with Scotland. Skelton utters threats against both and proclaims
the prowess of Henry VIII:

> Dulce meum decus, et sola Britanna salus.

The following year (1513) he was given full opportunity for
the expression of his patriotism. England was victorious in both
Scottish and French campaigns, and Skelton wrote a group of
victory-poems celebrating the victors in panegyrics and satirizing
the defeated in wild scurrility. The *Ballade of the Scottyshe King*
commemorated Flodden within a few days of the battle and was
speedily followed by the satire *Against the Scottes,* in both of
which abuse acquires the value of decoration as Skelton works
himself into a verbal fury against the 'tratlynge Scottes.' Towards
the end of the same year came the more dignified but duller
Latin responses, the *Chorus de Dis contra Scottos* and the companion poem celebrating the almost simultaneous French defeat
at Thérouanne, the *Chorus de Dis contra Gallos.* To the same
period belongs another anti-Scottish satire, the more personal
Against Dundas, which has audible echoes of the Flodden group.
The English poems of this group reveal Skelton as a master of
invective. A torrent of abuse flows from his pen and envelops
his opponents whether they are individuals or nations:

> Kynge Jamy, Jemmy, Jocky my jo

is all the respect paid to the worthy James IV of Scotland.
Yet this abuse is balanced by a fierce patriotism and tributes to
his patrons. Henry is 'Your souerayne lord, our prynce of
myght,' the Earl of Surrey, the victor of Flodden, is the 'White
Lyon' and 'rampaunt of moode.'

There is every indication that Henry enjoyed this invective—
he even spurred Skelton on to later flytings in a similar abusive
style. Skelton's fierce vigour had still plenty of opponents, and
this latest flood of graceless and undignified verse raised a storm
of protest from (the confession is his own) 'diuers people.' With
characteristic doggedness he wrote a reply, *Unto Diuers People
that remorde this Rymynge agaynst the Scot Jemmy,* in the same
short line metre but in language more dignified, taking refuge in
his patriotism and the treachery of the Scottish king, and
rounding on his detractors as traitors lacking 'true English blood.'

Commendations Skelton did have. In the year of the Flodden
poems (1513) Henry Bradshaw, a monk of Chester, completed
his *Life of St. Werburge,* àt the close of which he commends his
'litell book' to poets ancient and contemporary, Chaucer and
Skelton only two lines apart, and the rivals Barclay and Skelton
receiving equal praise:

> To all the auncient poetes, litell book, submytte the,
> Whilom flouryng in eloquence facoundious,
> And to all other whiche present nowe be,
> Fyrst to maister Chaucer and Ludgate sentencious,
> Also to pregnant Barklay nowe beyng religious,
> To inuentiue Skelton and poet laureate.[70]

For the opposition Barclay is once again the mouth-piece. His
five *Eclogues* were published about 1513-14, and in Eclogue IV a
long passage is directed against the recent developments of
Skelton's verse and his advance in courtly favour:

> Another thing is yet greatly more damnable:
> Of rascolde poets yet is a shameful rable,
> Which voyde of wisedome presumeth to indite,
> Though they haue scantly the cunning of a snite;
> And to what vices that princes moste intende,
> Those dare these fooles solemnize and commende.
> Then is he decked as Poet laureate
> When stinking Thais made him her graduate:
> When Muses rested, she did her season note,
> And she with Bacchus her camous did promote.
> If they hauue smelled the artes triuiall,
> Such is their foly, so foolishly they dote,
> Thinking that none can their playne errour note:
> Yet be they foolishe, auoyde of honestie,
> Nothing seasoned with spice of grauitie,
> With many wordes, and fruitlesse of sentence.[71]

What perhaps finally fired the resentment of Barclay and the
critics was the production, perhaps a little earlier than the Flodden
satires, of *Elynour Rummyng,* a Bacchic poem beside which *The
Jolly Beggars* might be celebrating a tea-party. The poem is
mediaeval in its attack on women—it has the choicest gallery of
women drunkards in English—and Renaissance in its abounding
vigour. It is as mordant as Juvenal's sixth satire, yet handled

70. Ed. C. Horstmann. E.E.T.S., p. 199.
71. Eclogue IV, ll. 679-702.

without any of the grim disgust against womankind of the Latin
satirist. One can see why Barclay and his fellow-churchmen
viewed this latest development of a court-poet with horror. To
them the poetry of Skelton was not merely repulsive; it was
discreditable to the Church. A priest, the rector of a country
parish, a churchman who had the ear of King Henry writing with
obvious relish bawdries of drunken old women—the situation was
intolerable.

Henry VIII did not concur. The following year (1514) Skelton
wrote three poems 'Be the Kynges most noble commandment'
Against Christopher Garnesche, a gentleman-usher of the court.
The flytings, like the flyting of Dunbar and Kennedy, are so
abusive, one suspects the quarrel was mainly on paper. The whole
affair has the appearance of an elaborate court jest. The self-
confident swagger of Skelton's lines and the easy manner in which
he refers to Henry confirm Skelton's favoured position at court:

> The honor of England I lernyd to spelle
> In dignyte roialle that doth excelle . . . .
> It pleasyth that noble prince roialle
> Me as hys master for to calle
> In hys lernyng primordialle.

Skelton's court poems of the period include his *Elegia in Margaritae
nuper comitissae de Derby funebre ministerium* (1516)—a highly
complimentary but perhaps quite sincere lament on his dead
patroness—and the undated *Calliope,* in which he complains (for
he was approaching sixty by now) of his advancing age:

> Though I wax olde,
> And somedele sere;

and in which he defends his court dress embroidered with the
name Calliope, promising the Muse his life-long service:

> Wyth her certayne
> I wyll remayne,
> As my souerayne.

Skelton's favour at court resulted in more than complimentary
poems and occasional pieces. From now on the interest in affairs
of the day, which had characterized several of the poems of the
preceding few years, became stronger, and Skelton grew more and
more to look on himself as an elder counsellor of the King. These

years coincide with the rise of Cardinal Wolsey, whom Skelton
regarded at first with the suspicion of an elderly churchman and
courtier towards a brilliant and aggressive junior, but later, as
Wolsey's influence over the King grew more potent, with genuine
alarm, and in the end with uncompromising hatred. This situation
at court finds an echo in Skelton's morality play, *Magnyfycence,*
of the years 1515-16.

The originality alone of *Magnyfycence* indicates that Skelton
wrote the play for counsel as much as for entertainment. All the
extant moralities of earlier date are essentially religious dramas
on stereotyped themes—Skelton's is the first morality on an
essentially secular theme. Never once is the court situation alluded
to; but under cover of mediaeval allegorical abstractions Skelton
offers advice to the King and comments on court life as he had
in his earlier *Bowge of Courte.* It is not difficult to see in the
good and evil counsellors of *Magnyfycence* parallels to the older
counsellors of Henry, like the Duke of Norfolk, one of the
Howards to whom Skelton was always faithful, and the newer
group headed by Wolsey. The attack implicit in this secularized
morality could not have passed without notice, but for a few years
Skelton's comments on current affairs were free from personal
references, and there is no record of any displeasure felt either
by Henry or Wolsey.

That Skelton at this period was dwelling in London is confirmed
by a lease granted by Abbot Islip and the Convent of Westminster
on 5 August 1518 to one Alice Newebury, of a tenement within
sanctuary, on the south side of the Great Belfry:

. . . in quoquidem tenemento Johannus Skelton laureatus modo
inhabitat.[72]

During the same year (1518) Skelton wrote an epitaph, like those
on Henry VII and the Countess of Derby, for a Westminster tomb,
but in a tone far different from the eulogies of the 1512 and 1516
poems—the *Devout Epitaph on Bedell, Late Belial Incarnate,* whom
H. L. R. Edwards has identified as William Bedell, treasurer and
receiver-general for Lady Margaret.[73] It would appear that
Skelton was not merely writing Westminster poems. His London

72. Westminster Abbey *Register Book* II, f. 146. Noted by H. F. Westlake. *T.L.S.,* 1921,
p. 699.
73. PH.D. Thesis, Cambridge.

residence was actually within the precincts of the Abbey, and it was probably to his tenement within the sanctuary that Skelton retired when only a few years later Abbot Islip received him as a fugitive from the vengeance of the Cardinal.

For the moment no thought of flight from the busy life of the court seemed to trouble Skelton. He spoke out fearlessly, whatever dispute his bluntness involved him in, and, though he had still his enemies, his friends remained loyal. One of these, Robert Whittington, schoolmaster, grammarian and, like Skelton, poet laureate, published in 1519 his *Opusculum* from the press of Wynkyn de Worde. It contained verses to Henry VIII and to some of the greater figures of his court and government—Wolsey, Brandon, the Duke of Suffolk, Sir Thomas More and John Skelton. Even in such distinguished company, Skelton is highly praised in some hundred and fifty lines of Latin elegiacs.

After some description of natural scenery, Whittington describes Apollo calling on the Muses to praise famous poets. They sing of Homer, Orpheus and other Greek poets like the tragedians and Pindar and Alcaeus; they then praise the Latin poets—Propertius, Ovid, Tibullus, Persius and Seneca. Apollo now commands the Muses to turn their eyes to Oxford, which has become his shrine like Delos or Tenedos, and above which he sees the Aeonian mount. There Skelton is one of his worshippers:

> Alma fovet vates nobis haec terra ministros
> Inter quos Schelton jure canendus adest
> Numina nostra colit.

The poem continues with an exaggerated series of metaphors and comparisons. Skelton's verses are sweeter than honey of Hybla, finer than Punic roses or Parian marble. He is more eloquent than Demosthenes, Ulysses or Nestor. He inspires all hearts as Tyrtaeus inspired the Spartans, or Homer's trumpet Alexander. He could recall souls from Acheron, soften the heart of lions, dispel the grief of Niobe. He could sing of the mysteries of the skies. The satyrs praise him and the dryads and sea-nymphs. So closes Apollo, and Whittington closes with a couplet of personal praise:

> Sat cecinisse tuum sit, mi Schelton, tibi laudi
> Haec Whitintonum; culte poeta, vale.

The humanist virtuosity of Whittington is ably demonstrated by the couplet which is spelt out by the initial letters of the hexameters:

Quae Whitintonus canit ad laudes tibi, Schelton,
Anglorum vatum gloria, sume libens.

Coming from a schoolmaster of the new-style humanist teaching, such praise is significant, even more significant than Erasmus' epigram of some twenty years earlier. Skelton was still in favour, as scholar, as poet, and as courtier.

His relationship with Whittington explains an adverse criticism of his poetry that has not aided his reputation. William Lily, the schoolmaster of St. Paul's and protégé of the humanist Colet, wrote a very uncomplimentary epigram on Skelton, that has been accepted too uncritically as conclusive evidence for the poet's unpopularity among the learned of the day:

Lilii Hendecasyllabi in Scheltonum eius
Carmina calumniantem
Quid me, Scheltone, fronte sic aperta
Carpis, vipereo potens veneno?
Quid versus trutina meos iniqua
Libras? dicere vera num licebit?
Doctrinae tibi dum parare famam
Et doctus fieri studes poeta,
Doctrinam nec habes, nec es poeta.

'And this,' says Fuller, who quotes the lines, 'I will do for W. Lily (though often beaten for his sake) endeavour to translate his answers':

With face so bold and teeth so sharp
Of viper's venom, why dost carp?
Why are my verses by thee weigh'd
In a false scale? may Truth be said?
While thou to get the more esteem
A learned poet fain would seem,
Skelton, thou art, let all men know it,
Neither learned, nor a poet.[74]

This has been accepted so long as a serious and representative piece of contemporary criticism that Skelton's fame has suffered by its continual citation. The story behind its composition is worth an enquiry.

In the very year that Whittington published his *Opusculum* with

74. Fuller's *Worthies*. 1662 Ed., p. 257.

the epigram to Skelton, William Horman, the vice-provost of
Eton, published from Pynson's press, for the use of his scholars,
a volume of *Vulgaria,* or English sentences interlined with speci-
men Latin translations.[75] The following year (1520) Whittington
replied with a rival volume of *Vulgaria* from the presses of
Pynson and Wynkyn de Worde.[76] Horman was furious, especially
since Whittington had already enraged him by producing (over
the nom-de-plume of Bossus) verses attacking his efficiency as a
teacher. The two masters of Eton and St. Paul's, Horman and
Lily, put their heads together and produced a volume of scurrilous
abuse—the *Antibossicon*—against their rival pedagogue. Whittington looked round for assistance, and found it in his friend
Skelton, who, as ex-tutor and author of such educational treatises
as the *Ars Ornate Loquendi* and a *Grammatica Anglica,*[77] and the
greatest satirist then alive in England, was more than qualified for
a schoolmasters' contest of abuse, whether in the vernacular or in
humanist Latinity.

Little now remains of the quarrel. Bale lists among Skelton's
works an *Invecta in Guil. Lilium* and quotes the opening line:

Urgeor impulsus tibi, Lilli, retundere.

The expression *retundere* implies that the verse was a reply to
verses of Lily. Wood cites Lily as having written an *Apologia
ad* {Joh. Skeltonum / Rob. Whittington} [78] for which Dyce 'sought in vain.'[79] Bale,
however, actually quotes Horman himself as one of his authorities,[80]
and there seems no doubt that Whittington and Skelton engaged
with Horman and Lily in a contest of mutual vilification. One can
only suggest now which side (if indeed any) won this battle of
schoolmasters. But the whole circumstances and background of
the quarrel robs Lily's epigram of any value as evidence of
Skelton's contemporary reputation. Whittington's laudatory
epigram, exaggerated though it is, probably better represents the
contemporary opinion. *'Doctrinam nec habes, nec es poeta'* is
the *tu quoque* of an angry schoolmaster, and not, as it has too long

75. Ed. M. R. James (Roxburghe Club, 1926).
76. Reprinted E.E.T.S. Ed. B. White.
77. cf. Bale's list and *Garlande of Laurell,* 1175, 1182, from which Bale derived his information.
78. *Ath. Oxon.* Ed. Bliss. I, 52.
79. Dyce I, xxxvii.
80. *Index Britanniae Scriptorum.* Ed. R. L. Poole and M. Bateson, p. 253. (Oxford, 1902.)

been accepted, the considered verdict of the humanists on Skelton.

While the quarrel of the schoolmasters was still entertaining the learned London circle, Skelton had already engaged a more serious adversary. The state of the church was disquieting. Luther's heresies of 1517 had run insidiously through Europe, and Skelton saw with dismay the spread of Protestant unorthodoxies in the English Church. Hussians, Arians, and now these latest, the Lutherans, were extending their influence, and the clergy paid heed only to the acquisition of riches and the building of regal palaces. More and more he found himself in sympathy with the older conservative statesmen like Norfolk, and churchmen like Warham, the Archbishop of Canterbury, while the King inclined to the more progressive admonitions of Wolsey. Skelton remained passionately loyal to the King, but his *Colin Clout* of 1519-20 reflects his pessimism under the new order, and is a bitter attack on the prelates of the church for not giving a lead to the nation against luxury and heresy. The mediaeval abstractions of *Magnyfycence* give way to direct attack in his own short line metre, and warnings he had conveyed in morality form as an allegory are now concrete and ominous. The bishops must preach once more and awaken the nation, which at the moment is ruled

> . . . at the pleasure of one
> That ruleth the roste alone.

The references to Wolsey are veiled; but they do not remain veiled long. In 1520 war broke out again with France and the conservative group were dismayed at this culmination of the new foreign policy of Wolsey and the King. In 1521 Wolsey travelled to Calais and Bruges to negotiate with the Emperor and the King of France. Skelton attacks the embassy furiously in *Speke Parrot* (late 1521), and in *Why Come Ye Nat to Court?* (late 1522-early 1523)[81] he pilloried the Cardinal in the most incisive satire he ever wrote, a thousand of the most scathing lines ever addressed to any statesman:

> Why come ye nat to courte?
> — To whyche court?
> — To the Kynges court,
> Or to Hampton Court?

81. The problems of 'the Wolsey group' are discussed in chapter ix.

The attack touches every point—vulnerable or not—in the activities of the Cardinal, his presumption, his wealth, his arrogance, his origin, his ecclesiastical and his political policy. It is difficult to see why Wolsey did not take immediate offence, unless the poems were at first circulated privately in the Howard group. None of them were printed in the lifetime of either Skelton or the Cardinal, but even circulating in manuscript form they must have come eventually to the eyes of Wolsey.

Perhaps Skelton's connections with the nobility saved him for the time being. The spring of the year (1523) in which he had finished *Why Come Ye Nat to Court?* he spent with the Howards at their northern seat, Sheriff Hutton Castle, where he composed *The Garlande of Laurell,* a long allegorical poem on the model of *The Hous of Fame.* The poem is both an apologia for his own life and writings, and a piece of compliment to the ladies of the Surrey household. In the poem Dame Pallas and the Queen of Fame discuss his position among the great poets, who appear in the persons of Gower, Chaucer and Lydgate to welcome him into their ranks. Later Occupacyon reads out a list of his works, which is now of the utmost value in determining the Skelton canon; and as his sole personal poem *The Garlande of Laurell*[82] is of considerable biographical importance. In it Skelton has no doubts of his place among the great poets. In the latter part Skelton defends his style and his satirical verse, and hints at the fate of other poets who have dared to criticize their rulers:

> Ouyde was bannished for suche a skyll . . .
> Iuvenall was thret for to kyll.

He has unbounded faith in his own powers and the reading of his works by Occupacyon becomes a triumphal progress, till all the judges cry out:

> A thowsande thowsande, I trow, to my dome
> *Triumpha, triumpha!* they cryid all aboute.

This judgment on his verse, he proudly implies, must become, in spite of all adverse criticism, the final judgment of England. Any consideration of Skelton's life must pay particular attention to this illuminating allegory.

---

82. *The Garlande of Laurell* is discussed in detail in chapter III.

Towards the end of the same year (1523) Skelton turned for the last time to political satire. Once more the target of his ridicule was the hated Scots. Margaret of Scotland had been intriguing with the Duke of Albany for some time; on a renewed outbreak of the war with France, Albany sailed for Scotland and invaded England, but the efforts of the generals Surrey, Dacres and Darcy compelled him to retire discomfited. In late 1523 or early 1524 Skelton completed this final attack on the Scots— *Howe the Douty Duke of Albany, like a cowarde knyght, ran away shamfully, with a Hundred Thousande Tratlande Scottes and faint harted Frenchmen, beside the Water of Tweede.* Here the muddier reaches of Renaissance English are dredged for invective to cast at the Scots:

> O ye wretched Scottes
> Ye puaunt pyspottes . . .
> And ever to remayne . . .
> In lousy lothsumnesse
> And scabbed scorffynesse
> And in abhominacion
> Of all manner of nacion.

For all his sixty-odd years Skelton was maintaining his vigour, if only in vituperation.

Skelton's last major poem is a sturdy defence of the Church against the new Lutheran heretics. In 1527 two young students of Cambridge, Thomas Arthur and Thomas Bilney, had been compelled to recant their heresies against the Virgin. Skelton in the *Replycacion* attacks them and all similar heretics in shrill and scolding verses. It is evident that critics complained of this poem and challenged the right of a poet to enter the field of theological dispute. The challenge brought from Skelton some of his finest fighting poetry—the Confutation attached to the *Replycacion,* where Skelton, anticipating by over fifty years Sidney's *Apologie,* claims for the poet

> . . . heuenly inspyracion
> In laureate creacyon.

There are innumerable sophists, doctors and philosophers without number

> . . . sed sunt pauci rarique poetae.

When he wrote this notable defence of his craft Skelton was

almost in his seventieth year. He had lived to see the Middle Ages break down and the foundations of the mediaeval church shiver; but his plea for the place and function of poetry is a Renaissance conception, undimmed either by his years or by the pessimism of old age.

Skelton's last years were darkened by the shadow of the Cardinal. An indication of his attitude to the policy of Wolsey is contained in Hall's *Chronicle* for the year 1523-24:

And in this season, the Cardinall by his power legatine, dissolued the Conuocacion at Paules, called by the Archebishop of Cantorbury, [i.e. the conservative Warham] and called hym and all the clergie to his conuocacion to Westminster, which was neuer sene before in England, whereof master Skelton, a mery Poet, wrote,

> Gentle Paule, laie down thy swearde
> For Peter of Westminster hath shauen thy beard.[83]

There is no other record of these verses, but they may well be authentic; the incident illustrates Skelton's resentment at Wolsey's abuse of his legatine power and at his high-handed treatment of dignitaries of the church.

How long Wolsey remained in ignorance of the successive attacks of *Colin Clout, Speke Parrot,* and *Why Come Ye Nat to Court?* one cannot tell. In the end he grew so angry that Skelton spent some part of the last few years of his life in the safety of the sanctuary of Westminster. The length of his actual imprisonment is difficult to determine. Probably the danger period was over in a few months.

Bale gives the only contemporary evidence:

Ob literas quasdam in Cardinalem Vuolsium inuectiuas, ad Vestmonasteriense tandem asylum confugere, pro vita servanda, coactus fuit; ubi nihilominus sub abbate Islepo fauorem inuenit.

Later writers have been inclined to decorate these bare details into a more spectacular dash for liberty—Wood adds a pursuit by the officers of the Cardinal.[84] One must not forget that Skelton's relationship with the Prior and the Abbot of Westminster was very cordial, and that he had no need to dash to sanctuary— he was already during his London years an occupier of a tenement

83. Hall, *The Triumphant Reign of Henry VIII.* Ed. C. Whibley. London, 1904. I, 287.
84. *Ath. Oxon.* Ed. Bliss: 51.

within the precincts.   There is no necessity to presume that he had ever given up the rooms he occupied within the sanctuary in 1518.[85]   The lease of the tenement in that year to Alice Newebury does not imply Skelton's departure—other cases may be cited from the Abbey Muniments of property changing hands without the original tenant being disturbed.

For example, Thomas Lylbourne occupied a tenement within the sanctuary during the same period.   In 1518 the tenement was leased to one Wm. Hubbard[86] and in 1522 to John Hubbard[87]— Lylbourne was living there at both dates.   In 1525 this same tenement was leased to John Barbour with the note 'in which Thomas Lylbourne late dwelt.'[88]   In 1529-30 it was leased to Barbour's widow, and Lylbourne is noted as again in residence.[89] Clearly a change in lessee made no difference to the position of the occupier, and Skelton probably never abandoned his tenancy of the Westminster house.   When the fury of the Cardinal reached the danger point, probably in 1523-4 after his discovery of *Why Come Ye Nat to Court?*, Skelton simply retired to the safety of his Westminster tenement and the patronage of Abbot John Islip.

Perhaps he was already repenting of his rashness.   There are several indications that, in spite of his anti-Wolsey satires, he had expectations of advancement from the Cardinal, and made some attempt to reinstate himself in Wolsey's good graces.   His three poems written between 1523 and 1528 have all dedications or verses to Wolsey, and unless one discounts these passages as forgeries or printer's additions,[90] one must infer that Skelton at last decided to play for safety.   *The Garlande of Laurell* concludes with a dedication to Henry and to Wolsey.   This dedication was not printed in Fauke's edition of 1523, appearing first in Marsh's edition of the complete poems in 1568; but since the poem contains several passages where the poet protests against his work being misinterpreted, and even asks Fame to erase one of his books from the list of his works, the repentant mood must have set in by 1523,

85.   cf. p. 33 of this study.
86.   Westminster. Abbey *Register Book* II, f. 147b.
87.   Ibid., f. 191.
88.   Ibid., f. 217.
89.   Ibid , f. 281b.   All these references are unpublished.
90.   e.g., J. M. Berdan.   *P.M.L.A.* loc. cit. denies the *Garlande* and *Albany* dedications but allows Skelton that of the *Replycacion*.   Brie (*Skelton Studien* loc. cit.) denies the latter in addition.

D

and the dedication may very well be genuine. Wolsey is reminded
of his promise of a benefice:

> . . . et fiat memor ipse precare
> Prebendae, quam promisit mihi credere quondam,
> Meque suum referas pignus sperare salutis
> Inter spemque metum.

Skelton is 'between hope and fear'—the hope of the promised
advancement, fear of the vengeance of Wolsey. He must have
realized by now that his patronage by the King was cancelled out
by Wolsey's domination over Henry; the volume is humbly
dedicated to both.

The change in front is surprising, but circumstances may have
been too strong for even a bold fighter like Skelton. A new
pessimistic note appears in the dedication:

> Twene hope and drede
> My lyfe I lede
> But of my spede
> Small sekerness.

The old confident swagger has disappeared and Skelton now lacks
the 'sekerness' to be anything but a humble suppliant.

The Duke of Albany of 1523-24 concludes with a similar
dedication. Dyce has suggested that this *Lenvoy* should be assigned
elsewhere—possibly to *The Garlande of Laurell*.[91] This would still
date it at 1523 and would only support the argument for a change
of front about this time; both poems were written within a year of
each other. Skelton in the *Albany* dedication commends his book
to the Cardinal and reminds him again of his promise of advancement:

> *Lenvoy*
> Go, lytell quayre, apace,
>   In moost humble wyse,
> Before his noble grace,
>   That caused you to deuise
>   This lytell enterprise;
> And hym moost lowly pray
>   In his mynde to comprise
> These wordes his grace dyd saye
>   Of an ammas gray.
>
> *Ie foy enterment en sa bone grace.*

91. Dyce ii, 83; i, xliii.

The third dedication to Wolsey is an even humbler petition—that to the *Replycacion* of 1528. This poem was published complete with the dedication by Pynson,[92] who died in 1530, and it is a reasonable assumption that a poem published within three years of composition was printed as the poet wrote it. This almost certain authenticity of the 1528 dedication strengthens the case for those of 1523 and 1523-4. In this final dedication Wolsey is addressed in grandiloquent but obsequious Latin:

Honorificatissimo, amplissimo, longeque reverendissimo in Christo patri, ac domino, domino Thomae &c. tituli sanctae Cecilae, sacrosanctae Romanae ecclesiae presbytero, Cardinali meritissimo, et apostolicae sedis legato, a latereque legato superillustri, &c., Skeltonis laureatus, ora.reg., humillimum dicit obsequium cum omni debita reverentia, tanto tamque magnifico digna principe sacerdotum, totiusque justitiae aequabilissimo moderatore, necnon praesentis opusculi fautore excellentissimo, &c., ad cujus auspicatissimam contemplationem, sub memorabili prelo gloriosae immortalitatis, praesens pagella felicitatur.

The humble suppliant of these lines is a different Skelton from the jaunty self-confident poet of *Why Come Ye Nat to Courte?* It is evident that the old man had found the Cardinal too strong an opponent, and even his former favour with the King was powerless to help him. Nothing came of the petitions to Wolsey, and Skelton spent the following two years, probably peaceably enough, in his tenement in the sanctuary of Westminster. Even if he never again proceeded beyond its boundaries, life there was not so restricted as might be imagined. Men like William Cornysshe, the musician of the Chapel Royal children, who had set to music several of Skelton's lyrics, had tenements within the sanctuary.[93] There was even a tavern, called the Hole Tavern, under the Great Belfry, which in 1521-2 had been leased to one William Staverton, citizen and grocer of London. One can imagine worse ways of spending the final years of a crowded and belligerent life.

Skelton died in Westminster on 21 June 1529.[94] He was buried

92. Brie, loc. cit., assumes the dedication to have been added by Pynson for its advertising value.
93. Westminster Abbey *Register Book* 1, f. 49, f. 116, f. 15, contain leases of this tenement to Cornysshe and his wife. Cornysshe had died in 1524.
94. Bale loc. cit.

in the chancel of St. Margaret's, Westminster, and the inscription was placed on his tomb:

> Joannes Skelton, vates Pierius, hic situs est.

Bale records that he left several children, and that on his death-bed proclaimed that he regarded their mother in the eyes of God as his legal wife:

> . . . se nusquam illam in conscientiam coram Deo, nisi
> pro uxore legitima tenuisse.

Skelton left no will; but administration of his goods was granted to William Mott, the curate of St. Margaret's. The record of the administration is preserved in Somerset House, for the year 1529:

> Magister Johannes Skelton poeta laureatus:
> decessit xvjto nouembris. anno domini praedict. in domo regri. coram magro. Roberto Bennet archiuio. compart. mr. Williamus Mott curatus ste. Margarete Westm. et peciit administrat. bonorum infra Iurationem existen. sibi committi, cui in forma Iuris Iurat. dominus commisit administrationem huiusmodi saluo Iure etc. deinde ext. Inuentam. eorundem bonorum etc.[95]

No time was lost in appointing a successor to the vacant living at Diss. For the last time the name of John Skelton figures in the records of his diocese. For the 17th of July the *Institution Book* has the entry:

> Dns. Thomas Clark clericus institutus fuit personaliter in ecclesia paroch. de Dysse Norvicen. Dioc. per mortem naturalem magistri Johannes Skeltonne ultimi Rectoris.[96]

So ended the life of this unconventional cleric. His had been a very full career, rich in experience among high and low, a life of bustle and excitement and general good fortune, terminating in a few years of seclusion and tranquillity, and dedicated for almost half a century to the Church and to poetry.

95. Somerset House, *Book Bracy*, f. 6.
96. Norwich Cathedral *Institution Book* xvii, f. 9b.

CHAPTER III

MIDDLE AGES AND RENAISSANCE

1. *The Legacy of the Middle Ages*

THE CAREER OF SKELTON FALLS SO NEATLY INTO WHAT FOR
England was a period of transition from the decaying forms of
the Middle Ages to the novelties of the Renaissance that, unless
he had•been exceptionally conservative or blindly progressive,
he could not fail to show the influences of both modes of thought.
Seldom has a poet borne the marks of a transition age so clearly
as Skelton. He is a Mr. Facing-Both-Ways, difficult to fit
into the classifications of his time, at one moment surprisingly
Renaissance in his attitude and his verse-forms, at another
uncompromisingly mediaeval. Education at a mediaeval university
untouched by the Humanism of the early fifteenth century,
and a position at a court that had not yet accepted the fall of
feudalism as a reality, had provided him with the background
common to the majority of mediaeval poets; but the passionate
sincerity and originality of his mind, his evident sympathy with
the aspirations of the new rising middle class, his sturdy defence
of English as a language for verse, an apology for poetry worthy
of Sir Philip Sidney, and verse-forms as vigorous as they are
novel, are all signs that Skelton was a true child of the Renaissance.

The mediaeval elements in his verse are the simpler to isolate.
In a poem of the early Renaissance the theme is often threadbare
from long use, the newer spirit betrays itself only in an unconventional attitude, a changed conception or a new lyrical quickening.
Originality of thought does not imply originality in subject-matter,
and in poets of the period a Renaissance spirit may be discovered,
of which it is not always easy to find evidence other than the
treatment of their topics. By the time Skelton wrote even his
earliest verses, the patterns of mediaeval verse had long since been
standardized. The later Middle Ages reproduced with scrupulous
fidelity the conventions of the Rose, the Daisy, Fortune and her
false Wheel, the Lament, the Testament, the Temple of Venus,
the Seven Deadly Sins, the Dream Allegory with its traditional

May Morning and its personifications from the *Roman de la Rose*, the Court of Love and its innumerable developments—all the colourful axioms of feudal idealism. Even in the admittedly mediaeval works of Skelton perhaps the most surprising fact is not how many of these conventions he has accepted, but how few.

The early poetry of Skelton was written for a courtly audience which had been brought up on the literature of feudalism. On the battlefield the foot soldier with his firearms had rendered the mailed knight of the romances obsolete, and the spread of international trade had given the commercial class a status that was to effect in the latter years of the fifteenth century a complete social revolution, but the long-winded and unhurrying poetry of the feudal age persisted into the sixteenth century to earn the grave approbation of a nobility which scarcely realized that their civilization and their literature were dead.

The earliest poem of Skelton is written to a well-worn mediaeval formula, that of the Falls of Princes, which may be traced in a clear line through the works of Boccaccio in the *De Casibus*, of Chaucer in the *Monk's Tale*, of Lydgate in his *Falls of Princes*, down to the *Mirrour for Magistrates*, in the earlier editions of which is included Skelton's poem *Of the Death of the Noble Prince, Kynge Edward the Fourth*. The King died in the year 1483 and this is probably the date of the verses.

The poem is in the form of a monologue by the dead King. He laments the transitoriness of mortal things:

What creature is borne to be eternall?

He rails against mutability; one cannot depend on earthly prosperity. The mediaeval theme of Fortune is introduced; she gave him victory and smiled on him deceitfully. He stored his coffers with the money of the common people:

I toke ther tresure, but of ther prayers mist.

He enumerates the royal palaces he built at Nottingham and elsewhere:

Yet at the last I went from them all,
Et, ecce, nunc in pulvere dormio!

A further mediaeval stock theme is introduced—the Boethius lament of *Ubi Sunt?*

> Where is now my conquest and victory?
> Where is my riches and my royal aray?
> Wher be my coursers and my horses hye?
> Where is my myrth, my solas, and my play?
> As vanyte, to nought al is wandred away.

The prevalent horror of death is echoed.in the following verse
with its continuation of the *ubi sunt* motif. The 'wormis mete' is
the end for all men.

> Why, what cam of Alexander the greate?
> Or els of stronge Sampson, who can tell?
> Were not wormes ordeyned theyr flesh to frete?
> And of Salomon, that was of wyt the well?
> Absolon profferyd his heare for to sell,
> Yet for al his bewte wormys ete him also;
> And I but late in honour dyd excel,
> *Et, ecce, nunc in pulvere dormio!*

He commends his spirit to God and beseeches the prayers of the
commons, concluding with the final repetition of the melancholy
Latin refrain.

Though the poem is a jejune and apprentice piece of work, it
is illuminating to see what were the models Skelton chose in his
apprenticeship. The elegy is merely a patchwork of mediaeval
moralizings and gloomy lamentations on the mortality of man,
with so little individuality that Skelton has even been denied the
authorship by one recent writer.[1] There is no real warrant for
this. The elegy is the work of a young poet accepting his most
accessible models, the same as those that suggested a strikingly
similar elegy to young Thomas More.[2]

These models served once more for an elegy on *The Dolourus
Dethe and muche Lamentable Chaunce of the Most Honorable
Erle of Northumberlande* (1489).

The poem, which shows the influence of Chaucer, is written
in highly alliterated rime royal. Skelton opens by lamenting the
death of the earl, and calls on Clio for succour:

> Mine homely rudeness and dryghnes to expell
> Withe the freshe waters of Elyconys well.

Clio is accustomed to record the praises of famous men; she

---

1. F. Brie: *Skelton Studien.*
2. *The English Works of Thomas More.* Ed. W. E. Campbell, A. W. Reed, R. W.
Chambers, etc. London, 1931. ı, 335.

must give him inspiration to tell of the treason that killed the
earl.   He attacks the cowards who abandoned him to his death
and the 'mayny of rude villayns' that slew him.   What wilful folly
made them rise against their lord?   Skelton tells the story of the
rising of the commons and Northumberland's expedition against
them.   Once again he uses the stock formula:

> O dolorus chaunce of Fortunes froward hande!

With an echo of Troilus' lyrical lament on the empty palace of
Criseyde, Skelton continues his complaint:

> O cruell Mars, thou dedly god of war!
> O dolorous tewisday, dedicate to thy name . . .
> . . . O Atropos, of fatall systers iii
> Goddes most cruel unto the lyfe of man,
> All merciles, in the is no pite!
> O homicide, which sleest all that thou can . . .
> Percy had knights and squires and was chief lord:
> Tyl fykkell Fortune began on hym to frowne.

If the poet had the power of the nine Muses he would have all
too little eloquence to praise the hero.   He wishes good fortune
to the 'yonge lyon,' the heir, and the poem concludes in the manner
of a mediaeval hymn with an appeal to the

> Perlese Prince of heuen emperyall,

and a verse that might have come from any mediaeval hymn to
the Virgin:

> O quene of mercy, O lady full of grace,
> Mayden most pure, and Goddes moder dere,
> To sorowful hartes chef comfort and solace,
> Of all women O flower withouten pere!
> Pray to thy Son above the sterris clere . . . .

The elegy on the Earl of Northumberland is less of a stock
lament than its predecessor.   Along with the railing against
Fortune, the echoes from Chaucer and from the mediaeval hymns
are current allusions and personal touches—'my wordes vnpullysht'
and 'my rude pen enkankered all with rust'—that save the poem
from the pure formality of the Edward iv elegy.   Its Latin
verse dedication to Percy,

> Qui Northumbrorum jura paterna gerit,

implies that it was written for the son of the dead earl, and so may claim more personal feeling than the former elegy on the King. Nevertheless, the Northumberland elegy belongs to the Falls of Princes tradition and shows little development of its mediaeval convention.

With these two laments may be considered the curious poem (of uncertain but probably early date) *Vppon a Deedmans Hed.* Skelton had received a skull from an 'honorable jentyllwoman' and this strange token resulted in a 'gostly medytacyon in English . . . comendable, lamentable, lacrymable, profytable for the soule.' Skelton cannot escape from the Middle Ages' fascinated horror of physical corruption. Death was not merely an allegorical figure, but a grim reality of wars abroad and plagues at home. The skull,

> With hys worme etyn maw,
> And hys gastly jaw
> Gapyng asyde
> Nakyd of hyde,
> Neyther flesh nor fell,

sets the poet brooding on the shortness of life. There is no escape from death:

> Oure days be datyd,
> To be chekmatyd
> With drawttys of deth,
> Stoppyng oure breth;
> Oure eyen synkyng,
> Oure bodys stynkyng,
> Oure gummys grynnyng,
> Oure soulys brynnyng.

The poem concludes with a short and conventional appeal to Christ. Nothing could be closer in spirit to the Middle Ages than these few macabre lines.

These three pieces are his purest examples of mediaeval thought and form. Elsewhere in his poetry the mediaeval elements, where they exist, are tempered by current ideas, or utilized as conscious archaism. It is significant that these formal conventional verses all belong to the earlier period of his poetry, in which he was still content to accept the traditions of the circle that formed his audience, and before he had developed his later individual style. As his sense of dissatisfaction with the life at court grew stronger, his poetry rapidly diverged from the accepted patterns. This departure from the tradition had two stages—at first he preserved the form of the old verse, while expressing the bitterest dissatisfaction with the society which it represented. This is exemplified by *The Bowge of Courte*. A few years later he abandoned both the form and the spirit of the mediaeval type in the new verse of *Phillip Sparow*.

The first stage in the departure was inspired by a theme that the Middle Ages had often enough handled—the disappointments of the life at court. There were many poets in the centuries between those of Virgil and of Aenius Silvius who had found court life unsuited to their talents. Skelton was not alone. His special claim to our attention is that he combined the theme of the courtier's life with the form of the dream allegory. Both the elements are unquestionably mediaeval; but there is little in the amalgam that belongs to the Middle Ages. In *The Bowge of Courte* the allegorical conventions are used for the purpose of covert but well-directed satire against the society of the time.

In the course of the fifteenth century the dream allegory had lost most of its original freshness. None of the Chaucerians except Henrison had preserved either the delicacy or the vigour of Chaucer's handling; yet the allegory became the accepted form for the more serious type of verse. The unrivalled opportunities it offered for internal ramifications was a danger which only a Chaucer or a Jean de Meung could surmount, and which produced in a less competent poet like Lydgate merely wearisome enormities. With the approach of the sixteenth century the dream allegory was revived seriously for the last time. Hawes combined it with scholasticism, Skelton turned it to satire. The form which had given such grace to the *Dit de la Fontaine Amoureuse* and *The Boke of the Duchess* became overburdened when it had to bear the weight of educational propaganda and pure satire. *The Pastime of Pleasure* retained the mediaeval vice of exhausting every aspect of every topic, without proportion and without perspective; *The Bowge of Courte,* by its very lack of this vice, by its satire and its attack on the civilization that had produced the allegory, denied itself the right to be considered a proper example of the genre. The mediaeval bottles were breaking with the wine of the Renaissance.

The Bowge of Courte belongs to Skelton's first period at court— the years of his tutorship to the sons of Henry VII. Because of its supposed indebtedness to Barclay's English version of *The Ship of Fools* (1509) it was formerly presumed to belong to the first years of the new reign.[3] But, as Brie has pointed out,[4] Locher's Latin translation of Brandt's *Narrenschiff* was published in 1497 and it is much more likely that the poem was written shortly afterwards. When Skelton returned to the court at the beginning of the reign of Henry VIII his style was no longer that of the Middle Ages. The date of the poem can actually be established between the years 1497 and 1500, as one of the two extant copies (that in the National Library of Scotland) has the following colophon: 'Thus endyth the Bowge of courte./ Enprynted at westmynster By me/ Wynkyn the worde./' Now Wynkyn de Worde took over Caxton's press at Westminster but moved to premises of his own in Fleet Street at the end of 1500. His books with the Westminster imprint are therefore pre-1500.[5] Accepting 1497 as one limiting date, one can narrow down the date of composition to a couple of years. E. Gordon Duff suggests (on typographical evidence) 1499 as the date of publication,[6] and one cannot be more than a few months out in assigning the composition of the poem to 1498.

The poem, which is written in rime royal, opens with Skelton calling to mind how older poets could write with a serious purpose:

> Dyuerse in style, some spared not vyce to wryte,
> Some of moralyte nobly dyde endyte.

He is prompted 'to aforce the same,' but Ignorance discourages him. While his mind is wavering he falls asleep in the port of Harwich,

> In myne hostes house, called Powers Keye.

3. cf. C. H. Herford, *Studies in the Literary Relations of England and Germany in the Sixteenth Century*, pp. 351 ff.; Cambridge, 1886. Albert Rey, *Skelton's Satirical Poems in their relation . . . to Barclay's Ship of Fools.* (Bern Dissertation 1899) *passim.* A. Koelbing, *Zur Charakteristik John Skelton's.* Stuttgart, 1904, p. 69 ff.
4. *Skelton Studien, sub. The Bowge of Courte.*
5. E. Gordon Duff, *A Century of the English Book Trade.* London, 1905. p. 173.
6. E. Gordon Duff, *Fifteenth Century English Books.* London, 1917. p. 128.
I am indebted to Professor A. W. Reed for these last two references. cf. H. S. Sale, *M.L.N.,* pp. 572-4.

He dreams that a ship anchors in the port, laden with royal merchandise. The poet joins the crowd that flock to the ship and is told that it is called *The Bowge of Courte*—literally the rations or allowance for an officer at court, and so a metaphor for the rewards of serving a prince. The owner of the ship is Dame Saunce-pere and the merchandise that she carries is called Favour. The poet is upbraided by her chief gentlewoman, Daunger, for approaching so near. To this the poet replies that his name is Drede and that he wishes to buy some of her ware. Daunger leaves him indignantly and a second gentlewoman, Desire, bids him be of good cheer and come forward without fear. She laughs at his plea of poverty, lends him a jewel, Bone Aventure, wherewith to procure entrance to the ship, and warns him to secure the friendship of 'she that styreth the shyp.'

> Fortune gydeth and ruleth all our shyppe:
> Whome she hateth shall ouer the see boorde skyp;
> Whom she loueth, of all plesyre is ryche,
> Whyles she laugheth and hath lust for to playe;
> Whome she hateth, she casteth in the dyche,
> For whan she frouneth, she thynketh to make a fray;
> She cheryssheth him, and hym she casseth away.

The poet joins with the others on board in supplicating the good offices of Fortune. So ends the prologue.

The poem develops as a series of interviews between Drede and a group of seven allegorical figures, who represent the vices of court life. Just when the poet imagines that Favour will never depart from him he sees on board these

> Full subtyll persones, in nombre foure and thre.

They are the friends of Fortune and the poet makes advances towards them. The first to address him is Favell, the personification of deceitful flattery, already so brilliantly portrayed in *Piers Plowman*.

Favell praises the poet lavishly in the manner of a deceitful courtier:

> Ye be an apte man, as ony can be founde,
> To dwell with vs, and serue my ladyes grace;
> Ye be to her yea worth a thousande pounde;
> I herde her speke of you within shorte space . . .

Favell has defended him when other men would have slandered:

> I can not flater, I muste be playne to the.

He assures the poet that he is favoured by Fortune. To this speech the poet replied with gratitude, but with some reserve because

> Methoughte, of wordes that he had full a poke.

As Favell goes he is met by Suspecte, or Suspicion. The poet hears them whispering together of him.

Suspecte now comes forward and cautions the poet against Favell:

> He wyll begyle you and speke fayre to your face . . .
> Spake he a fayth no worde to you of me?
> I wote, and he dyde, ye wolde me telle . . .
> But I wonder what the deuyll of helle
> He sayde of me, whan he with you dyde talke:
> By mine auyse, vse not with him to walke.

Suspecte pledges him to keep his silence and the poet promises never to discover his counsel, ironically questioning him why he had not kept it to himself all the time. Suspecte departs with a mysterious promise to tell the poet more.

The next figure to come forward is Harvy Hafter, the type of the subtle rogue at court, with a more clearly individualized personality than those of the other six allegorical figures, and probably drawn from a court figure known to the poet.

> He gased on me with his gotyshe berde;
> Whan I loked on hym, my purse was half aferde.

Harvy Hafter greets the poet boisterously, singing lines from popular ballads to show that he realizes that Drede is a poet. What a pleasure it must be to have such knowledge! Though Harvy Hafter is a 'homely knaue,' he bids the poet welcome:

> But ye be welcome to our householde.

For a moment Skelton has forgotten his allegory and the ship has become the reality—the royal household. Harvy Hafter departs with the promise to let the poet know if anything is ever said against him.

The poet sees him join with Dysdayne and hears the two of them plot his downfall. Dysdayne is painted as a pure allegorical abstraction:

> Enuye hathe wasted his lyuer and his lounge,
> Hatred by the herte so had hym wrounge,
> That he loked pale as asshes to my syghte.

Dysdayne approaches and follows his plan of picking a quarrel
with the poet—perhaps with such a complaint as the older courtiers
of the train of Henry VII may have made against Skelton:

> It is greate scorne to see suche an hayne
> As thou arte, one that cam but yesterdaye,
> With vs olde seruants suche maysters to playe . . .
> We be thy betters, and so thou shalte vs take,
> Or we shall thé oute of thy clothes shake.

At this point out rushes Ryotte, the drunken courtier, whose
appearance and manners are minutely described—bleared eyes,
ragged hose and coat, a feather in his hat, an empty purse, and a
flow of ribald language. He demands to know who the poet is,
and Skelton once again forgets his ship allegory and sees himself
in the court he was growing to hate:

> Forsothe, quod I, in this courte I dwelle nowe.
> Welcome, quod Ryotte, I make God auowe.

Ryotte outlines the life he invites the poet to join. One must
abandon study and keep good company:

> This worlde is nothynge but ete, drynke and slepe.

He offers to play dice with the poet, but, discovering nothing
in his purse but a buckle, he makes for the stews:

> To wete yf Malkyn, my lemman, haue gete oughte.

No sooner has Ryotte departed than the poet sees whispering
in a corner the figures of Dysdayne and Dyssymulacyon. The
portrayal of the latter is in sharp contrast with the picture
of Ryotte. Dyssymulacyon, like Dysdayne, is a mediaeval
abstraction:

> Than in his hode I saw there faces twyene;
> The one was lene and lyke a pyned goost,
> The other loked as he wolde haue me slayne.

Dyssymulacyon hints darkly at slanders against the poet—the
allegory is dropped for a moment:

> For all our courte is full of dyceyte,

and after some ingenious verses in which he suggests much but reveals nothing, Dyssymulacyon departs and leaves the stage free for the final figure of Disceyte:

> Yf I had not quyckly fledde the touche,
> He had plucte oute the nobles of my pouche.

As Disceyte tells how he saved the poet's life, Drede sees 'lewde felawes' approaching to slay him. Rushing to the ship's side he awoke and

> Caughte pen and ynke, and wrote this lytell boke.

The poem concludes with the hope that no one will be displeased since it is all 'substance of slumbrynge.' But he finishes off with the caustic lines:

> But yet oftyme suche dremes be founde trewe:
> Nowe constrewe ye what is the resydewe.

This pessimistic sketch of court life is more than the satirist's stock material. The convention is better seen in the *Eclogues* of Alexander Barclay, who, no courtier himself, freely adapted the traditional complaints of Aeneas Silvius' *Miseriae Curalium*. Skelton, however, wrote from his own embittering experiences of court life. The ship of Fortune was for him no mere piece of formalism, but a symbol of his progress and, it may be surmised, of his decline in favour. *The Bowge of Courte* of 1498 must be associated with his break from the courtier's life and his entry in the same year to holy orders.

His method of portraying the characters of the vicious courtiers shows a curious blend of the abstract sketches of the Middle Ages with the rotund characterizations of the new age. Dysdayne and Dyssymulacyon both in name and in appearance are hastily conceived, and their only human characteristic is their speech. Ryotte, on the other hand, is an excellent piece of realism, a thoroughly repulsive portrait of a drunkard, while the sketch of Harvy Hafter is so individual that one suspects Skelton of victimising one of his raffish opponents.

One further literary species may be discovered influencing the poem—the 'Fool' literature that grew from the *Narrenschiff* of Sebastian Brandt. This German verse-survey of the numerous varieties of 'fools' was published in 1494 and was rapidly translated into other languages—notably into Latin by Locher, who

published in 1497 his *Stultifera Navis,* and into English by
Barclay, whose translation, from Locher, appeared in 1509 as
The Ship of Fools. What was in Brandt a mediaeval collection
touched with humanist pedantry, became in Locher a Renaissance
attack on the extravagances of the age.[7] As there is no reason to
suppose that Skelton knew German, he must have read the poem
in Locher's Latin. Both the mechanism and the motive of *The
Ship of Fools* are discoverable in *The Bowge of Courte.*[8] The
Narrenschiff becomes the ship of Fortune and the fools that
crowd into it are the fools of court favour. The sketch of Ryotte,
in particular, corresponds to a whole class of riotous fools in the
original ship. Skelton has put together with considerable ingenuity
his various motifs. The poem is strikingly lacking in the
mediaeval padding that one might have expected, and *Narrenschiff*
allegory and court satire combine into an incisive unity quite
unmediaeval in compactness.

More than twenty years later Skelton returned to dream
allegory in *The Garlande of Laurell* of 1523. In the intervening
period his verse had been so markedly characterized by Renaissance
freedom from earlier authorities that the choice of a mediaeval
model must have been deliberate. *The Garlande of Laurell* was
written in Sheriff Hutton Castle, while Skelton was a guest of
the Howard family, and the form of the poem acknowledges the
old-fashioned taste of an aristocratic household. Only half a
dozen years before its appearance a Howard had been born who
was to naturalize in England the poetry of the Italian Renaissance.
But when Skelton read his leisurely allegory to the Howard
ladies, this future Earl of Surrey was a child of six; the elders
preferred to acclaim the verse of their own generation.

The *Garlande* was published by Faukes in October, 1523, a few
months after its composition, and is the only poem of Skelton
that appeared in print during his lifetime. Perhaps the publicity
that the poem had gained from its appearance before a noble
audience and the sense that it was an *Apologia pro Vita Sua*
induced this unusual step. It must have been written about the
beginning of 1523, because Thomas Howard, Earl of Surrey

---

7. cf. Pompen, *English Versions of the Ship of Fools.* London, 1925.
8. cf. C. H. Herford, *Literary Relations,* p. 352 ff.

and husband of Elizabeth, to whom the poem is dedicated, became General-in-chief of the Scottish campaign in February, 1523, and spent the spring and summer raiding the Borders. Sheriff Hutton Castle was the most northerly seat available for the family, and it is to be presumed that Skelton was a guest of the Howards during this period. This date is confirmed by the mediaeval astrological dating in the opening verse. Mars is described as 'retrogradant.' The Retrogression of Mars occurs at intervals of a little over two years, and that which Skelton witnessed has been calculated for April, 1523. The early months of 1523 may be accepted as the date of composition.[9] The poem is partly a piece of personal glorification, partly a graceful compliment in rime royal to the Countess of Surrey and her ladies.

After the astrological dating, Skelton muses on the changes of Fortune and as he is drowned 'in this dumpe' he rests in the Forest of Galtres, to fall into the conventional sleep of the dream allegory. He sees a vision of a pavilion in which Dame Pallas and the Queen of Fame are disputing his claim to be admitted to the court of Fame. The poem develops as a series of pros and cons from the two disputants.

Fame announces the claim of Pallas to have her servant Skelton admitted to the court of the Queen. She finds in him some deficiency but

> Sith he has tastid of the sugred pocioun
> Of Elyconis well

it is fitting that Pallas should defend him.

Pallas replies; and through her lips we hear the voice of John Skelton defending himself against his critics. She defends his satires of the previous few years:

> And if so hym fortune to wryte true and plaine,
> As sumtyme he must vyces remorde . . .

and cites Ovid and Juvenal as poets whose comments on

---

9. cf. Helen Stearns, *The Date of the Garlande of Laurell*, *M.L.N.*, 1928. The mathematical calculations to establish the dates of the Retrogressions of Mars are noted in this article and in *Skelton's Quarrel with Wolsey*: William Nelson, *P.M.L.A.*, June, 1936. Further calculations are given by H. L. R. Edwards, *P.M.L.A.*, June, 1938, pp. 608 ff. These three calculations (all done by mathematical colleagues of the writers concerned) differ among themselves. We are in such matters in the hands of the scientific expert. Nelson (loc. cit.) then suggests that 'Skelton undoubtedly relied on the inaccurate astronomical tables of the time.' Edwards (loc. cit.) considers that 'Skelton has deliberately antedated the retrogradation for his allegoric ends.' When the search for a precisely accurate date necessitates such assumption, we are safer to be content with 'the early months of 1523.'

E

public affairs brought them into danger. The Queen mentions
Demosthenes as a genuine candidate for honour and to this Pallas
asks why Aeschines had none. Fame defends herself, but Pallas
complains that fame nowadays comes only to those who work evil:

> Some haue a name for thefte and brybery;
> Some be called crafty that can pyke a purse;
> Some men be made of for their mokery;
> Some careful cokwoldes, some haue theyr wyues curs.

Why should a poet not have promotion? Fame admits her
arguments and announces that if Skelton can produce any works
that justify his claim to be a poet he will not be banished from
the 'laureat senate.' This is what Pallas has been waiting for.
Aeolus—the trumpeter of *The Hous of Fame*—blows a blast to
summon

> What poetis we haue at our retenewe.

This ends the first section of the poem.

The second section opens with a description of the aspirants
to fame:

> On euery syde
> They presid in faste; some thought they were to longe;
> Some were to hasty, and wold no man byde;
> Some whispered, some rownyd, some spake, and some cryde.

Orpheus and Amphion harp so melodiously that the oak stump
against which Skelton is leaning starts back and he sees around
the tent of Pallas a thousand poets. Phoebus, their leader, sings
a mediaeval complaint on his loss of Daphne; when the complaint
is ended the 'poets' move by in procession to provide Skelton with
one of these poetic catalogues beloved by the Middle Ages. They
pass in disordered ranks, Homer with Cicero, Lucan with Virgil,
Terence followed by Seneca and Boethius, Boccaccio linked
strangely with Macrobius, Plutarch with Petrarch, and Propertius
with Vincent of Beauvais. At the end of the line come the three
great English poets, Chaucer, Gower and Lydgate, who address
Skelton with 'godely chere.'

Gower encourages him with praise:

> Ye haue deserved to haue an emplement
> In our collage aboue the starry sky.

Chaucer announces that all three will bring him before the court of Fame, and Skelton replies with his tribute to the poet he revered:

> O noble Chaucer, whos pullysshed eloquence
> Oure Englysshe rude so fresshely hath set out!

Lydgate appoints Skelton to be 'pronothary'—the mediaeval candidate who publicly defended his thesis. He is brought by the three to the Palace of Fame. Here Skelton turns aside from his narrative to give an elaborate mediaeval set-piece, the description of the palace with its diamonds and jaspers and sapphires. To these splendours come pursuivants from all corners of the world, with tidings like those in Chaucer's house of Rumour:

> With, How doth the north? what tydyngis in the sowth?
> The west is windy, the est is metely wele:

After listening to these rumours, Skelton is presented to Occupacyon, the 'regestary' of Fame. She bids him welcome:

> Welcome to me with all my hole desyre!
> And for my sake spare neyther pen nor ynke;
> Be well assurid I shall aquyte your hyre.

Skelton inserts another digression, introduced naïvely enough by Occupacyon:

> Let vs somwhat fynde
> To pass the tyme with, but let vs wast no wynde.

She leads him into a field where there are a thousand gates inscribed with the names of all nations, and one is described in detail—the gate called Anglia. Beyond the gates he sees a crowd, and re-echoes the 'felde ful of folke'. with the authentic accent of Langland:

> Some fayne themselfe folys, and wolde be callyd wyse,
> Some medelynge spyes, by craft to grope thy mynde,
> Some dysdanous dawcokkis that all men dispyse,
> Fals flaterers that fawne thé, and kurris of kynde.

The vision of knaves disappears and the scene mysteriously changes to a garden like the garden of the Rose. Apollo sings to Flora and the Muses while:

> Dryades there daunsid vpon that goodly soil.

A more personal interlude follows. Skelton has a question

to ask of Occupacyon. She anticipates him. He wishes to know
the name of his poetic opponent. After a few lines of cryptic
Latin attacking this 'vatis adversarius,' the name 'Rogerus
Statham' is given in code.[10] The interlude was doubtless directed
against one of the other guests—probably a relative of Mistress
Geretrude Statham, to whom a complimentary lyric is addressed
some lines later. It illustrates well the occasional quality of
the whole poem.

Occupacyon and the poet now mount 'by a wyndyng stayre' to
the chamber of the Countess of Surrey, who announces to her
ladies:

> A cronell of lawrell with verduris light and darke
> I haue deuysed for Skelton, my clerke.

As the ladies busy themselves with the embroidery of the laurel
chaplet, Occupacyon addresses Skelton:

> Beholde and se in your aduertysement
> How theis ladys and gentylwomen all
> For your pleasure do there endeuourment,
> And for your sake how fast to warke they fall:
> To your remembrance wherefore ye must call
> In goodly wordes pleasauntly comprysid,
> That for them some goodly conseyt be deuysid.

The poet takes up his pen and pays compliment to the Countess
of Surrey, and to each of the group of ladies that make up the
house party, in a set of graceful lyrics which are not equalled in
English again till the publication of *Tottel's Miscellany*. Their
fresh Elizabethan quality is in vivid contrast with the mediaeval
monochrome of their background.

Wearing his new chaplet of laurel, the poet is brought before
the Queen of Fame. All marvel at its beauty. The Queen 'gaue
on me a glum,' and demands Skelton to justify his position. The
poet calls on Occupacyon to read the list of his books to establish
himself as a poet. Here follows an important, if scarcely poetic,
section of the *Garlande,* the list of the works of Skelton. In a
vainglorious spirit—far different from that in which Chaucer
had drawn up a similar list in his 'retracciouns'—he establishes
the canon of his works, many of which are known only as names

10. The code was first worked out by Henry Bradley in *Two Puzzles in Skelton. The
Academy*, Aug. 1896 (1265), p. 83.

in *The Garlande of Laurell,* and, perhaps less intentionally, he lets drop biographical hints that are of the utmost importance in reconstructing his career.

When the list is finally read out, Skelton is acclaimed by all the 'oratoris and poetis':

A thowsande thowsande, I trow, to my dome,
Triumpha, triumpha! they cryid all aboute;
Of trumpettis and clariouns the noyse went to Rome;
The starry heuyn, me thought, shoke with the showte:
The grownde gronid and tremblid, the noyse was so stowte;
The Quene of Fame commaundid shett fast the boke;
And therwith sodenly out of my dreme I woke.

The poem closes with a *Lenuoy* and a dedication.

The allegorical conventions do not sit too happily on Skelton. The best part of the *Garlande* is the group of lyrics where he openly abandons this model. His audience demanded a poem in the old tradition, and all the elements that made up the old tradition are reproduced with an air of elaborate patience. Here are all the set pieces of the allegory, but the machinery that operates them has grown a little rusty. The vision of the Field and of the Garden of Apollo are introduced abruptly and dismissed without apology. Even the language of the poem is so consciously aureate that its out-moded dignity and elaboration must have possessed a charm for the original audience. Skelton had the manner of the poem imposed on him, but he was not imposed on by his material. He had been writing too much vital verse in the previous few years to believe that there was a future for allegory.

The mediaevalism of Skelton was a very partial affair. The two elegies, and the skull poem, and some of his formal hymns— these are perhaps his only pieces of pure mediaeval verse. Generally, when he wrote in the forms of the passing age, the idiom of his own generation breaks through. *Phillip Sparow* is a mediaeval Mass of the Birds, with long catalogues of authorities and tributes to the Romances, *Elynour Rummyng* is mediaeval in its attack on women, and *Magnyfycence* uses the morality form. Yet all of these works are unmistakably Renaissance in their handling and inspiration. Skelton has sometimes been regarded as one of the last of the mediaeval English poets. The older spelling of his English alone gives his work a superficial air of archaism that will not be found in *Tottel's Miscellany,* only some thirty years later. The archaism is mainly in appearance. Lydgate and Occleve belong to Chaucer's world, and even Hawes is sincere in his use of old-fashioned verse. Skelton belongs to his own changing age; the marks of the transition are everywhere apparent in his verse. There is less community of feeling than perhaps Skelton himself realized between Chaucer, Lydgate and Gower—the poets' 'collage' of *The Garlande of Laurell*—and their cocksure protégé at the court of Fame. It is in Skelton, rather than in Wyatt and Surrey, that one discovers the beginnings of the English Renaissance.

2. *The New Age*

The poets of the reign of Henry VIII fall naturally into an older and a younger group. Between them lies the barrier of Italy. Barclay, Hawes and Skelton were untouched by the Italian Renaissance, the mainspring of the poetry of Wyatt and Surrey. Yet when Skelton is contrasted with his contemporaries, their work appears old-fashioned and conventional. The explanation is not that Skelton felt the influence of Italy. He quotes scraps of German, French, Latin and Greek, but Italian never. He had been abroad in France, but he had not joined the growing number of Englishmen who completed their education with an Italian journey. In *The Garlande of Laurell* he mentions Boccaccio, Poggio and Petrarch as if they had never written a word except in Latin. The *De Casibus* he may have read; it is almost certain he was unfamiliar with the *Rime,* although Petrarch's work was to be the overwhelming influence in English in the coming few years. What claim, then, has he to be considered a Renaissance poet?

To Skelton's contemporaries he was ahead of his time and his poetry was sometimes uncomfortably unorthodox. To the poets of *Tottel's Miscellany* the memory of the old poet laureate was rapidly becoming a legend, commemorating the *Merie Tales* of a poet now old-fashioned; by the time of Spenser and of the later Elizabethans, the poetry of Skelton had fallen into oblivion. Yet had the Elizabethans scanned his work, they would have found there many of their own usages in practice and something of their own doctrine already formulated. The ferment of the Renaissance affected Skelton, as it affected Wyatt and Surrey and their successors. Though he had none of their sense of exaltation in the glory of an opening era, and probably never fully realized that he was on its threshhold, his poetry is touched with Renaissance freedom. His liberation from set forms, his innovations in satire and in the lyric, his attitude to social problems and his conception of the function of a poet are all characteristics of the early Renaissance in England..

His conception of the poet's place in society is that of Sidney in the *Apologie for Poetrie*. Like Sidney, he refutes the 'platonic-puritan' attack of his own day on poetry. The second part of the *Replycacion*, written almost sixty years before Sidney's *Apologie* contains a defence of poetry strikingly parallel to that of the later critic. Poetry to both Skelton and Sidney was one of the highest functions of the brain of man. The poet may aspire to any subject, affirms Skelton against his critics:

> Ye say that poetry
> Maye nat flye so hye
> In theology,
> Nor analogy,
> Nor philology,
> Nor philosophy . . .

This is exactly the charge to which Sidney replies. To him poetry was greater than all the other branches of learning: 'Now therein of all sciences I speake still of humane (and according to the humane conceit) is our *Poet* the *Monarch*.'

Poetry occupies such a high position because it is by its very nature something divine. Sidney's second argument for poetry is its divinity—the Romans called the poet *vates,* which is both poet and seer: 'So heavenly a title did that excellent people bestowe upon this hart-ravishing knowledge.' Skelton claims the same inspiration, not the classic-mediaeval inspiration from the Muses, but the Platonic Renaissance conception of divine energy:

> There is a spirituall,
> And a mysteriall,

And a mysticall
Effecte· energiall,
As Greekes do it call,
Of suche an industry,
And suche a pregnancy,
Of heuenly inspyracion
In laureate creacyon . . .
God maketh his habytacion
In poetes whiche excelles,
And soiourns with them and dwelles . . .
We are kyndled in suche facyon
With hete of the Holy Gost,
Which is God of myghtes most,
That he our penne doth lede,
And maketh in vs suche spede,
That forthwith we must nede
With penne and ynke procede.

To both Sidney and Skelton the type of the divine poet is David
the Psalmist. To Sidney he is the *Vates*: 'And may I not
presume a little farther, to shewe the reasonablenesse of this word
Vatis, and say that the holy *David's* Psalms are a divine Poeme?
. . . Lastly and principally, his handling his prophecie, which is
meerly Poeticall.' Skelton justifies all flights of poetry by the
same example:

Kyng David the prophete, of prophetes principall,
Of poetes chefe poete . . .
Than, if this noble kyng
Thus can harp and syng
With his harp of prophecy
And spirituall poetry . . .
Why haue ye than disdayne
At poetes, and complayne
Howe poetes do but fayne?

These last three lines are a remarkable anticipation of yet one
more of Sidney's defences. As a further charge made against
poetry, Sidney quotes the puritan-platonist complaint 'that it
is the mother of lyes.' His defence rests ultimately on the
Aristotelian theory that poetry deals with the ideal rather than
with the factual. Such a defence was beyond the reach of Skelton.
Yet to the ethical protests, 'Howe poetes do but fayne,' he responds
with ethical defences, and shows that he was thoroughly aware of
the implications of this moral criticism. Mediaeval ethics accepted

poetry only so far as it supported Christian doctrine, and both Skelton and Sidney are striving for a recognition of the poet as an artist alone. Both men had to make concessions to gain this freedôm—they both claim that poetry *is* beneficial to religion and the state. The assurance is but a sop to a moral Cerberus. Their recognition of the essential—that poetry cannot be bound hand and foot to ethics—shows that they are both moving, the one haltingly, the other triumphantly, along the path to the new freedom of the spirit. There is nothing remarkable in this attitude in Sidney. But that Skelton in 1528 should in his last poem approach so closely to the Renaissance thought of the late sixteenth century is a miracle of insight. Half a century of English criticism was to follow before the publication of the *Apologie*—Wilson, Ascham, Gascoigne, Puttenham and Webbe all struggling towards the *Aufklärung*. Here in Skelton lay the kernel of the new aesthetic.

One of the points in which Skelton agrees most closely with the Renaissance poets is in his vigorous use and defence of the English vernacular. The mediaeval school regarded English as a vulgar tongue, incomparable with Latin as a medium for poetry. Even in Skelton's own day, this was the normal attitude among educationists and poets. Hawes, in *The Pastime of Pleasure*, apologises for his rude and barbaric English and regrets that he does not write in Latin; if English must be written, the style should be 'eloquent':

> So that elocucyon doth ryght well claryfy
> The dulcet speche frome the langage rude
> Tellynge the tale in termes eloquent.
> The barbary tongue it doth ferre exclude
> Electynge wordes whiche are expedyent
> In latin or in englysshe after the entent,
> Encensynge out of the aromatyke fume
> Our langage rude to exyle and consume.[11]

Indeed, as late as 1544, Ascham is to be found apologizing for English in the preface to *Toxophilus*: 'Although to have written this boke either in Latin or Greke . . . had been more easier and fit for mi trade in study . . .'

As the Renaissance spread from Italy to France and then to England, the poets of all three countries rose to the defence of the

11. *Pastime of Pleasure*, ll. 917 ff.

vernaculars. In Italy the defence that had begun with Dante was continued by Bembo and clearly enunciated in the *Dialogo delle Lingue* by Speroni. In France the poets of the Pleïade formulated the same principle in the famous *La Deffense et Illustration de la Langue Françoyse* of du Bellay (1549). The vernacular movement was to have its finest expression in the poetry of Spenser, who had first been taught respect for the English tongue by his schoolmaster, Richard Mulcaster. Mulcaster's *Elementarie* (1582) struck a decisive blow for English against the pleas of the classicists, and Skelton's conception of English is that of the later schoolmaster. Mulcaster's work was written almost at the same time as the *Apologie for Poetrie*; it is illuminating to see how Skelton once more anticipates by some fifty years doctrines considered inseparable from the Renaissance.

In *Phillip Sparow,* his first poem in the 'new style,' he is still apologetic:

My style as yet direct
With Englysh wordes elect.
Our naturall tong is rude
And hard to be enneude
With pullysshed termes lusty;
Our language is so rusty,
So cankered, and so full
Of frowardes, and so dull,
That if I wolde apply
To wryte ornatly,
I wot not where to fynd
Termes to serue my mynd.

He proceeds with some acute criticism of the language of Gower, Chaucer and Lydgate. Gower's English is too archaic, Lydgate's is too diffuse:

It is dyffuse to fynde
The sentence of his mynde.

Chaucer, on the other hand, wrote English simply and clearly:

His termes were not darke,
But pleasaunt, easy, and playne.

This was written about 1508. Skelton echoes the apologetic tone of Barclay, but there is nothing in Skelton of Hawes' championship of Latin. His clear appreciation of Chaucer's superiority is evidence of his accurate valuation of the vernacular. A few years sufficed to show him that he was on the right path. *The Garlande*

of Laurell of 1523 concludes with a defence of the English tongue
against Latin. The tone is now no longer apologetic but openly
defiant:

> Go, litill quaire,
> Demene you faire;
> Take no dispare,
> That I you wrate
> After this rate
> In Englysshe letter;
> So moche the better
> Welcome shall ye
> To sum men be:
> For Latin warkis
> Be good for clerkis;
> Yet now and then
> Sum Latin men
> May happely loke
> Vpon your boke,
> And so procede
> In you to rede,
> That so indede
> Your fame may sprede
> In length and brede.

This downright defence is exactly that of Mulcaster:

> I do write in my naturall English tongue, because though I make
> the learned my judges, which understand Latin, yet I mean good to
> the unlearned, which understand but English . . . He that under-
> stands no Latin can understand English, and he that understands
> Latin very well, can understand English farre better, if he will
> confess the truth.[12]

In spite of his old-fashioned classical training, Skelton grasped
more clearly than anyone else of his generation the superiority of
English over Latin. His defence was no mere empty utterance.
He handled English with the verve and vitality of one enjoying
the use of a living language. Had he lived in the more doctrinaire
times of the later sixteenth century, these brief notes might have
been expanded into a preface which would not have appeared out
of date among the poetic manifestoes of the period.

Perhaps one reason for Skelton's support of the vernacular was
his appreciation of the changing social order. The rise of the
middle class that characterized the transition from the fifteenth
to the sixteenth century is nowhere more apparent than in his

12. Mulcaster: *Positions*, 1581, ed. Quick, p. 2.

verse. Skelton in his most typical moods is a popular poet. In spite of his court position and his many copies of formal verses, he is the mouthpiece neither of the court nor of the nobles. He wrote for the public ear, not learned poetry like *The Pastime of Pleasure,* but popular pieces—savage public satire like *Colin Clout,* coarse bawdry like *Elynour Rummyng,* and invective against the Scots, whom the people hated and feared. He expresses the sentiments of the commons because he had lived among them, sharing in their life and feelings, and listening to their complaints:

> Thus I, Colyn Cloute,
> As I go aboute,
> And wandrynge as I walke,
> I here the people talke.

Much of *Colin Clout* is an appeal from the unprivileged classes: 'Men say,' 'the communalte dothe reporte,' 'howe the commons grones,' 'the people iangle'—these are typical phrases from the poem. The old order of the nobility comes in for severe criticism:

> But noble men borne
> To lerne they haue scorne,
> But hunt and blowe an horne,
> Lepe ouer lakes and dykes,
> Set nothyng by polytykes.

Here, then, is another Renaissance trait. Skelton is fully aware of the changing social structure. With a certain glib facility he could unashamedly write court poetry by request, complete with the full complement of mediaeval allusions for noble audiences, and perhaps with more sincerity than most poets of his time. But in his parish of Diss and on his rides through England, he had seen situations that deepened the note of passion in his satirical verse. Everywhere the commons were critical of the state of society; they found a ready ally in the pen of Skelton. If the old order was changing, Skelton was to be on the side of the new; his vigorous, unpretending style has in it much of the spirit of this critical and not yet cultured bourgeoisie. His appreciation of the age of social change expressed itself in the types of poetry he wrote. No longer is poetry to be the entertainment of a small cultured class. Just as he supported English against Latin, so he developed popular poetry at the expense of the learned and the recondite. Poetry must leave the calm of the cloister and the pageantry of the court, and come out into the everyday world to learn the ways of men. The scope of poetry must be widened to include politics, national affairs, corruption in the church, revelry at the ale-house. Nothing could be too high or too low. This sense of the universality of poetry is something that had been lacking in English since the death of Chaucer.

When one adds to these factors his genuine, though cautious, humanistic leanings, and his originality both in satire and in lyric, it cannot be doubted that he felt the power of the Renaissance. His Humanism will be considered later. His originality is every- where apparent. The direct attack in his satire is new. His breathless verse-form is new. His lyric has often the candour and passion of the Elizabethans:

> For I haue grauyd her wythin the secret wall
> Of my trew hart, to loue her best of all!

Lines like these anticipate some of the best work of the later Renaissance.

Middle Ages and Renaissance jostle each other uneasily in the poetry of Skelton. They seldom mingle and they never combine. In the days of the Elizabethans a balance was to be achieved between the older and still valuable aristocratic culture and the new rude vigour of the citizen class. Elizabethan drama could assimilate the best of both; Skelton came too early for such a balance to be possible. He alternates violently from one manner to the other, fully cognizant only of their differences, most of his sympathy on the side of the new. His significance at this period of English literary history is that he was the first poet to catch the transitional spirit of his times and express the aspirations of a new society. It is this consciousness of the new age that distinguishes him from the other poets of his time and brings him occasionally so close to the poets of the later Renaissance. Yet neither his fellow-poets nor his successors realized his real importance. Each school regarded him as infected with the heresies of the other. So, condemned both as rebel and as reactionary, he fell rapidly into neglect. By the end of the century, when new Italian modes captured the ears of English poets and critics, few remembered that Skelton had been an innovator, and no one realized that his poetry had been the opening of the early Renaissance.

CHAPTER IV

WOMAN AND THE LYRIC

THE ATTITUDE OF LITERATURE TOWARDS WOMEN CAN SOMETIMES be a useful criterion of a civilization. Between the type of mind that conceived the Wife of Bath, the 'Wedo,' the Good Women, the figure of Joan Beaufort, or the ideal subject of *The Garment of Good Ladies* and the creator of Rosalind and of Lady Macbeth, there lies a gulf that can be explained only by the change of a whole mode of thought. It is difficult to believe that the private relationships of men and women have differed very greatly in any age. In their accepted public attitudes towards women, Middle Ages and Renaissance differed profoundly. Skelton has left so many poems in which women figure, as subjects both for commendation and for satire, that this group of verses forms a further indication of his strangely indeterminate position between the two ages. The verses vary in type, from the boisterous *Elynour Rummyng* to his personal realistic lyrics, and from the conventionalized praise of *Phillip Sparow* to the graceful compliments of the *Garlande of Laurell* lyrics.

The Middle Ages saw woman only as a sinner or a saint, a monster sent to lead men's minds to hell or a virgin goddess to raise them to heaven. To the mediaeval church everything connected with sex was corrupt, procreation was a sinful necessity legitimate only for laymen, and the ideal life lay in communion with God, implying celibacy for the priesthood and virginity in the convent. Between these extremes there was no official compromise. Marriage was a concession granted to the ordinary man and woman which prevented their ever aspiring to the higher life. This attitude produced two corresponding literary types, the pattern of which only a few exceptional characters like Criseyde evade successfully. Woman in mediaeval lyric and romance is either idealized beyond the reach of humanity or degraded beneath its contempt.

The idealized type was the standard of all courtly love poetry, and the adultery on which the whole tradition rested detracted

70

in no way from the idealization. Hymns to the Virgin and lyrics
to the beloved both use the same ecstatic and exaggerated style,
the hymns borrowing endearments from the love poetry, and the
songs borrowing in return the language of adoration.

> She is the clerness and the verray light
> That in this derke worlde me wynt and ledeth

sings Chaucer of a queen who was but his patroness.

> My swete moder, my par amour

so the infant Christ addresses the Virgin in one mediaeval
religious lyric.[1]

At the other end of the scale was the tradition that had grown
out of Juvenal's Sixth Satire and had developed through the
repressions of ascetic churchmen—woman as Mother Eve, the
author of man's downfall, her physical attractions a snare against
which the ingenuous spirit must be ever on its guard.   Even
these physical attractions served only to conceal her depravity.
Mediaeval authors analyze with bitterness what to them was the
inherent lust and ugliness of womankind.   *The Wife of Bath's
Prologue* is based on a succession of such diatribes as the *Epistola
Valerii ad Rufinum de non ducenda uxore* and the *Liber Aureolus
Theophrasti de Nuptiis,* both favourite reading for the mediaeval
misogynist.   From these Latin attacks developed Jean de Meung's
complaints of Le Jaloux in the *Roman de la Rose*:

> Ha! se Theophrastes creüsse,
> Ja fame espousée ne eüsse!
> Il ne tient pas home por sage
> Qui fame prent par mariage,[2]

and the further abuse in Deschamp's *Miroir de Mariage*. Through
Langland, Lydgate and Occleve the tradition of bitter satire on
the depravity of woman continued to the beginning of the
sixteenth century, where, at the very gateway of the Renaissance,
one finds similarly morose attacks in *The Ship of Fools,* in
Dunbar's *Twa Mariit Wemen and the Wedo* and the *Elynour
Rummyng* of Skelton.   It was a tradition that died hard.

Renaissance literature accepted women as women.   Poets like
Spenser and Drayton might idealize them in Petrarchan hyperboles,

1. Chambers and Sidgwick. *Early English Lyrics.* 141.
2. ll. 8975-8.

and satirists like Marston attack them with fury, but Stella and
Delia were on the same human plane as the poets themselves.
The change in attitude was reflected not only in literature. One
of the marks of the Renaissance educationist was his insistence
on the necessity for women's education. Vives developed the
theme in his *De Institutione Feminae Christianae,* while, in a
quieter but more practical manner, Sir Thomas More educated
his daughters to be a match for the scholars of their time, an
achievement that had considerable influence even in his own day.
In such an atmosphere idealization and thoughtless abuse were
equally out of place.

The French lyric of the Middle Ages had varied from the
idealized adultery of the Court of Love poetry to the idealized
debauchery of the pastourelle. These essentially Gallic formulae
less often found a place in the corresponding mediaeval English
lyrics. Yet, beyond a handful of perfect things like *Alysoun,*
the love-song of the English Middle Ages seldom achieved either
depth of insight or personal revelation. These qualities came
easier to the Renaissance poet, who belonged to a society
tolerating and later encouraging the expression of romantic love.
The new attitude towards women gave them greater freedom
and a position of equality with their humble petitioners. The
Renaissance poet could frame his appeal with a passion and a
directness hitherto the exception. Even a complimentary poem
to a lady took on, with its candid appeal, the air of a love poem.
Skelton shows no passages of greater contrast in any of his works
than in the *Garlande* when he commends the Countess of Surrey
in allusive mediaeval rime royal, and then turns to praise the
younger women in the new graceful, direct Renaissance style.
They become real women and not stately patronesses worshipped
from afar.

Phillip Sparow falls into two sections, the first a mock Mass
of the Birds on the death of the sparrow,[3] the second a 'Commendacion' of Philip's mistress, Jane Scroupe. The commendation
is written like the rest of the poem in Skeltonic short lines, which
are divided almost into stanza form by a recurring Latin refrain:

> *Hac claritate gemina*
> *O gloriosa femina*

3. This section is discussed in chapter vii.

followed by lines from the 118th Psalm. Skelton calls on Arethusa
and Apollo, and protests against Envy. He hopes:

> That I may say
> Honour alway
> Of womankynd!
> Trouth doth me bynd
> And loyalte
> Euer to be
> Their true bedell.

The poem then proceeds, with a mediaeval wealth of detail, to tell
of the idealized beauty of Jane:

> Of her features clere
> That hath non erthly pere.

Her grey eyes, her bent brows, the white and red of her cheeks,
'her lyppes soft and mery' are all dwelt on with grave elaboration.
Two stanzas commend 'a warte vpon her cheeke,' which is set
there 'lyke to the radyant star.' She is all flowers at once:

> She is the vyolet,
> The daysy delectable.
> The columbine commendable,
> The ielofer amyable . . .
> This blossom of fresh colour . . .
> She florysheth new and new
> In beaute and vertew.

The poem moves on to commend her 'fyngers small,' her slender
waist, and has a realistic moment that is reminiscent of Suckling:

> But whereto shulde I note
> How often dyd I tote
> Vpon her prety fote?
> It raysed my hert rote
> To se her treade the grounde
> With heles short and rounde.

Formalism descends once more as the poet describes her dress
and her kyrtle. He laments the inadequacy of his praise and the
'Commendacion' closes with the final Latin refrain.

Except for an occasional Cavalier-poet touch, there is little in
the poem beyond the commonplaces of the Middle Ages. The
catalogue of a lady's features may be paralleled in a dozen of
the commoner French Court of Love allegories; the Latin refrain

F

has a religious quality that suggests the hymns to the Virgin, and this impression is heightened by the continual use of lines from the 118th Psalm. Skelton had no personal feeling for the young Jane Scroupe, and the poem is a piece of compliment for her elders' eyes, who were doubtless as content with its seraphic hyperboles as Sir Robert Drury was with the eulogies of *The Second Anniversary*. It is a charming tribute, but of little importance beside the first part of the poem or the more personal lyrics of Skelton.

In sharp contrast with these almost religious 'Commendacions' of a young girl is the lively satire of *Elynour Rummyng*. Both poems are in the same tumbling Skeltonic short line, and it is probable that *Elynour Rummyng* was the immediate successor to *Phillip Sparow,* the earliest poem in this metre. *Phillip Sparow* was written shortly before 1509, when it was mentioned in *The Ship of Fools*. Neither it nor *Elynour Rummyng* has the 'Orator Regius' endorsement, which begins to appear on poems from 1512. *Elynour Rummyng* must therefore belong to c.1509. The contrast between it and *Phillip Sparow* is startling; yet each runs true to its mediaeval type. The hymn-like adoration of the 'Commendacions' is perfectly consistent with the unholy delight in the drunkenness of *Elynour Rummyng*. Both Elynour and Jane were what the Middle Ages had made them, and if Skelton's humorous treatment indicates a sneaking sympathy for the old ale-wife, which he certainly never felt for the red and white school-girl, it is only because he was deserting his mediaeval models for his own observations of real humanity.

The poem opens with a repulsive but humorous description of Elynour:

> A comely gyll
> That dwelt on a hyll . . .
> Her lothely lere
> Is nothynge clere,
> But vgly of chere,
> Droupy and drowsy,
> Scuruy and lowsy,
> Her lewde lyppes twayne,
> They slauer, men sayne.

As if the poem had been a counterblast to the detailed portraits

of the allegory, every feature of Elynour passes under review.
Her nose is crooked, her eyes are bleared, her Lincoln Green is
forty years old.

> She dryueth downe the dewe
> Wyth a payr of heles
> As brode as two wheles.

'But to our tale!' exclaims the poet in the first passus:

> She breweth noppy ale,
> And maketh thereof port sale
> To trauellars, to tynkers,
> To sweters, to swynkers,
> And all good ale drynkers.

This passus describes the ill-conditioned wenches who run to
her brewing:

> Some wenches come vnlased,
> Some huswyues come vnbrased,
> Wyth theyr naked pappes,
> That flyppes and flappes . . .
> A sorte of foule drabbes
> All scuruy with scabbes . . .
> Suche a lewde sorte
> To Elynour resorte
> From tyde to tyde.

The second passus is concerned with the foul brewing of the ale.
Hens run along the mashfat:

> And somtyme she blennes
> The donge of her hennes
> And the ale together;
> And sayeth, Gossyp, come hyther,
> This ale shal be thycker,
> And flowre the more quicker.

The third passus tells of their payments. Some have no money and
bring their hose, their shoes, their husbands' hoods, wedding rings,
spinning wheels, salt, meal, or rabbits—all for a drink of the
wonderful ale. Skelton comments on the drinkers with the
ironical amusement of Chaucer:

> Some go streght thyder,
> Be it slaty or slyder;
> They holde the hye waye,
> They care not what men say . . .
> Some, lothe to be espyde,
> Start in at the backe syde.

In the remainder of the poem Skelton draws a mordant series of sketches of the women drinkers. 'Dronken Ales' is full of the gossip of the London streets:

> There hath ben great war
> Betwene Temple Bar
> And the Crosse in Chepe.

Mad Kit follows, and Margery Mylkeducke with legs

> As fayre and as whyte
> As the fote of a kyte.

Maude Ruggy is so ugly,

> Ones hed wold haue aked
> To se her naked . . .
> All foggy fat she was.

As figure after figure is added to the gallery, the scene grows more and more riotous. Sybbyll drinks:

> With a sory face
> Wheywormed about

and retires sick from the orgy:

> Than began the sporte
> Amonge the dronken sorte,

till the poem closes abruptly:

> My fingers ytche;
> I have wrytten to mytche
> Of this mad mummynge
> Of Elynour Rummynge.

The poet ends with mock solemnity in Latin, inviting all women drunkards and sluts to read his poem:

> Omnes foeminas, quae vel nimis bibulae sunt, vel quae sordida labe squaloris, aut qua spurca foeditatis macula, aut verbosa loquacitate notantur, poeta invitat ad audiendum hunc libellum.

Elynour Rummyng owes much to Langland, whose picture of the ale-house in the sketch of gluttony gave Skelton the form of the poem. There is a similar gallery of drunkards:

> Tymme the tynkere and tweyne of his prentis,
> Hikke the hakeneyman and hughe the nedeler.

There is a similar scene of riot and dissipation:

> There was laughyng and louryng and 'let go the cuppe,'
> And seten so til euensonge and songen vmwhile,
> Tyle glotoun had y-globbed a galoun and a Iille.[4]

Skelton transformed Hikke and Hugh and 'Clement the cobelere' into the drunken sluts of his Flemish canvas, with something of

4. *Piers Plowman*, passus v, ll. 304 ff.

the physical loathing of the earlier anti-woman tracts. There is a certain perverted humour, too, in his enjoyment of deformities that belongs to earlier times. Yet in the brilliance and clarity of his sketches he is ahead of Langland's mere character-labels. Each repulsive figure is individualized in a few strokes of deadly satire. Of all his poems *Elynour Rummyng* was probably the most detrimental to his subsequent reputation. Pope's 'beastly Skelton' is derived almost solely from a judgment of *Elynour Rummyng* that ignored its gusto and vitality.

The remainder of Skelton's verses to women are less dependent on traditional measures. He has a group of lyrics that are purely personal in their inspiration. In his lifetime they were probably regarded as a coherent group, since shortly after his death, five of them were published together in a pamphlet entitled *Diuers Balettys and Dyties*. Brie attempted to mould them into the narrative of an early love-affair, but they do not appear to have been written all to the same lady. That they belong to the earlier part of his career is suggested by their intimate tone and by the dedication of one to Mistress Anne of the Key in Thames Street, which suggests his first London period.

The first, *Womanhood, wanton, ye want,* is for Mistress Anne, and is an indignant protest against the lady:

Why so koy and full of skorne?

The poet repays his rejection with interest:

But one thyng is, that ye be lewde:
Holde youre tong now, all beshrewde!

He closes with the sardonic dedication:

To mastres Anne, that farly swete,
That wonnes at the Key in Temmys Strete.

This was not his only poem to the fair Mistress Anne. *The Garlande of Laurell* mentions at least one other that has been lost:

The vmblis of venyson, the botell of wyne,
To fayre maistres Anne that shuld haue be sent,
He wrate thereof many a praty line,
Where it became, and whether it went.

Similar in spirit to *Womanhood, wanton* is *My Darlyng Dere,* a song of a deluded lover, set to a not unpleasing jog-trot rhythm:

What dremyst thou, drunchard, drousy pate!
Thy lust and lyking from thé gone.

The third of a boisterous trio is made up by *Manerly Margery,
Mylk and Ale,* wherein the lady makes indignant mock protests:

> Be Crist, ye shall not, no hardely;
> I will not be japed bodely:
> Gup, Cristian Clowte, gup, Jake of the vale!
> With, Manerly Margery Mylk and Ale.

Manerly Margery was set to music by William Cornysshe, who
became Henry VIII's Master of the Chapel Royal children. The
music, along with that of Skelton's hymn *Wofully Arayd,* is
preserved in a contemporary volume of settings.

The Auncient Acquaintance is a song to a lady who had deceived
her husband. The poet claims that the ancient acquaintance
between the lady and himself allows him to speak freely:

> Yet so it is that a rumer begynneth for to ryse,
> How in good horsemen ye set your hole delyght,
> And haue forgoten your old trew louyng knyght.

Skelton describes the anger of her husband and counsels her to
be more secret in future and:

> Play fayre play, madame, and loke ye play clene,
> Or ells with gret shame your game wylbe sene.

The two remaining poems are of a more serious cast, and of
more poetic value.

Knowledge, Aquayntance, resort, fauor with grace seems to
be a genuine love poem. It begins with a description of the
effects of love, that

> Deadly wo and payne
> Of thoughtful hertys plungyd in dystres.

He praises the lady's features; she is the star of the evening:

> Radyent Esperus, star of the clowdy nyght,
> Lode star to lyght these louers to theyr porte.

The lyric continues in happy phrases with Elizabethan fervour:

> Remorse haue I of youre most goodlyhod,
> Of youre behauoure curtes and benynge,
> Of your bownte and of youre womanhod
> Which makyth my hart oft to lepe and sprynge,
> And to remember many a praty thynge;
> But absens, alas, with tremblyng fere and drede
> Abashyth me, albeit I haue no nede.
>
> You I assure, absens is my fo,
> My dedely wo, my paynfull heuynes;
> And if ye lyst to know the cause why so
> Open myne hart, behold my mynde expres:

I wold ye could! then shuld ye se, mastres,
How there nys thyng that I couet so fayne
As to enbrace you in myne armes twayne.

Nothyng yerthly to me more desyrous
Than to beholde youre bewteouse countenance:
But hatefull absens, to me so enuyous,
Though thou withdraw me from her by long dystaunce,
Yet shall she neuer oute of remembraunce;
For I haue grauyd her wythin the secret wall
Of my trew hart, to loue her best of all!

There is here such a contrast with the boisterous rhythms of
Manerly Margery and *Womanhood, Wanton* that one must assume
a very different recipient, a nobler lady, less accessible for a
scholar. She is probably the subject of *Go pytyous hart,* which is
subscribed 'At the instance of a noble lady.' In this poem Skelton
bewails the cruelty of fortune, that compels him to conceal
his love:

One ther is, and euer one shalbe,
For whose sake my hart is sore dyseasyd;
For whose loue, welcom dysease to me!
I am content so all partys be pleasyd:
Yet, and God wold, I wold my payne were easyd!
But Fortune enforsyth me so carefully to endure,
That where I loue best I dare not dyscure.

Both these poems are strikingly personal and have a sincerity
that seems to point to some real experience of the poet, perhaps
some ill-concealed passion of his early court days. Their most
surprising quality is their direct statement, their absence of
traditional compliment and of surplusage. In this they correspond
with the later satires of the poet—they have a hard, clean quality
that is in advance of the love-poetry of his age, an anticipation
of the lyrics of the end of the century.

This same disciplined movement may be discovered in several
of *The Garlande of Laurell* lyrics. Here there is no question of
a love affair. The eleven lyrics are simply compliments. Four
are in the rime royal of the *Garlande* itself and continue its
mediaeval manner, comparing each lady with famous Biblical and
classical heroines. The remaining seven are in a variety of metres,
and are mainly stanzaic—the verse to Margery Wentworth is a

variation of the rondeau.   Some of Skelton's most delightful
passages occur in these complimentary poems:

To maystres Jane Blenner-Haiset

What though my penne wax faynt,
And hath smale lust to paint?
Yet shall there no restraynt
Cause me to cese,
Among the prese,
For to encrese
Yowre goodly name . . .

The verses to Isabel Pennell have a particularly fresh charm:

By saynt Mary, my lady,
Your mammy and your dady
Brought forth a godely babi!

The poem continues with echoes from a mediaeval spring song
and anticipates the bird-calls of Nashe and the other Elizabethans:

Sterre of the morow gray,
The blossom on the spray,
The fresshest flowre of May . . .
It were an heuenly helth,
It were an endles welth,
A lyfe for God hymselfe,
To here the nightingale,
Among the byrdes smale,
Warbelynge in the vale,
Dug, dug,
Iug, iug,
Good yere and good luk,
With chuk, chuk, chuk, chuk!

The compliment to Isabell Knyght is courteous and graver:

But if I sholde aquyte your kyndness,
Els saye ye myght
That in me were grete blyndnes,
I for to be so myndles,
And cowde not wryght
Of Isabell Knyght.
It is not my custome nor my gyse
To leue behynde
Her that is bothe womanly and wyse . . .

This direct approach, which he has transferred from satire to
lyric, he keeps quite distinct from the more involved mediaeval
manner of the first four pieces. The old court-poet's verses have
not the passion of later lyrists—he was now over sixty years of

age—but they are touched with their sincerity and grace. Something of the incisiveness of his public utterances finds its way into the compact phrases of his lyric.

More important is their anticipation of things to come. Skelton's lyrics are scattered throughout his work, and both that dispersion and their scantiness make it easy to miss their total effect. They have all the discipline of metre, the athletic phraseology, the spring-like freshness and occasionally the insight of the Renaissance lyric. Only the best lines of Wyatt and Surrey are superior to

> Her that is bothe womanly and wise.
>
> Sterre of the morow gray.
>
> Thoughtful hertes plungyd in dystress.
>
> I haue grauyd her wythin the secret wall
> Of my trew hart, to loue her best of all!

Skelton can use the English vernacular with a better sense of its accent than Wyatt, who often fumbles a line like:

> With his hardiness takes displeasure.

Compared with such a line (and there are many such in Wyatt) Skelton's metre marches with military precision. Yet, in spite of his anticipation of the later lyrists, it does not appear that he had any influence on their verses. Lyric for Skelton was a side-line, and in the later Renaissance it was forgotten that he had written even one.

His poems on woman have a wide range of expression, both mediaeval and new-fashioned, and they form a considerable section of his work. Yet she was not for him, as she could be for the Elizabethan sonneteers, a subject of real importance. He never completely grew away from the mediaeval attitudes of adoration and contempt, never really trusted the Renaissance literary humanizing of woman. The expression of passionate love lay for ever beyond him. He was married 'in the eyes of God,' and, it can be believed, married happily, but his marriage produced no poetry.[5] In these poems on woman he is not always a mediaeval poet, but he never ceases to be a mediaeval thinker. One has to realize that behind all his early Renaissance characteristics lie traditions, some of which he never dreamt of questioning.

5. But Koelbing claims as Skelton's some verses 'On the Parting from his Wife,' first printed by Gray Birch in the *Athenaeum,* 29 Nov. 1873.

CHAPTER V

SKELTON AND THE HUMANISTS

1. *The Springs of English Humanism*

THERE ARE CERTAIN WIDELY USED TERMS LIKE ROMANCE AND beauty that call for a periodical re-definition. With changes of period and of nationality, the meaning of Humanism has similarly altered, and even the fifteenth century, which enunciated its fundamental principles, cannot offer, any more than can the present day, a concise definition of that great movement. Before tracing Skelton's relations with the Humanist movement it is as well to realize the complexity of the conception, and the alterations which it underwent even in the lifetime of the poet.

Humanism was the product of the Italian Renaissance. The individualistic instinct of the Quattrocento turned to the classics and Italy re-discovered a literature that gratified both her artistic instinct and her sense of patriotism. The Church was not so enthusiastic. Pagan morality and pagan poetry were too closely linked in the pages of Ovid and Martial, and even a messianic eclogue did not make Virgil a complete Christian. In spite of the Church's disapproval the early Italian humanists eagerly studied the classics and found there a nobler latinity, a finer poetry and an educational ideal that they strove to put into practice. Early humanist teachers like Vittorino da Feltre, who founded a school in Mantua under the patronage of the Gonzagas, and Guarino da Verona, head of a similar school in Ferrara, reconciled their interest in classical antiquity with their Catholic doctrine, and the latter particularly had a great influence on the earliest English followers of the movement.

For these teachers Humanism was the beginning of a new era. Barbarism at last was at an end after the darkness of the Middle Ages. Scholastic philosophy was to give way to individual inquiry, and mediaeval prolixity to classical conciseness. They could not realize that in a few decades Humanism was to develop along several divergent lines and have results that even the most far-seeing could not have prophesied. In Italy it abandoned Christianity. In Germany it split Christianity into two irreconcilable divisions. In England, after toying for a few years with Ciceronianism and mere stylistic exercises, it settled down to apply humanist education to the needs of daily life; this practical form in turn fell under the influence of the now transformed Humanism from Germany to lend a ready support to the Protestant Reformation; till in the end English Humanism, hardened in its arteries and somewhat stiffened in its joints, passed from Protestantism to Puritanism and looked askance at the Italy from which the whole movement had sprung.

The transitions from the earliest variety of Humanism to the further stages were natural enough. While many of the finest Italian scholars remained within the Church, the attraction towards freedom of thought was irresistible, and the study of the classics developed in Italy a secondary semi-pagan Humanism. Italian writers, conscious that they were heirs in the direct line to the Roman heritage, found it easy to adopt with classical poetry classical philosophical systems, which could be Christianized to any required degree or left almost transparently pagan. Neo-Platonism flourished under such humanists as Politian, Ficino, and Pico della Mirandola, and the Platonic Academy of Florence, founded in 1438 under Cosimo di Medici and reaching its peak under his brilliant grandson Lorenzo at the end of the century, opened men's eyes to a world of philosophic thought beyond the authority of the Schoolmen. Though the Academy itself strove to reconcile antiquity with Christian dogma, it was a reawakening that led in many cases to scepticism.

Humanist influence grew every day. Lorenzo di Medici gathered round him an erudite circle of scholars and poets. Leo x patronized the new group and won his reward in elegies and orations. The state required her scholars, for diplomacy still demanded elegant Latin correspondence and resounding public orations. Yet in spite of this high position, by the middle of the sixteenth century the humanists in Italy were in disgrace, openly charged with self-conceit, with profligacy and with irreligion. It is true that they remained within the Church, and an open declaration of atheism was for economic reasons unusual. But an age that read Machiaevelli's *Il Principe* with approbation pursued their enquiries undeterred by mere Christian scruples, and Burckhardt[1] records several sharp passages between church authorities and humanists who had too openly declared for rationalism.   Piero Valeriano, writing in 1527 and inspired no doubt by the imperialist sack of Rome, gives in his *De literatorum Infelicitate* a gloomy picture of the miseries of a scholar's life, where but a few years previously the status of the humanist had been unchallenged.   The tide of their popularity receded, but their influence was deep and lasting, both in Italy and in the wider civilization of Europe.

In Germany the situation was radically different.   The transition to classical modes of thought was easy for a nation like Italy that had never really ceased to regard Latin as a native tongue. Germany in the fifteenth century was still mediaeval, and universities like that of Cologne were strongholds of scholastic philosophy and education.   Beyond Christianity Italy could look back to a civilization older still, the complex organization of the Roman Empire, in which the bolder and more enquiring spirits of the Italian Renaissance saw an age akin to their own.   Germany looked beyond Christianity and saw only barbarity.   Her cultural roots seemed to strike no deeper.   The old Teutonic gods and early Germanic poetry represented pre-Christian darkness, whereas Virgil had remained continuously familiar and Iupiter Optimus Maximus guarded in extant temples a mythical golden age. The new creed was more difficult for the Teutonic peoples, and in its transition from Italy it lost much of its literary tone and gained a greater depth of moral significance.   Rudolph Agricola (d. 1485), whom all the German followers claimed as their forerunner, is typical of the early days of Humanism in Germany. Born in Holland and educated successively at Groningen, Erfurt, Louvain and Cologne (the study of whose scholastic philosophy he always regretted), he spent some years in the Ferrara circle, returning in 1479 with a command of Ciceronian Latin and—what was then far more uncommon—of Greek.   Already he was a humanist with a difference.   Studies in Hebrew and Divinity and religious verse reveal the transalpine bias towards a Christian outlook even in humanist exercises.   Principles came before

1. *Die Cultur der Renaissance in Italien*, trans. S. C. Middlemore, II, VI, iii.

mere knowledge. Such a view is already far removed from the Humanism of Italy, and it is only a step to the writings of the greatest German humanists, Melanchthon and Ulrich von Hutten and Erasmus himself.

Side by side with the growth of a moralistic outlook developed an impatience with the older scholastic philosophy and a revolt against the intolerant theology, the mediaeval logic and the monasticism that accompanied Scholasticism, and the ignorance that all too often it concealed. The younger German scholars rose in open warfare and despised even the degrees of the universities, till the University of Cologne was driven to expel humanist reformers from her class-rooms. The feud came to a crisis when one of the younger humanists, Reuchlin, whose interest in Hebrew literature had been stimulated by Pico della Mirandola, defended the Talmud against the attacks of Johan Pfefferkorn, a Jew who was strongly supported by the Theological Faculty of the University of Cologne. Reuchlin was attacked by the Dominicans and the case was carried to Rome, where in the end Reuchlin lost, in spite of a majority verdict for him. The controversy became the common battlefield in the fight of Humanism against Scholasticism, and all Europe was involved. The English humanists—More, Fisher, Linacre, Grocyn, Colet, Latimer, Tunstall—rallied to the side of Reuchlin. The formal victory appeared to be with the older scholars, till the publication in 1516 of the famous *Epistolae Obscurorum Virorum* reversed the position and changed their victory into a rout.

In these epistles the 'obscure men'—the scholastic philosophers of Cologne and of every other university in Europe—are parodied in a series of letters supposedly addressed to Ortwin Gratius, don of the University of Cologne. The *Epistolae Obscurorum Virorum* had a European success. More wrote enthusiastically of their brilliance to Erasmus, and not even the official disapproval of the Church could kill their popularity. They clinched the victory for Humanism. In the letters the scholastic theologians are held up to ridicule, with their ignorance of Greek and their complaints against scholars *'non graduates.'* A passage from Ovid is expounded in four different ways—*'Scilicet naturaliter, litteraliter, historialiter, et spiritualiter; quod non sciunt isti poetae'*[2]—a parody of the allegorical expositions of Scriptures and the classics. The obscure men solemnly discuss whether the chicken in the egg is flesh and so forbidden on Friday.[3] They complain of Virgil and Pliny in atrocious Latin (*'noves auctores'*!) and of the humanists' *'novum Latinum.'*[4] One of the obscure men writes:

Et isti humanistae nunc vexant me cum suo novo latino, et annihilant illos veteres libros, Alexandrum Remigium, Ioannem de Garlandia, Cornutum, Composita verborum, Epistolae magistri Pauli Niavis,[5]

enumerating one by one the text-books of mediaeval latinity, which the advanced humanists had brushed aside with impatience. The *Epistolae Obscurorum Virorum* raised laughter over all Europe, and the victory for the reformers was complete, though the Universities of Paris and Cologne and Louvain did not realize their defeat for many years—by which time the tide of European thought had passed them by. The work is a valuable criterion for distinguishing one of the varieties of Humanism—the patriotic and scholarly German type that rejected mediaeval pedantry.

For the moment one must leave German Humanism to prepare itself for the Reformation and turn back over half a century to the beginnings in England. The movement attracted at first men whose interests were more in the formal aspects than in the intellectual and spiritual. Of the first important figure, Humphrey, Duke of Gloucester (d. 1447), it is not unfair to say that he came on Humanism by accident, without realizing the influence his activities would have on English scholarship. A patron and a book buyer rather than a scholar, he corresponded with Italian students and was familiar with the work of Guarino. His love of learning was genuine, and his example gave an impetus to the purchase and presentation of Latin and Greek volumes at a time when they were particularly necessary. His patronage and interest in the rising culture was continued under such men as Thomas Beknyton (d. 1465), Bishop of Bath

2. *Epistolae Obscurorum Virorum*, ed. Stokes, 1, 28.
3. ibid. 1, 26.   4. ibid. 1, 46.   5. ibid. 1, 7.

and Wells, Thomas Chaundlers (d. 1490), Chancellor of the University of Oxford and an early promoter of Greek studies, and John Whethamstede (d. 1465), Abbot of St. Albans and a donor of books to Glastonbury College, Oxford.[6]

The direction once given, the development of Humanism was accelerated, and in the second half of the fifteenth century the gathering of printed books and manuscript volumes and the journey to Italy to study with Guarino or other teachers became the method by which humanist ideas were carried towards England. This newer period of study and research was essentially an affair of the individual. The Universities of Oxford and Cambridge, though never such strongholds of Scholasticism as those of Cologne, Louvain, and the Sorbonne, were still untouched by the newer learning, and their official recognition of the teaching of Greek, the knowledge of which was becoming almost synonymous with Humanism itself, did not come till half a century later. England was still far behind, but the keener students turned instinctively southwards.

The newer group were students who found in Italy a spiritual homeland. Most of them were pupils of Guarino—Tiptoft, Grey, Free, Gunthorp and Flemming all owe their learned ideals to the Ferrara teacher. Yet just because their interest was that of the individual student, these men had less influence than the later English humanists, and their names are obscure beside those of Colet and More and Latimer. John Tiptoft (d. 1470) was friendly with Italian humanists and presented gifts of books to Oxford; his translations from Cicero won the praises of the industrious Leland. William Grey (d. 1478) returned from Italy with about six hundred books and manuscripts which he presented, as Duke Humphrey had done before him, to Balliol College. John Free (d. 1465) made translations, and on his Italian journey studied not only Latin and Greek but Hebrew and science and medicine, and on his return he kept up his friendship with Guarino by correspondence. The succession was carried on by John Gunthrop (d. 1498), whose career presented the now standard features of study under Guarino and the gift

6. For detailed studies of these early scholars cf. W. Schirmer, *Die Englische Früh-humanismus.* Leipzig, 1931. R. Weiss, *Humanism in England during the Fifteenth Century.* Oxford, 1941.

of a library to the two English universities, and Robert Flemming, who produced a volume of Latin poems including a short epic for Sixtus IV.

The whole group dissipated their learning in mere latinist exercises—elegant letters to Guarino and poems such as those of Flemming—with the result that their eventual influence was not so great as that of Duke Humphrey. Though for them the major interest in the Renaissance was that of language and style, and though they had no direct influence on the universities, they gave English education direction, and they established Italy as the point from which all the newer ideals of the sixteenth century were to spring.

In England a newer Humanism was at hand. That of the early Renaissance in Selling, Linacre, Grocyn, Latimer, More, Tunstall, Colet and Wolsey had little use for mere exercises. Humanist latinity was for them only a means to an end, and the subject was of more importance than the manner; to the ambitious Wolsey a humanist education was the *sine qua non* for a life of action. William Selling (d. 1494) studied in Italy and introduced Greek to his monastery at Canterbury, linking his Humanism with practical educational ideals. The literary studies of Thomas Linacre (d. 1524) were merely an adjunct to the practice of medicine—he published the pioneer edition of Galen. William Grocyn (d. 1519) lectured on Greek at Oxford and at London and numbered young Thomas More among his pupils. Grocyn's bias was towards Biblical criticism, where again the native feature of later English humanists is evident, the urge towards action.

The development was not yet at an end, and before the story of English Humanism is complete one must turn once again to Germany. There Humanism had found from the beginning an ethical and national note of its own, and this, allied to the anti-scholasticism so apparent in the *Epistolae Obscurorum Virorum,* soon divorced German Humanism from the Humanism of Italy and sometimes even from Humanism itself. This is not the place for a history of the Reformation. The new movement can be seen from afar in the early German humanists. The opposition to the scholastic philosophy and theology in the

Epistolae Obscurorum Virorum, the insistence on German nationality against the influence of a 'supercilious' Italian culture, the transalpine ethical bias and the spirit of independence of the Renaissance itself all combined to widen a breach that Luther was to render irrevocably open. Beatus Rhenanus praises Erasmus as the equal of Cicero; Ulrich von Hutten and Johann Reuchlin both pride themselves on being Germans as well as humanists. When in the end the Reformation came it is clear that in Germany Humanism had become inextricably entangled with religion—and with a completely new religion. In Germany, and later in England, Reformation and Humanism seemed to have joined hands for ever against the Catholic Church. The later German humanists like Melanchthon at Wittenberg and Zwingli at Zürich were responsible for the remodelling of German education on lines that combined the ideals of the new age—at once Germanic, humanist and Protestant—where classical teaching and evangelical doctrine ran together to found a recognizably national education. So the movement, which in Italy had developed into irreligion, ended in Germany as Protestant-Humanism.

Not all the German humanists were Protestant. Erasmus, the greatest of them all, like most of the English humanists up till the very moment of the Reformation, based his Humanism upon Catholic theology. He is the nearest of all the continental scholars to the English humanists, and his relations with them were intimate and cordial. He first came to England at the invitation of Lord Mountjoy in 1499, soon becoming friendly with the Grocyn-Linacre circle, and subsequently was a periodical visitor to England. For some years he lectured in Greek at Cambridge. In many ways Erasmus, Germanic though he is, is typical not of German Humanism but of the practical and less theological Humanism of England.

By the turn of the century Humanism had been established as the strongest force in the intellectual life of England. The Venetian printer, Aldus Minutius, in his introduction to a translation of Linacre's, praised Britain as its real centre—so rapid had been the development in the previous half century. It produced its own system of education under the guidance

G

of almost every great humanist of the early sixteenth century. Colet, Erasmus and Richard Croke—to mention only a few of them—all lectured on humanist subjects; Wolsey founded his school at Ipswich and his Cardinal's College at Oxford; Colet founded St. Paul's School; Linacre helped to found the Royal College of Physicians. Erasmus produced his translation of the New Testament, the *Novum Instrumentum,* in the year that saw the publication of *Utopia,* in which More pictured the ideal state governed and disciplined by humanists. In England the movement was producing tangible results. When the Reformation did come to England, these results were too firmly established to be altered in character as they had been in Germany. The Reformation combined easily with the now established English Humanism and achieved a balance in such men as Spenser that remained stable until the Puritans rejected many of its purely intellectual and cultural aspects. In the early years of the sixteenth century humanism as it was exemplified in men of such diverse character and accomplishments as More, Colet, Linacre and Erasmus was one of the finest elements of the English Renaissance.

Humanism was not a rigid doctrine, even in any one country. There were irreconcilable differences in the Humanism of Vittorino da Feltre, of Melanchthon, and of Sir Thomas More, though all three recognized no prouder title than that of humanist. It was a variable quality that might be combined with any degree of scepticism, Catholicism, Protestantism, even Puritanism, and still remain nominally Humanism. Yet, in spite of the diversity of beliefs among its followers there remain common factors transcending all their mutual differences which bring one as close as is possible to a definition of the movement.

The great common element was the renewed interest in the classics. The fall of Constantinople let loose on Europe a flood of Greek manuscripts and teachers of Greek, and men saw in the authors of Greece and Rome at once a model and an inspiration. Prelates of the Church like Warham set out in their old age to learn Greek, and men bought 'brown Greek manuscripts' and accumulated volumes with an almost religious reverence. Side by side with the interest in antiquity grew up a desire for choice latinity. Humanists wrote to each other in elegant Ciceronianisms, and only the wiser of them saw the danger to their native vernaculars. Perhaps one of the healthiest features of the English movement was the comparative disregard of Latin elegance and the tenacious hold on the native tongue.

The return to the classics implied a denial of the thought and education of the Middle Ages. The *Parva Logicalica* of Petrus Hispanus, the *Doctrinale* of Alexander, and similar text-books of mediaeval learning acquired the same disreputable reputation among the advanced humanists as university degrees. One of the obscure men quotes a humanist lecturer with indignation: One poet, this scholar had said, was worth ten Masters of Arts, and the Masters were not masters of the Seven Liberal Arts but of the Seven Deadly Sins, and knew nothing of the *Parva Logicalica!* This violent reaction had not been a characteristic of the older Italian students like Vittorino; the more level-headed English scholars, like Richard Croke, recognized the value of the older studies. Even in their darkest hour the English universities never incurred the contempt that fell upon Cologne; English scholars lectured gladly at Oxford and Cambridge, and Skelton prided himself on his university degrees.

2. *Skelton and the Humanists*

The question of Skelton's relationship with this movement has been discussed in several studies and the results have been widely divergent. There has been a tendency to set him too rigidly on one side or the other, critics either praising him as a humanist for his knowledge of the classics, or condemning him as a mediaeval scholar for the lapses in that knowledge. Several accept him as a humanist without question;[7] another writer sees in him an anti-humanist and proclaims 'that the humanists disliked Skelton might almost be posited *a priori*';[8] another argues for his being a purely mediaeval poet and scholar;[9] while a later writer suggests a *via media* by making Skelton a late product of the continental Renaissance.[10] Critics have clearly had difficulty in assessing his real position.

7. All the German writers on Skelton—Thümmel, Bischoffberger, Brie, and Koelbing.
8. J. M. Berdan, *Early Tudor Poetry*, p. 218.
9. R. L. Dunbabin, *M.L.R.*, 12, 129ff., 257ff.   10. L. J. Lloyd, *M.L.R.*, 24, 446.

These discrepancies are largely due to the absence of any attempt to differentiate between the varieties of Humanism in the early Renaissance period. The position of Skelton is interesting. He had no contacts that can be discovered with the fully developed Humanism of More or Colet, but he has distinct affinities with the older school, the pupils of Guarino of the previous century. The downright denials of Skelton's Humanism come from placing him in too sharp contrast with his contemporaries. It has not always been realized that in some respects Skelton lagged a couple of generations behind his times. Humanism had roughly three levels in English, the patrons like Humphrey, the student-researchers like Free and Tiptoft, and the more recognizable humanists of the early sixteenth century. Skelton has many features in common with the middle group.

One must guard against the temptation to think of Humanism with boundaries rigidly definable and to deny the title of humanist where some of the standard beliefs or accomplishments are absent. There were not a few men of the early Renaissance who could in honesty be only partially humanist, when the vogue of Humanism cut across their major loyalties to state or religion. Skelton could sympathize with humanist education—he had been tutor to a humanist king—and yet recognize valuable elements of discipline in the older schooling; he could write humanist poems and yet be afraid of the disruptive tendencies of the new doctrine; he could regret the passing of the Middle Ages at the very moment he was writing verse instinct with the spirit of the Renaissance. At a time when the state of society and the fundamental beliefs of the age are in process of irrevocable alteration, there is some excuse for being cautious and even for being a little blind. One cannot condemn Skelton off-hand because he did not grasp all the implications of Humanism, and accepted it only partially. Some of its implications he saw more clearly than many of his contemporaries and fought fiercely and often stridently against a movement that was to alter for ever the religion of the country.

One result of the revived interest in the classics was the re-awakened enthusiasm for education. One and all the humanists read Quintilian and several in the early sixteenth century wrote treatises of their own on the educational ideals of the day. A list of some of these reveals that the educational interest was not confined to one country. Erasmus, a Dutchman, wrote the *De Civilitate Morum Puerilium*; Guillaume Budé, the French scholar, *L'Institution du Prince*; Vives, a Spaniard and a visiting lecturer to Oxford, wrote the *De Tradendis Disciplinis* on the decay of learning and was with More a supporter of women's education; the German Melanchthon has much of his educational theory in his *De Miseriis Paedagogorum*; and the series was rounded off by an Italian and an Englishman— Castiglione with his *Il Cortegiano* (1528) and Elyot with the fine Tudor idealism of *The Governour* (1531). Skelton's treatise for Prince Henry (and possibly Prince Arthur), the *Speculum Principis,* is rather earlier than any of these, and it has all too little of their humanist inspiration.

This rediscovered *Speculum Principis* is one of his most disappointing works. The title was so suggestive of a humanist treatise on the education of a prince that several writers have treated it as such in a consideration of his work. The manuscript of this piece, after disappearing from Lincoln Cathedral Library, has lain till recently unnoticed in the British Museum.[11] Any expectation that it would be a Renaissance 'Courtesy Book' has been proved to be unfounded. The *Speculum Principis* is Renaissance only in name. Skelton mentions it in *The Garlande of Laurell*:

> A tratyse he deuisid and browght it to pas,
> Callid Speculum Principis, to bere in his honde,
> Therin to rede, and to vnderstande
> All the demeanour of princely astate.

This claim is an overestimate of both the scope and the value of the *Speculum*.

After a dedication, the treatise outlines (with authorities quoted and docketed in the mediaeval manner) the virtues of a prince. Honour is preferable to the force of arms; Scipio's authority is cited for princes *'nobilitate litterarum bene praediti.'* Horace supports the same view. Listen to Aristotle's advice to Alexander; be patient. Above all, the prince requires virtue and knowledge.

11. B.M. Add 26, 787. Printed by F. M. Salter in *Speculum*, 1934, pp. 25ff.

Avoid riches, which are snares. After quoting from the second Psalm, the treatise laments that few princes have kept the path of virtue; let our princes take these as warnings and not as examples. *Non vt principis nostri occasionem emulandi; verum deuitandi capiant instrumentum.* The examples are then quoted of Zedekiah, Pilate and Manasses, and the treatise briefly outlines the life of Saul and adds a commendation of virtue, honesty, knowledge, learning and discipline. But the prince may object and point to his illustrious family history. Skelton excuses himself by citing Lucilius and Juvenal's *Difficile est satiram non scribere.* In spite of noble family, exile may overtake the prince; after a riming list of its horrors the poet announces that everything must suffer change—*cuncta sub sole sunt mutabilia.*

Now lest the treatise become too long and tedious for a prince to read, Skelton gives a list of riming precepts—surely a strange collection of warnings. Avoid gluttony; be temperate; avoid fornication and the deflowering of virgins; do not be afraid of marriage; love your wife; do not be ungrateful; listen to the other side of an argument. The list continues with more counsel—to avoid anger, to preserve faith, deliberate long and speak little, to honour doctors and consult philosophers and revere theologians; especially to love poets. Be humble, pious and gentle. Learn of misery from the lives of Caesar, Pompey and Alexander. Read books, histories and annals, and commit them to memory. The treatise closes with the date in astronomical terms and the note:

> Per Britonum vatem Skeltonida Laureatum. Apud Eltham,
> 28 Augusti, anno gracie, MCCCCCI.

This is far nearer Occleve than Castiglione; the tone is that of the *Regiment of Princes* rather than that of *Il Cortegiano.* On this treatise Skelton can put forward no claim to Humanism. There is nothing here but a bundle of moral tags and a few citations from mediaeval authorities like Juvenal and the Vulgate. One must look elsewhere for evidence of Skelton's contact with the humanists.

Writers who argue against Skelton's Humanism stress the silence of the records. Why, they demand, should he not be mentioned by the other humanists? One of them, William Lily,

indeed wrote an epigram against him. Even the praise by
Erasmus in the Dedication to his Ode *De Laudibus Britanniae,*
where Skelton is *literarum lumen ac decus* has been taken to
represent merely praise of Prince Henry that conceals actual
ignorance of the poet's work.[12] This argument is difficult to
maintain in the light of fresh evidence. The Lily epigram has
already been shown to be part of a schoolmaster's battle of
invective and not a serious charge against Skelton.[13] The praise
by Erasmus gains in value because of the recent discovery that an
ode to Skelton, which Dyce had assigned to Pico, was actually
written by Erasmus. It is true that in 1499, when Erasmus first
visited England and when he probably composed the ode, he was
not the public figure he was later to become on the publication
of the *Adagia*; but the testimony of Erasmus must be counted, and
even when allowance is made for Erasmus' skill in rhetorical
flattery, the poem is still a solid tribute to Skelton.[14] From the
title, *Carmen Extemporale,* it would appear that Erasmus and
Skelton had met, and from the references to Skelton as the Homer
and Virgil of Britain it is equally certain that it is Skelton's
poetry that Erasmus praises. Even if the praise is exaggerated it
is sufficient to disprove such assertions as 'that the humanists
disliked Skelton might almost be posited *a priori.*'[15]

If Skelton could be considered an admirable poet by a humanist
in 1499, the question must immediately arise, 'What did he know
of Greek?' By 1500 a knowledge of Greek was the first tenet
in the humanist credo. Skelton's point of view is curious. Some
Greek he knew. There are scraps of Greek in *Speke Parrot* and
occasional Greek phrases elsewhere throughout his poems. *'Calon,
agaton, cum areta,'* in the *Countess of Derby* elegy and a Latin
gloss like that in the *Replycacion, 'Energia Graece, Latine efficax
operatio,'* reveal some knowledge of Greek vocabulary. It is
probable that his acquaintance with Greek was never more than
slight. He did not receive the new language with the typical
enthusiasm of the humanists. When the older scholars in Oxford
banded themselves as 'Trojans' against the 'Greeks' and open

12. R. L. Dunbabin, *M.L.R.,* loc. cit.   13. cf. chapter II.
14. cf. chapter II, and I. A. Gordon, *New Light on Skelton, T.L.S.,* 1934, p. 636, and
subsequent correspondence.
15. J. M. Berdan, loc. cit.

warfare broke out between the two parties, Skelton wrote in *Speke Parrot*:

> In Academia Parrot dare no problem kepe:
> For *Graeci fari* so occupyeth the chayre
> That *Latinum fari* may fall to rest and slepe.

In another part of the poem he makes his position clear:

> Let Parrot, I pray you, haue lyberte to prate,
> For *aurea lingua Graeca* ought to be magnyfyed,
> Yf it were cond perfytely, and after the rate,
> As *lingua Latina,* in scole matter occupyed;
> But our Grekis theyr Greke so well haue applyed,
> That they cannot say in Greke, rydynge by the way,
> How, hosteler, fetche my hors a botell of hay!

Later in the poem he complains that small children can say 'Aveto in Graeco' who cannot run through their Latin conjugations. Skelton's point of view is easy to appreciate. He saw the end of the old learning, and noted with dismay the spread of Greek among young students before they had obtained a really working knowledge of Latin, which was still the international language of the learned world. He had no objection to Greek itself—if it were 'cond perfytely'—but the 'Grekis' against whom he rails could handle neither Greek nor Latin.

There is perhaps another reason for his stand against the too easy introduction of Greek. *Speke Parrot* is an attack on the policy of Wolsey, educational, political and diplomatic, and Wolsey was an ardent supporter of Greek, the founder of the Oxford lectureship. Nothing more was necessary to make Greek suspect in the eyes of Skelton. By the date of *Speke Parrot* anything associated with the Cardinal had a bitter flavour; perhaps in these lines his natural conservatism makes him view Greek with a caution that was only too eagerly accentuated by his hatred of Cardinal Wolsey.

Yet these quotations from *Speke Parrot* reveal an enthusiasm for education. He regrets the passing of the old scholastic education:

> Tryuyals and quatryuals so sore now appayre.

In an attack on Wolsey he sneers at his ignorance of these scholastic studies:

> But a poore maister of arte
> God wot, had lytell parte
> Of the quatryuals
> Nor yet of tryuials.

These passages show a mind profoundly concerned with the disappearance of these two divisions of mediaeval education—the Trivium of grammar, rhetoric and dialectic, and the Quadrivium of music, arithmetic, geometry and astronomy—before the advance of the new humanist studies, as an older-fashioned educationist to-day might complain of the decline of classical education and the advance of science. Skelton was not alone. The older Italian humanists had a great respect for mediaeval education; and Richard Croke, who was appointed Reader in Greek at Cambridge, delivered his inaugural oration in July 1519— some two years before Skelton wrote *Speke Parrot*—and in the very middle of an enthusiastic support of Greek, asserting its superiority over Latin, he puts forward as one of its greatest claims its utility in the study of the trivium and the quadrivium, which in spite of the contempt of many is of great educational value: 'He passes on to show the utility of the study [of Greek] . . . to commence with the trivium and quadrivium—which many "inflated with a vain pretence of knowledge" cavil at as trivial and sterile.'[16] If a humanist lecturer in Greek at Cambridge can find so much good in the mediaeval curriculum, Skelton may be allowed something more than mere obscurantism in his support of the culture under which he had been brought up.

This speech of Croke's brings into higher relief an essential difference between English and German humanists. Croke was in the very centre of the circle that produced the *Epistolae Obscurorum Virorum,* and an intimate friend of Hutten, one of its main authors. Yet although in the *Epistolae* he is mentioned several times as if he were a humanist exactly on the plane of Hutten, from his Cambridge oration it is clear that he sympathized with the German humanists in their attitude neither to mediaeval education nor to university degrees. In this he falls exactly in line with Skelton, who consistently lauds the trivium and quad-

16. J. B. Mullinger, *The University of Cambridge,* 1, 532, where the whole address is summarized.

rivium and takes a never-failing pride in his university degrees. The English humanist was at all times a more cautious and less disruptive personality than the humanist of Germany, and was more inclined to retain useful mediaeval elements that the continental scholar rejected impatiently as old-fashioned.

Skelton's classical reading has been on occasion held suspect, but his early translation of Cicero's Letters and of Poggio's version of Diodorus Siculus suggests a familiarity with the classics more than could be gathered from mediaeval collections of quotations. One cannot measure the extent of his knowledge simply by counting the number of times he mentions Latin authors. He has seventeen references to Virgil and only four to Cicero.[17] One writer has attempted to show that his classical reading was exclusively mediaeval.[18] A glance at the reading of an early humanist school invalidates this argument. The classical authors he does mention with commendation are not particularly mediaeval and could be found in any of the earlier humanist schools in Italy. The procession of famous authors in *The Garlande* contains the following classical names: Quintilian, Theocritus, Hesiod, Homer, Cicero, Sallust, Lucan, Persius, Virgil, Juvenal, Livy, Aulus Gellius, Horace, Terence, Plautus, Boethius, Maximinianus, Quintus Curtius, Macrobius, Plutarch, Propertius and Valerius Maximus. Elsewhere in his works he refers to Pliny, Ovid, Martial, Claudian, Statius, Plato, Catullus and Seneca. Even if he had not read them all—and the Greeks he must have read only in translation—the list is impressive. It is illuminating to compare the list with an average list of school books read in the first century of humanist education. These included the following: Phaedrus, Valerius Maximus, Virgil, Cicero's Letters, and the Catiline speeches, Ovid, Lucan, Sallust, Statius, Seneca, Claudian, Horace, Terence and Plautus for general education and poetry; Justin, Quintus Curtius, Florus, the Latin version of Arrian, Plutarch, Caesar, Sallust and Livy for history; Cicero, Quintilian, and the Church Fathers for oratory; Cicero, Seneca, Plato, Aristotle, Boethius and Augustine for philosophy.[19] These two lists reveal little discrepancy. Three-

---

17. cf. H. J. Lloyd, loc. cit.　　　　18. R. L. Dunbabin, loc. cit.
19. From W. H. Woodward, *Vittorino da Feltre and other Humanist Educators.* 179. 'A Review of the educational aims and methods of the first century of Humanism.'

quarters of the humanist authors occur in the Skelton list; the remainder were already known to the Middle Ages. There is nothing in the list of classical authors known to Skelton that suggests a mind exclusively mediaeval; the reading of Skelton and the reading of a pupil of Vittorino or Guarino were remarkably alike; the only real difference was Skelton's less enthusiastic interest in Greek. The coincidence of the two lists, and the absence from both of authors like Tacitus and Lucretius, who were familiar to the later humanists, support the suggestion[20] that Skelton's sympathies lay not with the humanists of his day but with the earlier humanists of the continent, whose break with the older scholarship was seldom abrupt or impatient.

That he had sympathies with *some* form of Humanism is undeniable. He uses the term 'humanity' frequently in the sense of culture and learning. To him it is something new. In *Speke Parrot* he talks of

Retoricyons and oratours *in fresh humanyte,*

and asks for the support of their suffrages. In his attack on Wolsey he complains of his lack of scholarship:

His Latyne tonge doth hobbyll,
He doth but cloute and cobbil
In Tullis faculte
Called *Humanyte.*

What Skelton thought of 'Tullis faculte' is clear from a few lines in *Phillip Sparow*:

Wolde God myne homely style
Were pullysshed with the fyle
Of Cicero's eloquence.

To Skelton, then, 'Humanyte' and Cicero's eloquence were something closely akin, as they had been for the Italian and the earlier English humanist. 'Humanyte' was for him a term of commendation, and it seems reasonable to argue that Skelton credited himself with the virtue and was in his own eyes a humanist. Ciceronian eloquence, however, was not regarded by the later English humanists as the chief or even as an essential part of Humanism, and Skelton's conservative leanings

20. cf. H. J. Lloyd, loc. cit.

towards an older and by this time out-of-date conception may go a long way towards explaining the apparent absence of relations between Skelton and the later English humanists. What Humanism he aspired to was in his own day quite old-fashioned.

Other arguments have been advanced against his claim to Humanism, notably that of religion. He was a conservative in religion, and this has been used to strengthen the argument for his mediaeval scholarship.[21] An argument from a man's religion in these years of the early Renaissance can prove nothing whatsoever concerning his scholarship. It has already been shown that the religious and the educational issues were distinct. Humanism could embrace any doctrine from orthodoxy to paganism. In the *Replycacion* Skelton attacked scholars who were humanists; he attacked them not as scholars but as heretics, objecting to their Protestantism and not to their Humanism. For Skelton, as for Erasmus and More, Reformation and Renaissance did not form one indissoluble whole.

Skelton is between two ages, and a genuine love of learning like that of the older continental humanists struggles with only partial success against a distrust of the newer philosophies and the religious difficulties they involved. On the one side is his classical reading, differing little from that of the pupils of Guarino; the testimony of Erasmus; his retention—in company with the more conservative English and Italian humanists—of the older 'solid' education; his confessed admiration for 'humanyte.' On the other is his blindness to Italy and perhaps his lack of enthusiasm for Greek. Cutting across these lines and confusing the issue are his private hatreds, of Wolsey, of Lily, of Lutherans, of all desecrators of the Church. As he grew older his prejudices hardened and his hatreds grew fiercer, till it becomes increasingly difficult in the criss-cross of 'humanyte' and mediaevalism to form a clear conception of where Skelton stood. Faced with the question of whether he was a humanist, he might be tempted to reply that he had always loved 'fresh Humanyte.' Presented with a curriculum from the school at Ferrara, he would have given it his complete approval, with the caution that so much Greek must not interfere with the pupils'

21. R. L. Dunbabin, loc. cit.

groundwork in grammar and rhetoric. But when he thought of his arch-enemy Wolsey endowing a college for the new learning and founding a chair of Greek, of Bilney misled by the Protestant-Humanism from Germany, he would have forgotten all the attractions of the new study and damned it outright. There, too, lies the danger for the modern critic of Skelton—one cannot be any more certain of his attitudes than he was himself. Humanism is not a tag which can be tied to one group of scholars and denied to another. It was a developing doctrine of surprising latitude. Skelton stands with one foot over its boundary.

In Skelton's own day his Humanism was old-fashioned. In a few years the progress of learning had passed him by. The humanist pattern became that of More, and even the memory of the early English student humanists was forgotten, till recent research revived an interest in their wanderings and aspirations. As Humanism gradually combined with Protestantism to become English Puritanism the reputation of Skelton waned. He had chosen the by-path in the belief that it was the highroad, but the main traffic of English culture had already taken a different route, and Skelton was left alone in his blind alley.

Chapter VI

THE FAITHFUL SON

Skelton's position in the humanistic world is undefined and even indefinable. He could claim a fair allegiance to the older school of humanists without compromising himself too far with the younger. But the second great movement of the Renaissance shifted Skelton never an inch from his orthodoxy. Towards the Reformation he showed nothing but repugnance, and towards the reformers nothing but implacable hatred. Yet a first glance at his poetry reveals what appears to be the influence of the new doctrines. His attacks on church and churchmen are often as bitter as those on persons and nations that he genuinely hated. Cardinal Wolsey, the prelates of the church, the nuns, the mendicant orders, the parish priest, all come in for their share of bludgeonings as hearty as any he dealt to the early supporters of Luther; but one must guard against the temptation to assign his attacks on the church to even unconscious sympathy with the reformed religion. To Skelton there was the difference of a whole mode of thought between mere reform and Reformation. To the end he was a faithful son of the mother church, critical of her servants and of many of the ways into which they had fallen, but never swerving for a moment from the central tenets of his faith and ready to use his poetic powers to defend her from the attacks of her critics.

When Skelton died in 1529 the Reformation was established in Germany, but in England the course of events had not yet advanced far enough to give official and royal sanction to the English Reformation, and reformers in England were represented by individuals who had found spiritual sanction for their breach in Luther's Wittenberg theses rather than by a nation encouraged from above to a political breakaway. Events in Germany, however, though several decades ahead of those in England, foreshadowed the issues and methods of the English Reformation.

Germany had found the temporal claims of the church particularly oppressive. The growing secularization of the clergy made

her more and more reluctant to see her revenues drained southwards to support a papacy that was both corrupt and alien. The
rank and file of the clergy had taken their cue from Rome, and
the literature of the century before the Reformation rings with
complaints against their corruption and their licentiousness. The
burgher of free Nürnberg, the questioning student of Erfurt or
even of scholastic and mediaeval Cologne, and the peasant of
Bohemia might never have visited Rome; but they listened to
dark and often authentic tales of the moral degradation of the
Eternal City, in which serious-minded Northerners found all too
often a complete separation of morality and religion. Nor was it
better at home. The priest had his concubine. The secular clergy
neglected their manifest duty and became fair game for the satire
of Brandt's *Narrenschiff*, Erasmus' *Encomium Moriae*, and dozens
of other attacks on the corrupt clergy of the day.

Devoutness was not entirely dead. It would not be difficult to
find throughout the whole period communities like the Brethren
of the Common Life of Deventer and spiritual clerics like Thomas
à Kempis. Catholic writers have tried to prove that these were
typical and not exceptional. 'It does not suffice,' writes F. M.
Gasquet, 'to speak in general terms of the "corrupt state of the
church".'[1] And this is undoubtedly true. Many of the charges
against the clergy must, in the light of subsequent research, be
considerably modified. But this 'subsequent research' is just
what the European countries of the Reformation period lacked.
It is of only academic importance now that a charge is only half
true if fifteenth century Germany believed it to be wholly so.
Often to-day we know more about the real facts of a historical
event than the average man of the time did. He judged, however,
not on what historical research has subsequently brought to light,
but on what he believed to be true. The Reformation began in
Germany not with men who had access to state papers and papal
archives and the records of Council and Convocation, but with a
people who were hostile to the temporal claims of the Pope and
severely critical of the corrupt state of the clergy.

The younger German humanists had begun not only to ridicule

1. F. M. Gasquet, *The Eve of the Reformation*, p. 392.

the forms of scholastic philosophy but even to enquire into the fundamental tenets of their faith. When the time came Luther found an enthusiastic group of scholars whose opinions marched perfectly in step with his own. A still stronger argument for the Reformation Germany found in her patriotism and her resentment against the interference of an Italian papacy. After the Diet of Worms of 1521, humanist and evangelical peasant stood solidly behind Luther and made the Reformation a national reality.

Such was the state of the church at the beginning of the six-teenth century. All thinking men realized the necessity for reform. But there was a sharp division on the method of reformation, and the religious history of the subsequent century is that of the struggles of the reformers like Luther and of the Catholic reformers, with whom Skelton so ardently sympathized, who looked for reformation from within. A century of counsel-taking, from the Council of Constance of 1414-18 to the Council of Rome of 1512, had producd little real change in the church, and the Catholic Reformation did not come till after the Council of Trent of 1545-64.

The Catholic reformers did not differ greatly from Luther in their attitude to the clergy. They wished to purify the church, reform clerical life, restore in the clergy some of the original church's enthusiasm for the salvation of man's soul. The dogma of the church they preserved intact. The reform they aimed at was as much a tradition as the reformer's rejection of the fundamental doctrines was a novelty. It had been called for generations back by the Wandering Orders—the Franciscans and Dominicans in particular—and by poets as far back as Gower, Langland and Chaucer. But occasionally these two schools of thought overlapped. The position of Erasmus was ambiguous to everyone but himself. He hated Lutheranism and monasticism with equal force, and preserved his faith to the end. Yet his translation of the New Testament, the *Novum Instrumentum* of 1516, was second to Luther's writing in promoting the Reformation, by striking a decisive blow at the infallibility of the Vulgate.

It was in such a critical period that Skelton wrote his poems on the church and her churchmen, and here our Janus looked in one direction only, and that determinedly backwards. It is strange that three men so different as Sir Thomas More, Erasmus, and John Skelton, who represent the Renaissance from angles so different and often so incompatible, should here travel one path so single-mindedly. All three stood for reform, but reform within the church, of her men and mechanism and never of her doctrines. More in his *Utopia* might imply a new faith in science along with an old faith in religion, Erasmus in his *Novum Instrumentum* might claim a more scholarly basis for the text of the Vulgate and in the *Encomium Moriae* might laugh at the follies of monasticism, Skelton in *Colin Clout* might charge the bishops with accusations later the common stock of the Reformation attacks; all three stood firmly for mother church and lived and died in her confession.

The first of Skelton's attacks is of least poetic value, but it expresses significantly his resentment at the licence of the parish priest. Some hunting priest had flown his hawk right into the parish church at Diss, where, while Skelton was celebrating Mass, it desecrated the Host itself. The result is the indignant *Ware the Hauke*. Skelton bursts out into characteristic abuse of 'Dominie Dawcocke,' but the poem goes far deeper than a mere personal attack:

> The pryest that hawkes so
> All grace is farre him fro;

and this although the offender is 'A parson benefyced.' His irreverence shocks the orthodox susceptibilities of Skelton, who gives a vivid description of the commotion—the hawk tearing off the altar cloth and coming to rest

> Upon my corporas face,

the falconers crying out, and the irreverent priest threatening to re-invade the church of Diss not with falcons but with hounds. The whole incident had been hushed up by bribery, and Skelton bitterly complains in the imagery of Langland:

> How be it, mayden Meed
> Made them to be agreed
> And so the Scrybe was feed—

and, turning to the prevailing laxity of church government, he utters a dark warning that shows he was only too aware of the signs of the times:

> Or els is this Goddis law,
> Decrees or decretals

H

Or holy sinodals,
Or els prouincials,
Thus within the wals
Of holy church to deale,
Thus to rynge a peale
With his hawkis bels?
Dowtles such losels
Make the church to be
In smale auctoryte;
A curate in speciall
To snapper and to fall
Into this open cryme;
To loke on this were tyme.

'To loke on this were tyme!' *Ware the Hauke* was probably written in the first decade of the sixteenth century. Later, as Skelton became increasingly alarmed at the menace to the church of the misdeeds of her own servants, he returned to the problem in *Colin Clout* in 1519, by which time Lutheran heresies were beginning to filter into England. But *Colin Clout* is not, as the *Replycacion* was to be, an attack on heresy; it is a solemn and passionate appeal to the prelates to preach to the people and reform the mother church before it is too late. Everywhere the people complain of laxity and corruption. Skelton but repeats their murmurs, those accumulated complaints of generations against the church, which provided a breeding ground for heresies of reform.

Such complaints had a long tradition in both clerical and secular writings. The Wandering Orders and the poets and pamphleteers of the Middle Ages had often enough castigated or satirized the failings of the church. But it would be a mistake to regard *Colin Clout* as simply a continuation of the mediaeval tradition of poetry calling for reform. Koelbing[2] quotes innumerable examples of similar indictments in the poetry before 1400, in the *Roman de la Rose,* in Gower's *Vox Clamantis,* in Chaucer, in *Piers the Plowman's Crede*; further in lesser known works—*God Spede the Plow,*[3] *The Husbandman,*[4] *The Mery Gest how the Plowman learned his Pater Noster,*[5] and the like, in several of which the indictment of the church is cloaked under a pastoral pseudonym.

2. Koelbing, *Zur Charakteristik John Skelton's,* p. 83 ff.
3. Ed. W. W. Skeat. E.E.T.S. 30.
4. Wright, *Political Songs,* p. 149. Rolls Series.   5. Hazlitt, 1, 209.

But the only pastoral element in *Colin Clout* is the name. The poem is thoroughly Renaissance in spirit and form and in method of approach, and cannot be regarded simply as another mediaeval complaint. The questions with which it deals are too much alive and its charges too specific. The problems that had caused grave shakings of learned heads in councils from those of Constance and Basel onwards find passionate expression in Skelton, who here represented the inarticulate complaint of the ordinary people. The ignorance, the arrogance, and the laxity of the prelates are held up to scorn in the language of burning indignation. Yet throughout Skelton is consistently orthodox; like all good churchmen of the day, he leaves dogma severely alone. Doubts were for weaker spirits; for him the faith that never questions.

The fundamental question is the struggle between lay and clergy:

> For the temporalte
> Accuseth the spiritualte;
> The spirituall agayne
> Doth grudge and complayne
> Vpon the temporall men,

and the general charges against the 'spiritualte' are quoted:

> All to haue promocyon
> That is theyr hole deuocyon.

The bishops are no better, caring little what occurs in their sees:

> In theyr prouynciall cure
> They make but lytell sure.

The bishops have become political figures and neglect their original charge of preaching:

> The temporalyte say playne,
> Howe bisshoppes dysdayne
> Sermons for to make
> Or suche laboure to take.

Skelton is afraid to name even the few exceptions. The church has forgotten the lessons of Thomas à Becket:

> Thomas *manum mittat ad fortia*
> *Spernit damna, spernit opprobia,*
> *Nulla Thomam frangit iniuria*
> But now euery spiritual father,
> Men say, they had rather
> Spende moche of theyr share
> Than to be combred with care.

The commons complain of their laxity and luxury—partridge and
pheasant in Lent and at night 'wanton warkes'—and of their
ignorance:

> Theyr lernynge is so small
> Theyr prymes and houres fall
> And lepe out of theyr lyppes
> Lyke sawdust or dry chyppes.

The priests are equally ignorant:

> Alas, for very shame!
> Some can not declyne their name;
> Some can scarsely rede,
> And yet he wyll not drede
> For to kepe a cure.

Simony and corruption hold sway, 'Myters are bought and solde,'
and the bishops sitting softly at home care nothing for the
spiritual welfare of the people.   The breaking up of foundations
has corrupted many a religious house.   The prelates (and especially
Wolsey) should learn humility from the example of Christ.   Skelton
proclaims himself a true follower of the church, but he realizes
that the opposition of the people had a real foundation.

The poem attacks the heretics, who are daily becoming more
common.   Some argue of predestination, some of Christ's incarna-
tion:

> And some haue a smacke
> Of Luther's sacke
> And a brennyng sparke
> Of Luther's warke . . . .
> And some be Hussyans,
> And some be Arryans,
> And some be Pollegians,
> And make moche varyans
> Between the clergye
> And the temporaltye.

The people complain of pluralities and dispensations and

> How prelacy is solde and bought,
> And come vp of nought.

The prelates rule even the king, so arrogant are they—and Wolsey
is hinted at again.   The bishops should preach:

> Ye bisshops of estates
> Shulde open the brode gates
> Of your spirituall charge,

And come forthe at large
Lyke lanternes of lyght
In the peoples syght.

Instead this essential work is done by masters of arts or friars, or by some doctor 'dronken as a mouse.' The friars preach merely for a living. The bishops occupy their time in saying Mass:

They occupye them so
With syngyng *Placebo*
They will no further go,

and do not defend the church against the recent attacks:

Such temporall warre and bate
As nowe is made of late
Agaynst holy Churche estate,

but they merely build fine houses with magnificent decorations.[6] The example of Wolsey is again suggested. Skelton refuses to judge these charges—the people make them and he simply repeats them—and he closes with a commendation of all zealous and devout churchmen:

Of no good bysshop speke I,
Nor good preest I escrye,
Good frere, nor good chanon,
Good nonne, nor good canon,
Good monke, nor good clerke,
Nor yette of no good werke,
But my recountyng is
Of them that do amys,
In speking and rebellyng,
In hynderyng and dysauaylyng
·Holy Churche, our mother,
One agaynst the other;
To vse suche despytyng
Is all my hole wrytyng.

All this is not just Langland redone. The personal tone, the directness of the attack, the specific charges against the upper clergy and the grasp of problems that troubled every thinking man at the beginning of the sixteenth century stamp *Colin Clout* not as a mediaeval complaint over the corruption of the clergy, but as a very live and intensely personal survey of contemporary evils. Whatever Skelton was, he was no trimmer. There is an inflexibility about the quality of his mind that made him often

6. cf. chapter VIII.

enough blind to newer conceptions, but this very stiffness of intellect implied an unusual vigour and an independence bordering sometimes on eccentricity. There is nothing subtle about the poetry of *Colin Clout*. Skelton charges like a rhinoceros. But its intensity gives it form, and the short tumbling lines are controlled by the dominant mood. Satire calls for a well-defined target and palpable hits. Whether the hits are justified or not may be a problem for ethics, but certainly not for poetry. Skelton did not pause to consider. He may never have seen life whole, but what he saw he saw steadily. The vigour of his poetry carries off the satire admirably. What might with less indignation have been a mere succession of short stumping lines became in his hands a fluid and passionate unity. There was nothing like it in the English poetry of his time; better satires have been written since, but none more sincere.

Perhaps its most astonishing feature is its clarity of vision. Skelton saw more clearly than most of his contemporaries where the progress and doubts of the last fifty years would end. The secularization of the church and the growth of speculation could have only one result. More could in his *Utopia* combine doctrines he knew were incompatible in a Renaissance Catholicism, Erasmus could retain his faith while he undermined the whole structure of the mediaeval church. Skelton admitted no such compromise. All who were not with the church, wholly and unquestioningly, were against it. He realized that one must be faithful or go under in the general cataclysm; he calls on the prelates for a renewed assurance of their faith years before the Council of Trent enjoined it in grave assembly.

Colin Clout reveals how Skelton could attack his own Church in exactly the same terms as the reformers, and yet turn on these reformers in still bitterer satire. There is nothing inconsistent in his attitude. Criticism from within the church by a faithful son was always legitimate and in this period it was especially salutary. The identical criticism from without was heresy—it was not meant to reform but to disrupt. Skelton in the *Replycacion* attacked the reformers with truculent savagery.

The *Replycacion* must be dated as late as 1528, and from a very fulsome dedication to Wolsey (which some have dismissed as a fabrication by Skelton's printer[7]) it has been suggested that The *Replycacion* is an attempt to win back Wolsey's lost favour with a poem of unimpeachable orthodoxy.[8] This may be possible, but the *Replycacion* is not a whit more orthodox than *Colin Clout*. The only difference is that in the one poem Skelton attacks the corruptions within the church and in the other he attacks her enemies. His attitude to the church is consistent throughout all his verse, and the Skelton of *Colin Clout* is the same poet as the Skelton of the *Replycacion*.

The main progress of the Reformation in England lies outside Skelton's lifetime. But no sooner had Luther set Germany and then Europe by the ears than his doctrines began to permeate through England, particularly after the publication of his three volumes of 1520, and though the treatises were publicly burnt at St. Paul's Cross on 12 May 1521,[9] and later at Oxford and Cambridge, these condemnations only accentuated the spread of Lutheran doctrines. A group of Cambridge scholars were converted to the reformed doctrines and held discreet meetings under the presidency of Robert Barnes at the White Horse Inn, which rapidly became known as 'Germany.'[10] Many who later became famous as reformers—Robert Barnes, Hugh Latimer, Thomas Bilney, Thomas Arthur—belonged to the confederacy. The authorities became panicky. Barnes was summoned before the bishops, condemned and imprisoned until he ultimately escaped to Germany. Wolsey discovered that his own Cardinal's College at Oxford had become a Lutheran centre and strong measures were taken both there and at Cambridge. Towards the end of 1527 Bilney and Arthur were summoned before the Chapter at Westminster on a charge of heresy. But for the moment their courage failed. Arthur recanted; Bilney recanted twice; and on Sunday, the 8th of December, the Feast of the Conception, they carried their faggot of repentance at St. Paul's Cross, and for the moment the authorities breathed freely again. It is to these events that Skelton refers in the *Replycacion*.[11]

7. cf. Brie, *Skelton Studien*.   8. Se Boyar, *M.L.N.*, Dec. 1913.
9. *Letters and Papers*, III, 485.
10. cf. J. B. Mullinger, *History of the University of Cambridge*, I, 572-3.
11. He may even have been present at their trial. Edwards (*P.M.L.A.*, 1938, p. 610) notes that a Master Skelton was a witness in 1528 to the abjuration of a heretic, Thomas Bowgas, in London.

The poem begins with a few lines of sympathy with the University of Cambridge, which has had to suffer these *degeneres filioli,* and Skelton summarizes his argument in highly decorative and (though Lily was not yet born) Euphuistic prose:

How yong scholars nowe a dayes embolned with the flyblowen blast of the moche vayne glorious pipplyng wynde, whan they haue delectably lycked a lytell of the lycorous electuary of lusty lernyng, in the moche studious scholehous of scrupulous Philology, countyng them selfe clerkes excellently enformed and transcendingly sped in moche high connyng, and whan they haue superciliusly caught

> A lytell ragge of rethorike,
> A lesse lumpe of logyke,
> A pece or a patche of philosophy,
> Than forthwith by and by
> They tumble so in theology,
> Drowned in dregs of diuinite,
> That they iuge them selfe able to be
> Doctours of the chayre in the Uyntre
> At the Thre Cranes . . .

The young men have not yet completed their studies and yet they dared to proclaim:

Howe that it was idolatry to offre to ymages of our blessed lady, or to pray and go on pylgrimages, or to make oblacions to any ymages in churches or els where.

Against such heresies, and especially the belittlement of the Virgin, Skelton is indignant:

> Wotte ye what ye sayed
> Of Mary, mother and mayed?
> With baudrie at her ye brayed;
> With baudy words vnmete . . . .

But for such heresies they were openly shamed at St. Paul's:

> Ye were fayne to beare fagottes;
> At the feast of her concepcion . . . .
> Ye are brought to, lo, lo, lo!
> Se where the heretykes go,
> Wytlesse wandring to and fro!

It would have been better if their mouths had been stopped before they could utter:

> Your sysmaticate sawes
> Agaynst Goddes lawes.

Skelton then remembers that some of these heretics even hold exhibitions at the university, the church was paying for such heretics.

> Some of you had ten pounde,
> Therewith for to founde
> At the unyversite,
> Employed whiche myght have be
> Moche better other wayes.

For they have strayed into various heresies of Jovinian, of Wycliffe, and of Luther:

> Ye soored ouer hye,
> In the ierarchy
> Of Iouenians heresy,
> Your names to magnifie
> Among the scabbed skyes
> Of Wycliffes flesshe flyes;
> Ye strynged so Luthers lute,
> That ye dawns all in a sute
> The heretikes ragged ray,
> That bringes you out of the way
> Of holy churches lay.

These heretics are doing great damage among the people, among whom the taint of Lollardy lingered, the renegade scholars have taught 'Lollardy learning' and have glossed the Scriptures to their own ends:

> Ye cobble and ye clout
> Holy Scripture so about,
> That people are in great doubt
> And fear leest they be out
> Of all good Christen order.

Better had they never been learned and remained devout! They are well checked by mother church, who will never countenance priests of such temper:

> Raylyng in your rages
> To worshyppe none ymages,
> Nor do pilgrymages.

The fathers of the church would never have tolerated such heresies:

> Saint Gregorie and saynt Ambrose
> You haue reed them, I suppose,
> Saint Jerome and saynt Austen,

and Skelton closes with the hint that unless they repent they may find themselves 'brent at a stake.'

Skelton's attitude to the Cambridge reformers is uncompromising. He was ready to accept the judgment of Westminster as the judgment of the whole church and beyond her judgment he refused to trespass. The poem is a natural development from *Colin Clout*. The scourge of the prelates has become the scourge of the heretics, and throughout both poems there persists the same savage delight in defending the church against all corrupters within and without. The second part of the *Replycacion* is a defence of poetry against the typical Renaissance and Puritan attacks—the uselessness of poetry and the 'lies' that poets tell. Skelton claims the inspiration of the poet, and it is clear that he had a clear conception of the function of poetry, poetry often justified, as *Colin Clout* and the *Replycacion* had been, by a moral purpose. To the mature Skelton such verse was of greater value, both artistically and ethically, than the allegorizings and mediaevalism of his own early verse and of much of his contemporaries. Skelton was throughout his career a religious poet. But the thought of his age did not lead to personal religion. To Skelton religion was an institution. In the days when that institution was threatened, he used all his powers to support the religion he knew and trusted.

From such strict orthodoxy and such unquestioning faith one cannot hope for a personal revelation. The religious lyrics of Skelton are what might be expected from a priest of his outlook, orthodox, impersonal, and rather old-fashioned. Their style is the style of the early fifteenth century rather than that of the beginning of the sixteenth, and this has led Brie to query their authenticity.[12] Doubts on authorship are always disturbing for the critic, and they must be answered before any further consideration can be given to the religious poems; they are a bare half dozen lyrics and the question is fairly easy to dispose of.

The religious lyrics of Skelton are found in three groups: 1. *Wofully Arayd* in two B.M. manuscripts, Fairfax 5465, and Harleian 4012, and on the fly-leaf of an old copy of Boethius (cf.

12. *Skelton Studien,* pp. 25 ff.

Dyce I, 141.). Only the Boethius version ascribes the poem to Skelton. 2. *Vexilla Regis Prodeunt* appears in Kele's *Christmas Carolles* (no date) with no name attached. 3. The remaining four—*Of Tyme,* and a trilogy of hymns, *Prayer to the Father of Heaven, To the Seconde Person,* and *To the Holy Gooste,* appear first in three small and almost identical octavo volumes with the title *Hereafter foloweth certayne bokes cōpyled by mayster Skelton, Poet Laureat, whose names here after shall appere.* A list of contents (all of fairly long poems like *Elynour Rummyng*) follows on the title page, but the four hymns are not mentioned in the list of contents, though they are printed in the subsequent text. This edition appears without a date in three versions with slight variations under the imprints of John Day, of Richard Lant, and of John Kynge and Thomas Marshe. The hymns later appear both in the text and in the list of contents in Thomas Marshe's collected edition of 1568. Dyce printed all six as Skelton's largely on the evidence of a verse in the *Garlande of Laurell,* where Skelton lists his religious lyrics:

> With, Wofully arayd, and shamefully betrayd;
> Of his makyng deuoute meditacyons;
> *Vexilla regis* he deuysid to be displayd;
> With *Sacris solemniis,* and other contemplacyouns,
> That in them comprised consideracyons;
> Thus passyth he the tyme both nyght and day,
> Sumtyme with sadness, sumtyme with play;

Brie argues that *Wofully Arayd* is attributed to Skelton in one manuscript only out of three; that one of them (Harleian 4012) is in a hand possibly belonging to 1475-1500; that the poem did not appear in Marshe's collected edition; and that the style is too early for Skelton. He suggests that Skelton's *Wofully Arayd* is lost, but was probably *based* on this extant version. The latter argument surely assumes more than Dyce himself did. There are perhaps grounds for querying the authorship, but they seem no stronger for denial than for ascription. The date 1475-1500 covers the period of Skelton's mediaeval verse, and is an argument for, rather than against, his authorship. The argument from style counts for nothing. We should have doubted any religious lyric of Skelton written in a style *other* than old-fashioned.

But Brie's arguments are weaker on the other poems. *Vexilla Regis* he simply denies: A *Vexilla Regis* by Lydgate exists; the style is that of *Wofully Arayd*. This is arguing from weakness to weakness. And the reason for the denial to Skelton of the four hymns is weaker still—that they do not appear on the title page of the first three editions is the sole argument adduced. But neither do the *Chorus de Dis contra Scottos* nor the *Chorus de Dis . . . . contra Gallos,* which are yet printed, like the four hymns, in the text, and which no one has denied to Skelton. All six poems are short and the non-appearance of their names on the title page of a diminutive octavo is easily explained. There was simply no room for them. The title page measures only about 3·5″ × 5·5″; the title is long and displayed over seven lines of black letter; the larger poems mentioned occupy another seven lines; there is a wood-cut above and below the type and one at each side, in the edition of King and Marshe in the B.M. The editions of Day and Lant have in addition the printer's device. Where on the page could a sixteenth century printer with his large black letter crowd *six* more titles—all of smaller poems?[13] The argument from the non-appearance in the title page takes no account of the limitations of early sixteenth century printing and is of no validity whatsoever. The four hymns are Skelton's. Indeed a later manuscript (B.M. Egerton 2642 f. 230) contains a copy of the verses *Of Tyme* ascribed without hesitation to Skelton.[14] If the bibliographical arguments against the four hymns are invalid the stylistic arguments have less weight, and considerable doubt may be cast backwards on the denial of *Vexilla Regis* and *Wofully Arayd*. When one adds to this evidence that the Fairfax manuscript, which contains *Wofully Arayd,* has the undoubted Skelton song *Manerly Margery* at only a few pages' distance, there seems no reason for doubting any further Skelton's authorship of the six hymns.

The most convincing evidence is the general tone of these religious lyrics. They are mainly hymns in the later mediaeval manner. Skelton passed the time 'sumtyme with sadness,' and

---

13. The title page is reproduced in the frontispiece.
14. This version contains a verse not printed by Dyce, who followed the editions. The Egerton additions I printed in *T.L.S.* 1936, 636.

called his hymns rightly 'contemplacyons.' There is little that was personal in the poems—only a few great spirits could achieve a direct personal relationship with God in the Middle Ages. 'Mediaeval religion,' writes one of the greatest authorities on the Middle Ages, 'is turned utterly towards God; the relationship of the soul to God is its whole matter. It is not humanitarian: not human, but divine scientia, fides et amor make mediaeval Christianity.'[15] Not till after the Reformation did ordinary men come into contact with their God. In the seventeenth century men with backgrounds so divergent as Donne and Bunyan could achieve personal relationship, but for Skelton, with his acceptance of mediaeval orthodoxy and indignant rejection of the Reformation in action and spirit, such a relationship could neither be achieved nor understood. This explains the difference between the impersonal tone of the hymns and the fiercely personal tone of *Ware the Hauke, Colin Clout,* and the *Replycacion.* These poems were religious, but they dealt with the externalities of the church—the corruptions of the clergy, the evils of simony, the luxury of the prelates, the heresy, the scandals and the gossip of college or convocation. About these Skelton could feel indignantly and personally. But on dogma he was dumb. So the religious lyrics are less characteristic, more of the age than of the man. Mediaeval religion demanded standardization of theological thought and achieved all too often only standardized devotion.

The only personal feeling is vicarious. But *Wofully Arayd* and *Vexilla Regis* deal with the sufferings of Christ. Here Catholic, poetic and artistic tradition allowed vivid personal treatment:

> Behold my body, how Jewes it donge
> With knots of whipcord and scourges strong;
> As stremes of a well the blode out sprong
>   On euery syde;
> The knottes were knyt,
> Right well made with wyt,
> They made the woundes wyde
> Now synge we, as were wont
> *Vexilla regis prodeunt,*

15. H. O. Taylor, *The Mediaeval Mind,* II, 582.

or in *Wofully Arayd*:

> Off sharpe thorne I have worne a crowne on my hede
> So payned, so stayned, so ruful, so red;
> Thus bobbid, thus robbid, thus for thy loue ded,
> Onfayned, not deynyd my blod for to shed;
>> My fete and handes sore
>> The sturdy nailis bore;
>> What myght I suffir more
> Than I haue don, O man, for thé?
> Cum when thou list, wellcum to me,
>> Wofully araide.

One remembers the emaciated Saviours of German carved cruci-
fixes and of Italian paintings of the Quattrocento. Skelton is here
writing in the mediaeval Catholic tradition that so often expressed
personal sorrow through artistic representations of the sufferings
of Christ.

But in the three prayers *To the Father of Heaven, To the Seconde
Person,* and *To the Holy Gooste,* there is nothing but impersonal
devotion. Even an individual poet like Dunbar, who could strike
such an original and personal note in his secular verse, was
traditional and impersonal in his hymns. There is no personal
feeling in

> Hale, sterne superne! Hale, in eterne
> In Godis sicht to schyne!
> Lucerne in derne, for to discerne
> Be glory and grace devyne;

It was the mediaeval manner, into which Skelton falls automatically:

> O radiant Luminary of lyght intermynable
> Celestial Father, potenciall God of myght
> Of heauen and earth, O Lord incomperable,
> Of all perfections the essential most perfyght!

Strange that an independent poet could write so like his contemporaries! But it was not strange to his contemporaries. To be
original in one's devotions was heresy; and the thought of heresy
even in others maddened him. Among all her devoted followers
the mother church had no more faithful son than John Skelton.

THE GOLIARD

IT IS ONE OF THE PARADOXES OF ORTHODOXY THAT THERE IS often more latitude inside than outside of its boundaries, and this is notably true of the Middle Ages. One step beyond orthodoxy and the penalties were severe—degradation, loss of caste, excommunication, in the end the stake. Let a man but preserve intact his allegiance to the spiritual demands of the church and he might satirize her clergy, mock her institutions, write sacrilegious parodies on her most sacred services, and pervert for his own secular use the verses and antiphons of missal and breviary. Devout churchman though Skelton was, militant churchman though he became, in his earlier poetry he did not hesitate to claim the orthodox churchman's prescriptive right to mockery even of religious services. There was in Skelton much of the Goliard, something of the independent *gamin* quality that had produced the rebellious satire and the sheer lyric of the *Carmina Burana*.

The Goliards were long since dead. The Arch-poet had died young in the mid-thirteenth century. The family of Golias became a glory to literature and an increasing scandal to the church, till she was forced to legislate against them, and by the time of Chaucer even the memory of the wandering scholars was dying out:

He was a janglere and a goliardeys—

Goliard has perhaps no more significance here than that of a merry rogue. Yet the spirit of the Goliards lived on. The original Goliards had been wandering clerks, on the road through wanderlust or lack of benefice, rebellious against an authority that left them to starve or provided support only at the price of stability and loss of freedom. They sang as rebels sang, of the things the church officially frowned upon, of love and Venus, of drinking and Bacchus, of youth and springtime; they satirized the abbot and the Pope; they wrote scandalous gospels and parodied the Mass;

1. This chapter is based partly on an article already published—Ian A. Gordon: *'Skelton's "Phillip Sparow" and the Roman Service Book.'* *M.L.R.*, October, 1934. I am indebted to the Editor for his permission to use the article.

they cited scripture for their own irreligious purposes. Though
the Goliards decayed and by the fourteenth century disappeared,
the tunes they sang and the patterns they created persisted. In the
first few years of the sixteenth century we find Skelton, tutor to
the king and beneficed clergyman, returning in *Phillip Sparow*
and the mock *Epitaphs* for John Clarke and Adam Uddersal to
the manner and spirit of the Goliards, to the intense annoyance
of equally orthodox but more susceptible clergymen like Alexander
Barclay.

When Skelton took up his office in Diss, he came in contact
with another priest, John Clarke. Clarke was an older man than
Skelton, who calls him 'old John Clarke, the holy patriarke of
Diss,' and it is possible that there was some professional jealousy
between the two priests. The old man died at the beginning of
1507 and with piety becoming his years left money 'to a pylgrym,
a priest, to be in prayer and pilgrimage, at *Rome* the whole Lent,
there to pray and syng for me and myn children, my fader and my
moder, *Rober* and *Cate, John Kew* and *Maut, Steven Brightled,*
and *John Payne,* the which I am in debt to.'[2] About the same time
there died in Diss another whom Skelton regarded with disfavour,
Adam Uddersal, the 'Holy Bailiff' of Diss. The death of the two
men gave Skelton an opportunity for a satire on their lives and
deaths in the form of an epitaph:

> Though this knaues be deade,
> Full of myschiefe and queed,
> Yet, where so euer they ly,
> Their names shall neuer dye.

The 'epitaph' on Clarke is called 'a devoute trental for old John
Clarke,' i.e. a Mass of thirty days' duration. It consists of some
sixty Latin lines praying for the damnation of his soul, followed
by a few lines in English. Clarke is depicted as a scoundrel:

> Non erat sibi similis:
> In malitia vir insignis;
> Duplex corde et bilinguis . . .
> Sepultus est amonge the wedes:
> God forgeue hym his misdedes!

2. cf. Blomefield, *History of Norfolk,* p. 17 ff.

Skelton remembers his old quarrels with the patriarch, who had insulted the established rector of Diss:

> Rectori proprio
> Tam verba retorta loquendo . . .

The patriarch had been a querulous old man:

> Dum vixerat is,
> Sociantur jurgia, vis, lis.

The epitaph continues with a mock appeal for priests to pray for his soul:

> *Fratres, orate*
> For this knavate
> By the holy rode,
> Dyd neuer man good . . .
> With, fill the blak bowle
> For Jayberdes sowle
> Bibite multum;
> Ecce sepultum
> Sub pede stultum . . .
> With, hey, howe, rumbelowe,
> Rumpopulorum,
> Per omnia secula seculorum.

The epitaph to Uddersal is on similar lines. The bailiff had extorted money from the common people:

> Namque extorquebat
> Quidquid nativus habebat.

Skelton looses a flood of invective against the dishonest officer and joins with the commons in cursing him:

> De Dis haec semper erit camena,
> Adam Uddersall sit anathema!

Both poems are mock prayers for the soul of the dead, interceding not for salvation but for damnation, and thoroughly goliardic in spirit.

> Anima ejus
> De malo in pejus
> Amen,

might have been a tag from the *Carmina Burana* themselves.

Phillip Sparow is the lament of Joanna Scroupe for the death of her sparrow, a trivial enough subject that became in Skelton's skilled hands telling poetry. It is tempting to see in it a parallel to Catullus' *Passer deliciae meae puellae,* but there is nothing of

J

Catullus in *Phillip Sparow,* nor was there meant to be. *Phillip Sparow* is a goliardic poem, a lament that mocks systematically the various offices for the dead from the breviary and the missal, and though it is written in English and the *Carmina Burana* in Latin, though it is his earliest poem in an original verse-form, Skelton never perhaps combined so well his half-appreciation of the Renaissance with his sympathy for the Middle Ages, here the Middle Ages of the Goliards.

The typical goliardic parody of the breviary and missal is either a hymn-parody:

> Vinum bonum cum sapore
> Bibat Abbas cum Priore,

which burlesques the *Stabat Mater,* or a drinkers' or gamblers' Mass, where the form of the Mass is preserved but the words are perverted and parodied. Novati[3] and Lehman[4] quote example after example: Bacchus becomes the Deity and the Introit of the Mass, *Introibo ad altare Dei,* becomes *Introibo ad altare Bacchi, amen* becomes *stramen, Dominus vobiscum* becomes *Dolus vobiscum, oremus* becomes *potemus,* and so the goliardic Mass pursues its riotous and sacrilegious course. Skelton never parodied the actual terminology of the service books. His usage is more subtle. The phrases and appropriate psalms and hymns are quoted with sly relish and followed up by the most inappropriate developments to form a grim but effective background to the mock lament for Phillip Sparow.

Skelton does not employ only the goliardic parodies of the Mass. These parodies themselves had been used by the singers of the *amour courtois,* who found in them yet another vehicle for the worship of Venus. In addition to Bacchus-Masses there were Venus-Masses, which gradually appear as the Mass of the Birds. The Mass of the Birds developed naturally enough. Doves had always been associated with Venus. What more natural than to include other birds than doves? Venus is worshipped in the language of religious devotion and in the forms of religious services. The anonymous Lovers' Mass of Bodleian Fairfax with the apparatus of Introibo, Confiteor, Misereatur, Officium, Kyrie,

---

3. F. Novati, *Studi Critici,* Turin, 1889.
4. P. Lehman, *Die Parodie Im Mittelalter,* Munich, 1922.

Gloria in Excelsis, Prose Epistle[5] and the rest represents the second stage in the development, from which it is but a short step to the Mass to Venus sung by the birds themselves. The Bacchus-Masses, the Venus-Masses and the Masses of the Birds show a shift of emphasis among their various elements, but the spirit and the religious attitude involved is the same throughout.

The Mass of the Birds occurs in several forms—in The Court of Love as a general service by the birds without any regular use of the missal, and in Jean de Condé's *La Messe des Oisiaus* as a point-to-point parody of the Mass from the *Introibo* of the nightingale to the *Ite, Missa est* of the blackbird. *Phillip Sparow* represents yet a further stage in the development of the Mass of the Birds. There is now no trace of the Court of Love convention which had associated the birds with Venus. Venus herself has disappeared. The birds gather to celebrate not a Lovers' Mass but the more appropriate *Missa pro Defunctis*—the Mass for the Dead led by Robin Redbreast. The goliardic spirit that runs through *Phillip Sparow* takes the form not so much of parody as of a consistent mockery of the services for the dead and the dying. Verses and antiphons and psalms from these services add piquancy to the lament and give to the poem a thread of sombre commentary. The *Officium Defunctorum* and the *Missa pro Defunctis* are impressive and solemn rites, and in spite of the underlying parody *Phillip Sparow* now and again catches something of their serious tone and breaks into almost unexpected poetry.

It is possible to analyse with accuracy the services of which Skelton made use in his most goliardic of laments; they are of four separate functions:

(i) The *Commendatio Animae,* where the soul of the dying man is commended to God with a short litany, a series of orations, and the reading of Psalms 117 and 118.

(ii) The *Officium Defunctorum*—the Office for the Dead—the most important parts of which are the services at Vespers and at Matins. They begin with the antiphons *Placebo Domino in regione Vivorum* and *Dirige, Domine, Deus meus, In conspectu tuo viam*

5. E.E.T.S., *Lay-folks Mass Book.* 1879, and E. P. Hammond, p. 210.

meam, and the head-words *Placebo* and *Dirige* are continually used as short titles for the Vespers and Matins in the Office.

(iii) Both of these services are from the breviary. In the missal is found the magnificent Mass for the Dead, the *Missa pro Defunctis,* with the Introitus *Requiem aeternam dona eis, Domine* and its Sequence the great hymn of the Day of Judgment, the *Dies Irae, dies illa.*

(iv) At the close of the Mass, if absolution is to be celebrated, the missal contains the order for the *Absolutio super Tumulum,* where the celebrating priest puts off the maniple and assuming a black cloak recites a short oration, after which a Responsory is sung—*Libera me, Domine, de morte aeterna in die illa tremenda.*

Skelton uses all these forms except that of the Matins, and *Phillip Sparow* is remarkable, even in goliardic poetry, for the way in which it uses first the Vespers in the Office for the Dead, then without indication or warning becomes the mediaeval Mass of the Birds—on this occasion naturally the *Missa pro Defunctis;* again without warning shifts into the absolution over the tomb; and then with a few lines on the coming of night returns to the close of Vespers in the Office from the breviary. After a section on the composition of a Latin epitaph, which owes nothing to the mediaeval parodies of the Mass but much to the mediaeval habit of erudition—for the poet cites dozens of authors in as many lines —come the 'Commendacions,' commendations not on the soul of Phillip Sparow, but with an understandable play on the word of the beauty of Joanna Scroupe, the supposed author of the first part. The poem ends with a defence against those churchmen to whom even the suspicion of goliardic poetry suggested scandal.

Skelton combined the spirit of the Goliard with the accurate knowledge of the well-educated priest. In an analysis of the poem and the usage it makes of the breviary and missal, nothing comes through so clearly as Skelton's accurate use of both, which a casual reading or unfamiliarity with the Roman service books is all too liable to obscure. The first part of the poem is spoken in the person of Joanna Scroupe, the young girl whose sparrow has been slain, and from the *Placebo* of the first line the mockery of the burial service continues unchecked. The first three hundred and

eighty-six lines use throughout the Vespers in the Office. The
borrowed passages run in pairs—in every case an antiphon followed
by the first lines of the following psalm, the whole rigidly keeping
to the order in the Office—and never, strange though it appears,
once parodying it, though the temptation to parody the psalms was
obvious enough. Dunbar's method in the *Dirige to the King at
Stirling* admitted no such self-denial. Indeed, Skelton remained
content to tell the mock serious tale, punctuating it throughout with
the key-phrases from·the Office in their precisely correct order.

The poem begins with the antiphon *Placebo;* the next couplet
replies with Psalm 114, *Dilexi [quoniam, exaudiet Dominus vocem
orationis meae]* :

> *Pla ce bo,*
> Who is there, who?
> *Di lex i,*
> Dame Margery;
> Wherefore and why, why?
> For the sowle of Philip Sparowe,
> That was lately slayn at Carowe . . .

It continues to describe the grief of the girl at the death of
Phillip :

> I syghed and I sobbed
> For that I was robbed
> Of my sparowes lyfe.
> O mayden, wydow, and wyfe,
> Of what estate ye be,
> Of hye or lowe degre,
> Great sorowe than ye myght se,
> And lerne to wepe at me!

There is no trace of verbal parody. After the antiphon *Heu, heu
me [quia incolatus meus prolongatus est]* follows Psalm 119, *Ad
Dominum cum tribularer, clamavi* :

> Of God nothynge else craue I
> But Phyllypes soule to kepe
> From the marees deepe
> Of Acherontes well,
> That is a flood of hell;
> And from the great Pluto.

These lines may perhaps be an echo of the 'Deliver my soul, O
Lord, from lying lips, and from a deceitful tongue' *[a labiis*

iniquis et a lingua dolorosa] of the second verse of the Psalm. The antiphon follows, *Dominus [custodit te ab ᴐmni malo*] and the poem quotes the appropriate Psalm 120, *Levavi oculos in montes,* but instead of the Lord who keeps Israel there follows a charming and delicate description of Phillip:

> It had a veluet cap,
> And wold syt vpon my lap,
> And seke after small wormes,
> And sometyme white bred crommes;
> And many tymes and ofte
> Betwene my brestes softe
> It wolde lye and rest;
> It was propre and prest.
> Sometyme he wold gaspe
> Whan he sawe a waspe,
> A fly or a gnat,
> He wolde flye at that . . .
> Lorde, how he wolde hop
> After the gressop!

We are shortly brought up with the antiphon *Si iniquitates [observaveris Domine]*:

> *Si in i qui ta tes*
> Alas, I was euyll at ease!
> *De pro fun dis cla ma vi,*
> Whan I sawe my sparowe dye!

Here Psalm 129, *De profundis clamavi,* is mocked for a couple of lines, and then is promptly dropped for:

> Phillip had leue to go
> To pyke my lytell too . . .
> Phillip wolde seke and take
> All the flees blake
> That he coulde there espye
> With his wanton eye.

This is turn yields, unexpectedly enough, to the solemn antiphon 'Despise not the works of thy hands, O lord' [*Opera manuum tuarum, Domine, ne despicias*], a strangely incongruous finish for the exploits of Phillip

> Vpon my naked skin.

Undeterred by incongruity, the poem quotes the correct Psalm 137, *Confiteor tibi, Domine, in toto corde meo,* and continues with the adventures of Phillip and Joanna's premonitions of his death, till the lament:

> *A porta inferi*
> Good Lorde, haue mercy
> Vpon my sparowes soule
> Wryten in thy bederoule!

Then comes the verse—this time perhaps more appropriate—*Audivi vocem* [*de caelo dicentem*], to which the response is 'Blessed are they that die in the Lord!'

Skelton follows correctly with the Magnificat—which is transformed into a fierce curse against Gib the cat:

> That vengaunce I aske and crye,
> By way of exclamacyon,
> On all the hole nacyon
> Of cattes wylde and tame;
> God sende them sorowe and shame!

The vengeance calls for one terrible fate after another:

> Of Inde the gredy grypes
> Myght tere out all thy trypes!
> Of Arcady the beares
> Myght plucke away thyne eares!

She remembers poor Phillip sitting

> Many tymes and oft
> Vpon my fynger soft

till the reader is brought up suddenly and dramatically with the 'Lord have mercy upon us,' the

> *Kyrie, eleison,*
> *Christe, eleison,*
> *Kyrie, eleison!*

of the Sarum breviary. The climax is so effective that one almost forgets that Phillip was only a sparrow, for the external form of the Office is continued in the following lines:

> For Phylyp Sparowes soule,
> Set in our bederoule,
> Let vs now whysper
> A *pater noster.*

The quiet Lord's Prayer is an excellent conclusion—and it is strictly in order. The rubric in the breviary for the Pater Noster after the Magnificat reads 'secreto'—'in a whisper.' So the first part closes with the Psalm from the Office, 'Praise the Lord, O my soul.' So far, Skelton's use of the Office has been a little derisive, but on occasion intensely dramatic. The sonorous phrases of the Office deepen the note of sorrow in the girl's lament, and the burlesque trembles on the verge of pathos—a transition the Goliards would have understood very well.

In the next section Skelton abandons the Office for the Dead and adopts a new ceremony—the Mass of the Birds. The change comes at line 387, but with the transition from the breviary to the missal Skelton changes his method. He makes no attempt to follow out the formulae of the Requiem Mass, as Jean de Condé had done, and as he himself had done in the earlier part of the poem. Only the general details of the Bird Mass are used and these in no special order. The birds are all summoned to the Requiem :

> To wepe with me loke that ye come,
> All maner of byrdes in your kynd;
> So none be left behynde
> To mornynge loke that ye fall
> With dolorous songes funerall.

The robin is the priest :

> And robyn redbreast
> He shall be the preest
> The requiem mass to synge,

and he is followed by a long list of assistants. The parrot reads the Gospel (the Oratio), and

> The mauys with her whystell
> Shall rede there the pystell

—the Epistle of St. Paul to the Thessalonians which is peculiar to the Mass for the Dead. The stock-dove, the peewit and other birds sing the versicles; the peacock sings the Graduale :

> The pecocke so prowde,
> Because his voyce is lowde,
> And hath a glorious tayle,
> He shall synge the grayle.

The puffin and the teal give alms, and the ostrich, because

> He can not well fly
> Nor synge tunably,

is made the bellman :

> Let hym rynge the bellys;
> He can do nothyng ellys.

Skelton's indebtedness to the mediaeval Bird Mass is clear. He uses the Mass and the birds, but he dropped the conventional love theme of the French and English poets, and refashioned the Bird Mass in the form of the Requiem.

He develops the Bird Mass further along original lines. At line 513 the phoenix is introduced after the other birds and given special duties that indicate, though there is no break in the verse, che introduction of a new service. The duties of the phoenix are those associated with the priest celebrating the Absolution over the Tomb, a continuation of the Mass for the Dead, but in itself a separate office. The phoenix blesses the hearse and censes it

> With aromatycke gummes
> That cost great summes.

He is dressed

> As a patryarke or pope
> In a blacke cope

and he is bidden to sing:

> He shall sing the verse
> *Libera me.*

Now the celebrating priest of the Mass does not, in fact, wear a black cloak, even for the Mass for the Dead. But in the rubric to the Absolution over the Tomb, are the following directions:

Finita missa, si facienda est Absolutio, celebrans . . . deposito Manipulo accipit pluviale nigrum, i.e., the celebrating priest puts off the maniple and assumes a black cloak. And at the close of the oration, the priest is directed to sing the Responsory *Libera me, Domine, de morte aeterna,* the 'verse' assigned to the phoenix in the poem.

The other details of the poem fit the rubric and verses for this Office with complete precision. The eagle is to be

> the sedeane
> The quere to demeane,

i.e., the *Subdiaconus* of the rubric, while

> The hobby and the muskette
> The sencers and the crosse shall fet;
> The kestrell in all this warke
> Shall be holy water clarke

assign three more duties mentioned in the rubric—the *Subdiaconus* bears the cross (*Subdiaconus . . . defert crucem*), and two acolytes carry the incense and the holy water (*praecedentibus duobus aliis Acolythis, uno cum thuribulo et navicula incensi, alio cum vase aquae benedictae et aspersorio*). These coincidences, with the citation of the significant Responsory *Libera Me,* leave no doubt whatsoever that the Mass for the Dead sung by the birds changes at line 513 for the succeeding Office—the Absolution over the Tomb. This ends at line 570.

In the next line (571) the poet is back again at the Vespers in the Office for the Dead. Evening is coming on:

> And now the darke cloudy nyght
> Chaseth away Phebus bright,
> Taking his course toward the west,
> God send my sparoes sole good rest!

And Skelton returns with telling effect to the close of the Vespers for the Office, with *Requiem aeternam dona eis, Domine,* the closing lines of the final psalm; to which the verse follows *A porta inferi;* the antiphon *Credo videre bona Domini* of the Sarum breviary and the verse *Domine, exaudi orationem meam* of the other forms of the Office; to end with the final words of the Office, the *Dominus vobiscum,* the command *Oremus,* and the *Oratio*— the oration with which the Office for the Dead at Vespers closes— *Deus cui proprium est misereri et parcere,* the special form of the oration used when the body was present in the church. And here, for the first time in six hundred lines, Skelton parodies the Office:

> On Phillips soule haue pyte!
> For he was a prety cocke
> And came of a gentyll stocke
> And wrapt in a maidenes smocke
> Tyll cruell fate made him to dy,

and Phillip is commended to the appropriate joys of his particular heaven in a few lines of parody on the words of the oration *sed iubeas eam* (i.e., the soul—*anima*) *a sanctis Angelis suscipi, et ad patriam paradisi perduci*:

> To Jupyter I call
> Of heuen emperyall
> That Phyllyp may fly
> Aboue the starry sky
> To treade the prety wren,
> That is our ladyes hen:
> Amen, amen, amen!

The whole conception is wonderfully clever and the use of the service formulae adds piquancy to an excellent piece of poetic workmanship. The use of the Vespers for the Dead, the change to the Requiem Mass and again to the Absolution over the Tomb are finely handled, while the final return to the Vespers from the Office is a piece of masterly technique. Even the Goliards did no better.

The remainder of the poem falls into two sharply contrasted sections; in the first (lines 603-844) Skelton decides to write a Latin epitaph for the dead sparrow, and here he gathers together a procession of his reading in the classics and the romances and the greater English poets before he composes his epitaph in Latin.

The final part is a new and independent section, the 'Commendacions,' where the last of the services is used, the Commendations for the Soul. But there is even less attempt than in the Mass of the Birds to follow the form of the breviary. Indeed, even the meaning of Commendations is altered. *Commendatio* in the breviary was a commendation of the soul to God. The 'Commendacions' in *Phillip Sparow* mean the praise of Joanna Scroupe. The use of the breviary is even more incidental and is confined almost to a running commentary derived from the psalm used in the *Ordo Commendationis,* Psalm 118. Starting with the couplet

> Beati immaculati in via
> O gloriosa femina,

he closes each verse-paragraph with four lines of Latin,

> Hac claritate gemina
> O gloriosa femina,

the invariable first couplet, and a second couplet consisting of a line from each of the sections in turn óf Psalm 118 followed by a line of Latin generally derived from the Vulgate psalms. One example will show the pattern:

> Hac claritate gemina
> O gloriosa femina,
> Bonitatem fecisti cum servo tuo, domina,
> Et ex praecordiis sonant praeconia,

where line three, as usual, is from Psalm 118, and line four is from the hymn of St. Thomas Aquinas sung at Matins on the Feast of Corpus Christi. This one example is sufficient to show that the structure of the 'Commendacions' is completely different from that of the lament and that there is actually no great connection between the two parts.[6] At the end of the 'Commendacions' (line 1238) Skelton makes a belated attempt to link them with the Requiem, and for a few lines he adheres once again to the breviary:

> Requiem aeternam dona eis, Domine!
> With this psalme, Domine, probasti me
> Shall sayle over the see
> With Tibi, Domine, commendamus—

this last being the final oration, Tibi, Domine, commendamus animam famuli tui, of the Ordo Commendationis Animae from the breviary. But, with the shift Skelton made in the meaning of 'commendation,' this new reminiscence of the service book has hardly the telling effect of the more sardonic first part. The 'Commendacions' read better as an independent poem. They differ in mood and in manner from the earlier lament, and they form a sequel rather than a continuation. Phillip Sparow is best regarded as two related poems, the first of which, containing the lament, the Requiem Mass, the Office for the Dead and the Absolution over the Tomb, is goliardic both in spirit and execution.

A retrospect of the Offices used reveals the thoroughness of Skelton's goliardic mockery. Phillip Sparow falls into five divisions, each a burlesque of one service: Officium Defunctorum (Breviary), 1-386; Missa pro Defunctis (Missal), 387-512; Absolutio super Tumulum (Missal), 513-570; Officium Defunctorum (Breviary), 571-602; Ordo Commendationis Animae (Breviary), 845-1260.

The poem is not a parody as Dunbar's Dirige to the King at Stirling is parody. There the Scottish poet burlesqued the Matins in the Office for the Dead, parodying each of the three Lessons and their Responses in turn, concluding with a Latin word-for-word parody of the close of the service, which closely resembles the rehandling of devotional language in the Drinking Masses:

> A porta tristitie de Strivilling
> Erue, Domine, animas et corpora eorum.
> Credo gustare statim vinum Edinburgi
> In villa viventium.
> Requiescant Edinburgi. Amen.

6. The 'Commendacions' have been discussed more fully in chapter IV.

This is not Skelton's method. The formulae of the various services remain unchanged. Perhaps they are not always even ridiculed. Instead they give a mock-serious background to the lament for Phillip that is at any moment liable to lose its mockery. There is no parody and no mockery in the close of the first three services:

God send my sparowes soule good rest!

Skelton was as serious over Joanna's loss and as sensitive in his handling of it as Catullus over Lesbia's, and his use of the Services for the Dead gives a formal note that has an attraction of its own.

Perhaps the most convincing proof that the poem was goliardic is the reception that it evidently had among the more unbending churchmen. The Goliards had long since fallen into disgrace, and the sight of a beneficed clergyman reviving the irreverence of the *Carmina Burana* was to the more conservative distasteful. In a passage already quoted from the *Ship of Fools,* Barclay contrasts the morality of his own writings with the 'wantonness' of *Phillip Sparow.* Skelton was stung into defence in the 'adicyon' or epilogue to the poem, which he later incorporated into *The Garlande of Laurell* with the introduction:

> Of Phillip Sparow the lamentable fate,
> The doleful destiny, and the carefull chaunce,
> Dyuysed by Skelton after the funerall rate;
> Yet some there be therwith that take greuaunce,
> And grudge thereat with frownyng countenaunce.

It is pretty clear that his offence was the burlesque of the 'funerall rate' and his return to the goliardic poetry so discredited in the eyes of most churchmen.

> Luride, cur, livor, volucris pia funera damnas?

'Why should one condemn the holy rites of a sparrow?' demands Skelton fiercely in the 'adicyon.' His orthodoxy was surely sufficient guarantee of good faith, and he himself later turned on those who strayed from Catholic fundamentals. The difference between Skelton and his critics was not radical. But Skelton had a sympathy with the roguish wandering clerics of the Middle Ages that found no place in the early Renaissance. Perhaps the sympathy was literary rather than real. He could be bitter enough against any actual abuse of privilege or of doctrine.

Phillip Sparow is a graceful and sensitive poem by a man not given either to grace or to sensitivity. One looks in vain for the 'wantonness' of Barclay's depreciation. The lament strengthened Skelton's reputation as a poet and did not in the end detract from his reputation as a churchman. It would be difficult to see how it could. The eclipse of the Goliards was only temporary—and Skelton went back to their best element—their poetry. That some of his contemporaries considered he had returned to their less worthy elements, their scurrility and abuse of the church, is a reflection on their critical powers and not on the poetry of Skelton. The goliardic poetry of *Phillip Sparow* is as much the product of a churchman as the devotional hymns and the attacks on Cardinal Wolsey. Its rehandling of a mediaeval form and mediaeval formulae combined with a usage of English and an alert intelligence that is typical of the Renaissance, make the poem one of the most individual things that Skelton ever wrote.

CHAPTER VIII

SKELTON AND THE MORALITY

IN THE 'GARLANDE OF LAURELL' LIST SKELTON CLAIMS TO HAVE
written three plays, only one of which has survived:

Of *Vertu* also the souerayne enterlude . . .
His *Commedy*, Achademios callyd by name . . .
Of *Magnyfycence* a notable mater,
How Cownterfet Cowntenaunce of the new get,
With Crafty Conueyaunce dothe smater and flater,
And Cloked Collucyoun is brought in to clater
With Courtely Abusyoun; who pryntith is wele in mynde
Moche dowblenes of the worlde therein he may fynde.

The survivor, *Magnyfycence,* written in 1516 when English drama
was still in its infancy, acquires an importance from its early date
that is not altogether justified by its intrinsic merits. By far the
longest, it is by no means the best of Skelton's works. He was no
dramatist, and the cut-and-thrust of his satire, which might have
added lively conversational passages to a play, is denied to the
morality form in which he worked. Yet in spite of these
disadvantages *Magnyfycence* represents an advance on previous
moralities, with their exclusive interests in topics religious and
moral. Skelton, without any apparent connection with the small
circle of dramatists writing under the eye of Sir Thomas More,
made with them the simple and yet revolutionary step of writing
secular drama.

The morality previous to 1500 bore all the marks of an origin
within the church and a development under its influence. Plays
like *The Castle of Perseverance* and *Mundus et Infans* combined
allegory with religious moralizing, and ignored both human character and dramatic action. Mankind in the moralities is a static
figure, and the dramatic conflict for the soul of man is a struggle
between abstract vices and abstract virtues, the most dramatic
moment the coming of Death to summon mankind to his appointed
end. Towards the end of the century, however, reality entered
and a new type of drama arose which had its beginnings in a

frankly secular play on a Roman theme, *Fulgens et Lucres* of Henry Medwall (c. 1495). At the beginning of the sixteenth century this minor revolt against the hitherto exclusively religious tone of the drama resulted in a completely altered attitude to the stage. It has been shown that the change originated with a group of which More was the driving force and his brother-in-law, John Rastell, the agent.[1] Rastell showed his sympathy with the new secularized drama by publishing *Fulgens et Lucres* in 1518, the year following his own scientific rehandling of a morality in *The Four Elements*. The secular interest was further developed in the plays of Rastell's son-in-law, John Heywood, whose interludes— discussion dramas like *The Play of the Wether* and comedies like *The Four PP*—represent one further remove from the conventional ethical discussions of the morality. As the tone of drama altered, open-air performances of *The Castle of Perseverance* type gave way to productions at court and elsewhere of the new secular morality and the interlude.

Skelton's drama of *Magnyfycence* falls between the old type and the new. It retains the old-fashioned form of the morality with a cast of allegorical abstractions, but, in its acceptance of the current secular tone it represents a striking advance on the older model. *Magnyfycence* is an allegory of contemporary history. Humanity or mankind becomes the individual prince Mag- nyfycence, and the virtues and the vices of the older morality become his good and evil counsellors. Like so many of Skelton's productions, the play is a blend of the old and the new, the form conservative, the theme entirely novel. No evidence has yet appeared connecting Skelton with the More circle, and it is probable that he had little, if any, contact with them. Yet it may well have been their recognition of the novelties in his morality that prompted John Rastell to print it in 1533, four years after the death of the poet, with the recommendation on the title page 'A goodly interlude and a mery.' The most distinctive and original dramatic work of Henry VIII's reign came from the presses of the Rastells, and the inclusion of *Magnyfycence* suggests that the More circle regarded it as similar in type to their own dramatic work, a piece of active rebellion against the restraints of the formal morality.

1. A. W. Reed, *Early Tudor Drama*. London, 1926.

In *Magnyfycence* Skelton's cordial relations with the noble family of the Howards, already noted, finds additional evidence. The Prince in the play is tempted by Fancy and Folly to abandon Measure, who represents prudence, and he is saved from ultimate ruin only by the intervention of Good Hope and Circumspection. R. L. Ramsay[2] has shown that the situation is an allegory of the state of affairs in England between 1509 and 1516. Magnyfycence represents Henry VIII, and the vices and virtues in the play are the two parties among the councillors—those, headed by Wolsey, advocating a campaign of showy extravagance, and those in favour of a more economical policy, of whom the chief was Thomas Howard, the Earl of Surrey. Victory at Flodden raised him to favour but the two parties split and the Howards were finally rejected in 1516, when Surrey (now the Duke of Norfolk) retired to the country. Wolsey, already a Cardinal, now became Chancellor, and his triumph was complete. This dating of the play at 1516 is confirmed by a reference (ll. 279-282) to a quarrel between Henry and Francis I immediately after the death of Louis XII in 1515:

For, syth he dyed, Largesse was lytell used.

The play is then a justification of Norfolk's policy of economy and watchfulness, and the first of Skelton's succession of satires on the Cardinal.

Magnyfycence is the earliest example in English of any dramatic form used for political satire and propaganda. Skelton had already in *The Bowge of Courte* adapted the dream allegory for the satire of court life. Once again he takes a purely mediaeval form, the morality, and handles it freely without conservative misgivings. 'Skelton's *Magnyfycence*,' writes A. W. Pollard, '. . . is on the older lines.'[3] This does not represent the whole truth. Into the apparently rigid mould of the old-fashioned morality Skelton has poured numerous elements that had never before found a place. The conservatism of his form is deceptive. Magnyfycence falls to temptation in the conventional manner, but under their allegorical names, his tempters may even be outline portraits of

2. *Magnyfycence*, E.E.T.S. edition. I am indebted to the excellent introduction for many subsequent details in this chapter.
3. A. W. Pollard, *English Miracle Plays, Moralities and Interludes*. Introduction lxvi.

K

actual councillors at court. Propaganda, satire, comment on contemporary politics and covert advice to a reigning monarch were all original material with which to build a morality.

The play is without act or scene division, but the development of the plot divides it into five clearly defined stages.[4] In the first of these the Prince is in prosperity, but one of the conspiring Vices wins his allegiance. The play opens with a discussion between Felicity (or Wealth) and Liberty (who represents license or prodigality)—should a prince preserve wealth and felicity or indulge his desires? An arbiter appears in the person of Measure (or Moderation), who claims dominion over both:

> Where Measure is mayster, Plenty dothe none offence;
> Where Measure lackyth, all thynge dysorderyd is:
> Where Measure is absent, Ryot kepeth resydence;
> Where Measure is ruler, there is nothynge amysse . . .

All three conclude the discussion amicably:

> There is no prynce but hath nede of vs thre.

The Prince, Magnyfycence, enters and sets Measure over both the others:

> For by Measure I warne you we thynke to be gydyd;
> Wherin it is necessary my pleasure to knowe:
> Measure and I wyll neuer be deuydyd.

The appeal of Liberty for 'Ioy and Myrthe' meets with universal disapproval. One detects the complaints of the older statesmen against the policy of Wolsey in Felicity's lines:

> Yet Measure hath ben so longe from vs absent,
> That all men laugh at Lyberte to scorne.

On the discomfited departure of Liberty, Magnyfycence piously condemns him:

> It is a wanton thynge, this Lyberte.

At this point, the first of the conspirators enters, Fancy, who proclaims that he is Largesse (or Liberality):

> Largesse, that all lordes sholde loue, Syr, I hyght.

He produces as his credentials a letter from 'Sad Cyrcumspeccyon.' Fancy ingratiates himself with Magnyfycence and slyly insinuates that Measure is beneath his dignity:

4. R. L. Ramsay's division is used.

Measure is mete for a marchauntes hall,
But Largesse becometh a state ryall.
What! sholde you pynche at a pecke of otes,
Ye wolde sone pynche at a pecke of grotes.
Thus is the talkynge of one and of other,
As men dare speke it hugger mugger:
'A lorde is a negarde, it is a shame.'
But Largesse may amende your name.

The second stage in lengthy static monologues introduces each of the conspirators in turn, and reveals their conspiracy against the Prince. Counterfeit Countenance delivers a long monologue exulting over the triumph of vice in England:

Counterfet maters in the lawe of the lande . . . .

To him enters Fancy with Crafty Conveyance to report the progress of the conspiracy. Magnyfycence is already beguiled and they have both been accepted into his household. A fourth conspirator, Cloaked Colusion, joins them, and they scheme that he, too, shall be introduced into the household under a false name. He is left alone on the stage to recommend himself to the audience in a monologue:

I am neuer glad but when I may do yll,
And neuer am I sory but when that I se
I can not myne appetyte accomplysshe and fulfyll
In hynderaunce of Wealth and of Prosperyte.

The final abstract court vice is now introduced, Courtly Abusion, for whose benefit Cloaked Colusion stages a mock quarrel with Crafty Conveyance:

COU. AB. What the deuyll! vse ye not to drawe no swordes?
CRA. CON. No, by my trouthe; but crake grete wordes.
COU. AB. Why, is this the gyse nowe adays?
CLO. COL. Ye, for surety; ofte peas is taken for frayes.

Courtly Abusion is left in his turn to deliver his introductory monologue in sprightly short-line stanzas:

What nowe? Let se
Who loketh on me
Well rounde aboute,
Howe gay and stoute
That I can were
Courtly my gere.

He is a spruce young fop who has introduced new fashion to the
country:

> All this nacyon
> I set on fyre;
> In my facyon,
> This theyr desyre,
> This newe atyre . . . .

The conspirators have now all been introduced and the plot
proceeds. Fancy rushes in to announce the fall of Measure.
Liberty is free! He remains on the stage to sing a song to his
hawk and sketch his own character:

> Of a spyndell I wyll make a sparre;
> All that I make forthwith I marre;
> I blunder, I bluster, I blowe, and I blother;
> I make on the one day, and I marre on the other;
> Bysy, bysy, and euer bysy,
> I daunce vp and downe tyll I am dyssy.

Folly enters 'in a foles case' and a clowning interlude ensues where
the two fools bargain for the sale of Folly's dog:

> FAN. Where the deuyll gate he all these hurtes?
> FOL. By God, for snatchynge of puddynges and wortes.

After some further clowning between Folly and Crafty Conveyance, Folly reveals his character to the audience. He makes fools
of all men—and he hints darkly at the folly of the Cardinal:

> Anone he waxyth so hy and prowde,
> He frownyth fyersly, brymly browde.

Fancy and Folly boast of their triumphs before the admiring Crafty
Conveyance and both depart to take up service in the palace.
Crafty Conveyance remains for his monologue.

Stage three: The time is now ripe for the final deception of the
Prince. He enters with the newly-honoured Liberty and the
older counsellor Felicity, who is protesting against the rejection
of Measure. Magnyfycence is now completely blind to all moderate
counsel. He announces that henceforth Felicity must be ruled by
Liberty and by 'Largesse,' who enters to claim his prisoner. The
stage is left clear for the vaunting monologue of Magnyfycence,
who in stately old-fashioned rime royal proclaims himself greater
than all the great princes of the past; Alexander, Caesar, Hercules,
Charlemagne all yield to him in honour. He repeats not the

mediaeval lament for their past glory, but the proud man's boast
of his own:

> I drede no daunger; I dawnce all in delyte:
> My name is Magnyfycence, man most of myght . . . .
> Of all doughty I am doughtyest duke as I deme;
> To me all prynces to lowte man beseme.

Courtly Abusion enters and swaggers before him, fascinating the
prince with fantastic fashions. The newcomer advised Magnyfycence to acquaint himself with Carnal Delectation and find
a 'fayre mistress,' whom Skelton describes in what seems a parody
of the aureate style:

> Fasten your Fansy vpon a fayre maystresse.
> That quyckly is enuyued with rudyes of the rose,
> Inpurtured with fetures after your purpose,
> The streynes of her vaynes as asure inde blewe,
> Enbudded with beautye and colour fresshe of hewe,
> As lyly whyte to loke vpon her leyre,
> Her eyen relucent as carbuncle so clere,
> Her mouthe enbawmyd, dylectable, and mery . . . .

Skelton continues the description with a sly mockery of the current
'high-style' poetry of a compliment. Magnyfycence is wholly
deluded by the suggestions of his new courtier. The discredited
Measure enters, but Magnyfycence rejects him angrily and flares
up into a temper as his new friends have tutored him to do:

> MAGN. Alas! my stomake fareth as it wolde cast.
> CLO. COL. Abyde, Syr, abyde; let me holde your hede.
> MAGN. A bolle or a basyn, I say, for Goddes brede!
> A, my hede! but is the horson gone?
> God gyue hym a myscheffe!

The Prince is now entirely in the hands of the conspirators. He
boasts once more of his security:

> I drede no dyntes of fatall Desteny.

But as he utters these words Fancy enters to announce that the
conspirators have cheated him. He wealth is gone and Felicity
is no more.

Stage four is the fall of Magnyfycence, emphasized by one of
the few stage directions: *Here* Magnyfycence *is beten downe and
spoyled from all his goodys and rayment.* Adversity enters to

complete the overthrow, followed by the grim figure of Poverty. Skelton draws a realistic picture:

> POU. A, my bonys ake! my lymmys be sore;
> Allasse, I haue the cyatyca full euyll in my hyppe!
> Allasse, where is youth that is wont for to skyppe?
> I am lowsy and vnlykynge and full of scurffe;
> My colour is tawny, colouryd as a turffe.
> I am Pouerte, that all men doth hate.
> I am batyd with doggys at euery mannys gate;
> I am raggyd and rent, as ye may se.

Poverty shows no sympathy with the lamentations of Magnyfycence:

> With curteyns of sylke ye were wonte to be drawe;
> Nowe must ye lerne to lye on the strawe . . .
> Syr, remembre the tourne of Fortunes whele.

Magnyfycence falls to uttering a mediaeval lament on the mutability of Fortune in terms that show Skelton remembering his almost thirty-year-old elegy for Edward IV.

> Where is now my welth and my noble estate?
> Where is nowe my treasure, my landes, and my rent?

One by one the conspirators return to jeer at the fallen Prince:

> LYB. What brothell, I say, is yonder bounde in a mat?
> MAGN. I am Magnyfycence, that somtyme thy mayster
>   was.
> LYB. What! is the worlde thus come to pass?
>   Cockes armes, Syrs! . . . .
> COU. COU. Ye, but trowe ye, Syrs, that this is he?
> CRA. CON. Go we nere and let vs se.
> CLO. COL. By Cockys bonys, it is the same . . . .

Stage five: The final scene of restoration is short. Magnyfycence is saved from killing himself by Good Hope. He is now a repentant tyrant and listens to the advice given by Redress, Sad Circumspection, and finally by Perseverance. The four characters finally left on the stage address the audience, rounding off the play with a 'moral' in rime royal stanzas on the mutability of Fortune:

> To day a lorde, to morowe ly in the duste:
> Thus in this worlde there is no erthly truste.
> To day fayre wether, to morowe a stormy rage;

To day hote, to morowe outragyous colde;
To day a yoman, to morowe made of page;
To day in surety, to morowe bought and solde;
To day maysterfest, to morowe he hath no holde.

Magnyfycence is restored to his palace and the play closes with
a pious prayer for the audience.

As a drama *Magnyfycence* has its moments of success. The
major defect is the long monologues with which each character
introduces himself to the audience. Sometimes these monologues
are edged satire—that of Courtly Abusion is rapier-keen—but
structurally they are a mistake. They slow the action till all sense
of drama is lost. The humorous scenes are excellent pieces of
rough fooling—Folly swindling Fancy over the price of a 'pylde
curre,' the battle of words between Cloaked Colusion and Courtly
Abusion are lively scenes for any stage. Fansy and Foly play
into each other's hands with the skill of practised comedians.
Here they are fooling Crafty Conveyance:

> FOL. Hem, Fansy! *Regardes, voyes.*
> (*Here* FOLY *maketh semblaunt to take a lowse from*
>   CRAFTY CONUEYAUNCE *showlder.*)
> FAN. What hast thou founde there?
> FOL.   By God, a lowse.
> CRA. CON. By Cockes harte I trow thou lyste.
> FOL. By the masse, a Spaynysshe moght with a gray lyste.
> FAN. Ha, ha, ha, ha, ha, ha!
> CRA. CON. Cockes armes! It is not so, I trowe.

Crafty Conveyance tears off his gown indignantly to the delight
of the two tormentors.

The graver scenes can on occasion be impressive. The fall of
Magnyfycence and the entrance of Poverty is a dramatic moment
admirably calculated, while the irony of the boastful monologue
of Magnyfycence on his invulnerable position at the very moment
when the conspiracy against him has succeeded reveals the hand
of a writer with a sense of dramatic presentation. The dénouement
of the play is statuesque. Standing figures round the fallen Prince
chant alternate verses like antiphons, in a scene that has rich
possibilities of dignified presentation. Except for the expository
monologues, the play is well proportioned and the construction
ordered—pride gives rise to conspiracy, conspiracy to the fall of

pride, the fall gives way to despair, and after despair comes restoration.

Characterization is best in the comic parts. Folly and Fancy are very nimble fools and their by-play darts round the heavier artillery of the others. The more serious parts have little contact with human character. The abstract quartet of confusingly similar court vices are, with the exception of the foppish Courtly Abusion, not clearly differentiated. Magnyfycence himself has human qualities, but his speeches are all public utterances. There is no intimate touch to humanize him or win our sympathy. Skelton came too early in the history of the drama to allow his characters to reveal themselves in action. Instead they announce their characteristics in set speeches, and this difficulty of exposition is a grave obstacle in the way of efficient characterization that no early dramatist was able to overcome.

If its allusions were to have any piquancy, such a topical play as *Magnyfycence* must have been produced immediately after composition. There is no record of any production, but it could have been produced only in two households—that of the Howards or that of the King. Skelton's *Garlande of Laurell,* written and recited in Sheriff Hutton Castle before the Howard family, shows how highly they regarded his public performances, and the consistent support of the Howard policy throughout the play was a solider compliment than the airy commendations of the *Garlande.* Yet what evidence there is suggests a production in court. Henry's love of dramatic performances needs no illustration. In spite of a passion for the elaborate and decorative masque he found the Interlude entertaining.

The allusions in *Magnyfycence* are aimed at the King. Skelton was at court from c. 1511 onwards, writing on occasion at the King's command, his pen always ready for defence and for advice. Some years after the play was written he could continue the attack on Wolsey unscathed—apparently secure in the King's support. *Magnyfycence* was therefore almost certainly written for production before Henry. The warnings of *Colin Clout* and *Speke Parrot* first find utterance in the scornful references in the play to Wolsey's low birth:

> A carter a courtyer, it is a worthy warke . . .
> A counterfet courtyer with a knaues marke.

To the court of Henry VIII the allegorical figures were easy to identify as court types if not actually as court personages. The moral was clear enough for those who had eyes to see:

> This mater we haue mouyd, you myrthys to make,
> Precely purposyd vnder pretence of play,
> Shewyth Wysdome to them that Wysdome can take.

This hortatory tone provides further evidence of a court production. Skelton would not have given advice to the Howards— they were only too well aware of their own policy. But to the poet Henry was blindly following the path to destruction and *Magnyfycence* was an effort to open his eyes 'vnder pretence of play.' The allegorical form and Henry's own friendliness to him gave Skelton a double immunity from any vengeance of the Cardinal.

Naturally there were critics. Some of the courtiers were *touché* by the innuendoes of his morality. It is fairly certain that the short satire *Against Venemous Tonges* is an epilogue to *Magnyfycence*. Some of its phrases and lines are direct references to the drama:

> Such tunges vnhappy hath made great diuision
> In realmes, in cities, by suche fals abusion;
> Of fals fickil tunges suche cloked collusion
> Hath brought nobil princes to extreme confusion.

The 'venemous tonges' are those of his critics at court shortly after the production of *Magnyfycence*. Skelton complains of slanders that have been uttered against him by some adversary to him unknown. He defends himself:

> He saith vntruly, to say that I would
> Controlle the cognisaunce of noble men
> Either by language or with my pen.

There was a time when women alone slandered:

> But men take vpon theim nowe all the shame,
> With skoldyng and skaundering make their tungs lame.

The poem concludes with a threat against his adversary regretting that the poet does not know 'what his name hight.' The name of his opponent is as much a mystery to us as it was to Skelton, but it is not difficult to see a connection between this defence of his writings against False Abusion and Cloaked Colusion and the veiled attack in *Magnyfycence* on the councillors of Henry, to whom he had already attached these very names.

Yet it would be a mistake to identify the characters of the play too closely with real people. Though they masquerade under allegorical names, they are not shadows, but they represent court types rather than individuals. Magnyfycence himself is not a portrait study of Henry VIII, and probably no individual courtier is represented. The play is an allegorical parallel to the situation at court and not merely disguised satire upon it. The King could view the pride and the downfall of *Magnyfycence* without feeling that he himself could be fooled so easily.

Whatever success it gained as drama, this novel rehandling of the morality was apparently a failure as propaganda. Henry accepted the play as entertainment without being seriously perturbed at its counsel and its serious intentions. It must have been a bitter disappointment for the Howard party to see Wolsey continue in favour, and the more conservative like Skelton realized that Henry had abandoned their policy. For the poet, however, *Magnyfycence* was only the beginning of the campaign. It will be seen how he abandoned allegory for satire and then turned to pure invective in a final attempt to warn the King of the dangers of retaining the Cardinal.

Chapter IX

THE WOLSEY GROUP

Skelton's satires against Wolsey form a clearly defined group of poems in an ascending scale of bitterness and outspoken expression. *Colin Clout,* which to contemporaries was the most famous of these outbursts, is in reality a general assault on the slackness of the higher clergy, and the comparatively few personal passages probably do not refer exclusively to Wolsey. But in *Speke Parrot* the satire is at once more cryptic and less apologetic, and Wolsey is now the sole victim of the poet's anger; while in *Why Come Ye Nat to Court?* Skelton in the end has come out into the open with a scathing personal attack on the public and private life of the Cardinal, whom he had first criticized merely as a churchman but who later became the object of his uncontrollable personal hatred.

The development of the satires requires, as with all occasional poems, a fairly precise date to be assigned to each, and until the order of the three poems can be determined and the events to which they refer tracked down, criticism of Skelton's development in satire may lead to serious misinterpretation. Fortunately, the poems are full of references to events of the time and may be dated as follows: *Colin Clout* in 1519-20, *Speke Parrot* towards the end of 1521, *Why Come Ye Nat to Court?* at the end of 1522 and during the first few months of 1523.[1] To the events of these years they form a running commentary from the point of view of the people and the older churchmen.

Wolsey's rise to a pre-eminent position in the state had been swift and unhampered. The man who in 1498 had been a master in William Waynfleet's school, and in 1506 a chaplain to Sir Richard Nanfan, entered the King's service, and Cavendish relates in his *Life of Cardinal Wolsey* how he first commended himself to Henry by his speed of action in an embassy. In the next few years his reputation became European and his adroitness in

---

1. These dates differ considerably from those assigned by Professor Berdan (*The Dating of Skelton's Satires, P.M.L.A.* 29, 499-516) and the evidence on which they rest is presented in full with the consideration of each poem.

diplomacy brought honours from home and abroad. In 1514 he became Bishop of Lincoln and later Archbishop of York. In 1515 he became a Cardinal and, obtaining the Great Seal, succeeded Warham as Lord Chancellor. In 1518 he became papal *legatus a latere,* and so short-circuited the superior office of Archbishop of Canterbury to the indignation of the more conservative clergy.

Skelton's three satires refer to the period from 1518, when Wolsey had become supreme in church and state, as Chancellor and Cardinal and Legate of the Pope. Skelton's first attack simply echoed the popular complaint—prelates should attend more to things of the spirit and less to affairs of the world. As Wolsey grew in power and interfered in church affairs both parochial and national, eventually dictating even to Convocation, and not content with leadership of the church, assumed virtual control of England's internal and foreign policy, Skelton's satire became more and more specific and increasingly virulent.

From his point of view he was perhaps justified. The events of these years were disquieting not merely to Skelton. Abroad Wolsey preserved England's independence by trimming a precarious balance of power among Europe's three most ᵛinfluential monarchs—Maximilian, the emperor of the Holy Roman Empire, Francis, the king of France, and Charles, the king of Spain. When in 1519 the death of Maximilian made Charles emperor in addition, the hegemony of Europe lay between Francis and Charles —and Wolsey took full advantage of the situation to support now one and now the other, till further diplomatic duplicity was out of the question. The Field of the Cloth of Gold in 1520 was a fine affair, but at the very moment Francis and Henry were entertaining each other with lavish spectacles, Henry was in touch with the emperor. Next year, in 1521, Wolsey met Francis in a conference at Calais—but took the opportunity to meet Charles at Bruges. The following year war broke out in May. Charles and Henry settled the general plan of the war at Windsor in June, and Wolsey lent his aid to raise a tax to pay for the war against France. Surrey, the Lord Admiral, conducted a campaign of devastation in France towards the end of 1522. Meanwhile France as usual created a diversion in Scotland, where Albany re-appeared and marched with the Scottish nobles and 80,000 men against Carlisle, to be bluffed into a truce and finally retirement by Dacre, the Warden of the East Marches. Wolsey's influence with Henry in these diplomatic moves was unlimited. Everywhere people saw his hand, and Skelton was not slow to echo the popular rumour.

But his hand was not merely in diplomacy. As early as 1518 he received a bull from the Pope to visit monasteries and nunneries,[2] and the clerical resentment at his reforms and suppressions gave the satirist full scope. In education his influence was pervasive. In 1517 the University of Oxford gave him the power to codify its statutes in spite of the opposition of Warham, and when the 'Trojans'—the supporters of the older education at Oxford—attacked the teaching of Greek it was to Henry and to Wolsey that the 'Greeks' appealed. Feeling ran high until More wrote a letter to the Senate warning them against opposing the King and Wolsey, who was especially enthusiastic over the new humanist study of Greek.[3] In 1520 Wolsey founded a chair of Greek at Oxford, and the path of preferment lay through a study of the new fashionable language.

Wolsey in the eyes of the public was at first merely a pushing churchman. But the rapidity with which he made himself pre-eminent in the state, his contemptuous attitude to Warham, the Archbishop of Canterbury, and to the older school of churchmen, his attacks on monasteries and foundations, his support of the new education, his extensive diplomatic entanglements and his regular meetings with foreign rulers, his rapid succession of church offices, his hope of the Papacy itself—all of these created a feeling of alarm in England, and especially in London, that provided a common motive for many poems, similar in spirit to Roy and Barlowe's *Rede Me and be not Wroth*[4] (1528), *Of the Cardnall Wolse*[5] (1521-22), and the satires of Skelton between 1518 and 1523.

In the first of his satires, *Colin Clout*,[6] Skelton presents himself

2. *Letters and Papers*, ii, 4399.
3. cf. H. C. Maxwell-Lyte, *History of the University of Oxford*, 236.
4. cf. Arber Reprint of Strasburg edition of 1528.
5. Furnivall, *Ballads from MSS.*, ii, 240.
6. For a fully detailed discussion of *Colin Clout* see chapter vi.

in the character of Colin Clout, the mouth-piece of the lay-folks, and continually emphasizes that he is speaking not of individual churchmen, but only repeating the popular complaints. The complaints are sweeping enough. The bishops are neglecting their duty, and the honest churchmen are 'loth to mell.' They are slothful and ignorant and can construe 'neither Gospell nor Pystle'; they live in ease, forgetful of the poor people who live in misery, and pay no heed to 'the people mones' and even pervert law in favour of churchmen. The truly religious men must beg and 'synge from place to place,' and even nuns must leave their nunneries, for foundations and monasteries are being broken up. The prelates should be 'lanternes of light,' but among them is one who will have a 'fatal fall.' The church is falling into disrepute because of Lutheran, Wycliffite, Hussian and similar heresies. The prelates now 'rule both Kynge and Kayser,' and noble lords pay tribute to them, in spite of the prelates' lowly origins. The bishops should not delegate their duties to Masters of Arts or friars—they should preach themselves, instead of allowing sermons to be delivered by an often ignorant clergy or by friars who preach simply for a living. The bishops do not even support the church's cause, but build royally and fill their halls with wanton tapestries. So runs the general complaint—one man rules the king; but his fortune may change, though at present nothing may be commanded but by permission of 'our presydent . . . . or els his substytute.' When such is the people's complaint 'somewhat there is amysse.' Skelton assures his readers of his own disinterestedness. He speaks only 'of them that do amys,' and if there be any who feel 'touched to the quycke' let them amend speedily. The bishops are represented as replying angrily—and revealingly—and the poem closes with a prayer to Christ to 'rectyfye and amende Thynges that are amys.'

The continually apologetic tone is significant. Skelton is speaking for the people and accuses no individual. But the references to 'our presydent,' to the tampering with monasteries and nunneries and foundations and to churchmen ruling the king point to a concealed attack on Wolsey, while 'his substytute' probably covers a reference to Thomas Ruthall, the Bishop of

Durham, who was his faithful henchman during these years. The
poem is surprisingly general in its language, and time and again
Skelton seems to avoid the possibility of uttering specific charges.

This air of generality coupled with references to Wolsey has
led Professor Berdan to suggest that the poem was written
piecemeal before Skelton began his attack on Wolsey and that
the Wolsey passages were grafted on as late as 1524-5.[7] *Colin
Clout* is mentioned in *The Garlande of Laurell* (1523) and so
must be earlier, but Berdan finds evidence for subsequent additions
in references to events that are apparently later than 1523. There
are four such crucial allusions. However, an examination of
contemporary records reveals that all four passages can be dated
before 1523, and so proves that *Colin Clout* must have been written
in its present form as a continuous and completed poem before
Skelton listed it in the *Garlande*.

These four disputable allusions must be examined in detail:
The breaking up of foundations: Religious men are compelled
to 'synge from place to place'; the nuns 'must cast up their blacke
veyles'; the people tell how the prelates

> . . . with foundacyons melles,
> And talkys lyke tytyuelles,
> Howe ye brake the dedes wylles,
> Turne monasteris into water milles,
> Of an abbay ye make a graunge.

Berdan takes these lines to be an allusion to the bull which Wolsey
procured in 1524 to allow him to use monastery funds to found
his Cardinal's College at Oxford.

Wolsey, however, had been casting his eyes at the monasteries
far earlier than 1524. In 1518 he procured a bull (dated 27
August) through the agency of Giglis de Silvester, Bishop of
Worcester and ambassador in Rome, the terms of which are nearer
to the Skelton passage. Silvester writes to Wolsey that he sends
the bull for the visitation of the monasteries, of the same tenor
as that obtained by the Bishop of Luxemburg for France. It
contains no provision for reforming the clergy, as that belongs to
the bishops, but he has often been struck by the necessity for
reforming the monasteries, although he considers those in his

7. J. M. Berdan, *The Dating of Skelton's Satires*, *P.L.M.A.* 21, 499ff.

diocese will complain.   Great care will be required in visiting
nunneries, as many errors will be found in them.[8]

It is unnecessary to assume an allusion to the 1524 bull when
one had already been granted in 1518; on these grounds one must
reject the suggestion that this passage was an addition to the
original poem.

Berdan takes the passage (ll. 162-186) on the fear of the honest
clergy to interfere with Wolsey, and on the extravagance of the
prelates as a reference to Wolsey's attempt in 1523 to extract
from Convocation by his legatine authority a fifty per cent. war
tax:

> But nowe euery spirituall father,
> Men say, they had rather
> Spend moche of theyr share
> Than to be combred with care;
> Spend! nay, nay, but spare.

The sense of the passage is against this.   It is a general attack on
the luxury of 'euery spirituall father,' who would rather spend
money on his private pleasures than be 'combred with care' of
preaching and leading the church.   These prelates will not even
defend the church against the criticism of the laity:

> But it is not worth a leke:
> Boldness is to seke
> The Churche for to defend.

The attack is on the spending of money for private luxury—
not on the extravagance of a war-loan—and this nullifies the
arguments for referring the passage to 1523.   It could belong to
any year in the previous decade.

Berdan cites as a later addition the description of the tapestries
with which the pleasure-loving prelates decorate their halls.
Skelton's description tallies exactly with a set which Wolsey
possessed in Hampton Court.   Here the evidence requires careful
examination.   Skelton's description can be no other than an
eye-witness's account:

> Arras of ryche aray,
> Fresshe as flours in May;
> With dame Dyana naked;
> Howe lusty Venus quaked,

---

8. This letter is calendared in *Letters and Papers*, ii, 4399, from B.M. Vit.B., iii, 231.

And howe Cupyde shaked
His darte, and bent his bowe
For to shote a crowe
At her tyrly tyrlowe;
And howe Parys of Troy
Daunced a lege de moy,
Made lusty sporte and ioy
With dame Helyn the quene;
With such storyes bydene
Their chambres well besene
With triumphs of Caesar,
And of Pompeyus war,
Of renowne and of fame
By them to get a name;
Nowe all the worlde stares,
Howe they ryde in goodly chares,
Conueyed by olyphantes,
With lauryat garlantes,
And by vnycornes
With their semely hornes;
Vpon these beestes rydynge,
Naked boyes strydynge,
With wanton wenches winkyng.
Nowe truly, to my thynkynge,
That is a speculacyon
And a mete meditacyon
For prelates of estate,
Their courage to abate
From worldly wantonnesse.

Some at least of these tapestries have been identified as a set still preserved at Hampton Court:

Of these six triumphs (Wolsey having duplicates of those of Time and Eternity) we at once identify three, namely, those of Death, Renown, and Time, as still remaining at Hampton Court in Henry VIII's great Watching or Guard Chamber; while the other three—of Love, Chastity, and Eternity or Divinity—complete the set of six designs, which are illustrative, in an allegorical form, of Petrarch's *Triumphs*.[9]

These tapestries tally so closely with those described by Skelton that they must be accepted as the same. They are listed in Wolsey's inventory as:

Hangings bought of the executors of my lord of Durham, 14 Henry VIII, containing the triumphs of Time, Death, Chastity,

9. Ernest Law, *A History of Hampton Court Palace*, 2nd ed., 1890, I, pp. 63-65.

L

Eternity, Cupid and Venus, and Renown or Julius Caesar and others *de filio producto*.[10]

Now 'my lord of Durham' is Wolsey's lieutenant, Thomas Ruthall, Bishop of Durham, who died on 4 February 1523.

Two interpretations are therefore possible. The description of the tapestries belongs to the original draft of the poem, which was written while Ruthall was alive, and the attack is an attack on Ruthall; or the description belongs to the period after 1523, when the tapestries were in the possession of Wolsey. In this case (and Berdan accepts the latter hypothesis) the whole passage must be a later addition.

There are as good reasons for accepting Ruthall as the object of attack. The whole poem is a general attack on the bishops and not simply on the Cardinal alone. Among the covert references to individuals is one to the deputy of Wolsey:

> . . . Without his presydent be by,
> Or els his substytute
> Whom he will depute.

This 'substytute' so singled out for attack is almost certainly the same Lord of Durham, who is represented by Brewer as Wolsey's drudge, and who accompanied him on most of his diplomatic missions. In a general onslaught on the luxury of the prelates— 'ye bisshops of estates'—there is no reason for assuming that Wolsey rather than the Bishop of Durham is the object of attack. Skelton seems to be describing the tapestries while they were still in the possession of Ruthall, and there is no evidence for the assumption that when he wrote the description they had passed into the hands of Wolsey. They may be accepted as part of the original poem, and another argument for piecemeal construction disappears.

Berdan finds evidence for other versions of *Colin Clout* in William Bullein's citation from it in his *Dialogue against the Fever Pestilence* (1564), where the lines of *Colin Clout*:

> Howe prelacy is solde and bought
> And come up of nought

appear as:

> How the Cardinall came of nought
> And his Prelacies solde and bought.

10. *Letters and Papers*, IV, 6184.

It is placing too great faith on the accuracy of quotation in the sixteenth century to base a theory of varying versions on a possible misquotation or corruption or a mere citation from memory. In conjunction with the three other pieces of evidence it was of some value, but when the other evidence for the later date disappears on close scrutiny, the fourth point becomes valueless in isolation.

There is, on the contrary, a very strong tradition that *Colin Clout* is Skelton's first attack on the Cardinal, and though the attack is not yet pointed and is more often on the prelates than on the virtual head of the church, the tradition of its priority must be allowed some weight in deciding the date of the poem. The view that *Colin Clout* is a single coherent poem and the earliest of the Wolsey group is strongly supported by the internal evidence. One compelling argument that it is one poem and not a collection of oddments circulated privately and later fitted together is the impression of unity that comes from a reading of the poem. Professor Berdan states that Skelton inserted the Wolsey passage and then 'erased the lines of cleavage.' The lines of cleavage have certainly disappeared—there is no trace of patchwork in the complete poem. It reads as a whole, and the passages hinting at Wolsey as integral parts of it.

The final and strongest argument for the poem's integrity is to me conclusive. The Wolsey passages are not strong enough or bitter enough to represent what ought, on Berdan's hypothesis, to be Skelton's later attitude—they are in the same disinterested tone as the rest of the work. In 1523 Skelton finished his bitterest attack on Wolsey in *Why Come Ye Nat to Court?* Every reference to the Cardinal has a poisoned sting. Why should Skelton after 1523 (in 1524-5, as Berdan suggests) return to a poem of perhaps 1519 and add, not more vitriolic passages, but obscure references for which he is at some pains to apologize?

> For no man have I named:
> Wherefore sholde I be blamed?

In 1523 he could 'name' his victim in the most objectionable terms. Why not in 1524-5? Indeed, it has already been shown[11] that by 1524 Skelton, far from renewing an attack on the Cardinal, was

11. p. 41 ff. of this study.

rather supplicating Wolsey in language which has at least the semblance of penitence. *Colin Clout,* then, is one single poem, composed within a fairly short and discoverable space of time. Skelton was artist enough not to throw together his poems as if from a rag-bag. As *Speke Parrot,* the second of the Wolsey series, was written in 1521, and Luther references demand that *Colin Clout* should be later than 1517-18, one may safely ascribe to it the date of 1519-20, and so establish it as the first of the attacks on Wolsey. So far the attack is apologetic, not exclusively devoted to the Cardinal, appearing side by side with stock pre-Renaissance complaints against the clergy. Skelton was only standing further back from his victim to sight his next shot more accurately, and in perhaps only a year's time every shot was going to find its mark with the uncompromising assault in *Speke Parrot.*

Speke Parrot has always been a baffling poem. Under the cloak of Parrot, a bird 'of a wonderous kynde,' Skelton continues the attack on the Cardinal, and by almost every device known to satire, innuendo and frontal attack, cryptic oracular utterance and direct charges he lays bare the weakness of Wolsey's policy. The date is again of importance if one is to steer aright through a poem of concealed topical reference. Berdan[12] dates the poem from mysterious numbers 33° and 34° at the end of the poem's sections, which he conjectures is Skelton's method of indicating the date of the composition. He suggests that Skelton dated the poem from the accession of Henry VII, in whose court he had served and whom he might still regard as his master. 33 Henry VII and 34 Henry VII would give the dates 1517 and 1518, which Berdan accepts as the date of the composition—the poem thus being a series of scattered and separate comments on the events of these years. But, like *Colin Clout, Speke Parrot* gives an impression of unity. The disjointed composition is intentional, and the attack centres so deliberately round one theme that one cannot agree that the arrangement is purely haphazard. The attempt to square the allusions in the poem with the years 1517 and 1518 breaks down, particularly in the Secunde Lenvoy, where what must be a reference to Wolsey on a mission to France is taken by Berdan to refer to a 1518 embassy of Charles Somerset, Earl of Worcester:

12. *M.L.N.,* xxx, 140-144.

With porpose and graundepose he may fede hym fatte,
Thowghe he pampyr not hys paunche with the grete seall:
We haue longyd and lokyd long tyme for that,
Whyche cawsythe pore suters haue many a hongry mele:
As presydent and regente he rulythe every deall.

Berdan interprets these lines as inapplicable to Wolsey because they appear to suggest that Wolsey had not the Great Seal. But the use of 'thowghe' is evidently concessive—he may feed himself fat with porpoise and grampus even if he did not already have the Great Seal—and the reference to the 'presydent and regente' can be to Wolsey alone. The poem is concerned not with an embassy of Somerset of 1518 but with a later embassy of Wolsey himself traceable to the year 1521.

An examination of the poem confirms the later date. It must have been written towards the end of 1521, for the references, as we shall see, are to Wolsey's meeting at Calais with Francis I and with Charles at Bruges in the autumn of that year. This date is confirmed and strengthened by Skelton's references to Greek.

The Latin dates throughout the poem agree exactly with the progress of Wolsey's embassy.[13] He left Dover on 2 August 1521 and left France for England on 28 November. In *Speke Parrot* we find that he is abroad *(Penultimo die Octobris)*; he is 'ovyr the salte fome' *(in diebus Novembris)*; he is invited to return—'he may now come agayne as he wente' *(15 Kalendis Decembris,* i.e., 17 November, a few days before his return); the King is warned against him in Latin verse *(Kalendis Decembris)*; and the rest of the poem is a general attack on Wolsey after an embassy with

> So myche consultation almoste to none entente.

Wolsey is invited to return:

> 'the way he went;
> From Calys to Dover, to Canterbury in Kent'

—another indication that the Calais embassy of 1521 is intended.

The second section confirms the later date. In it Skelton attacks the progress of Greek studies. In 1516 Bishop Fox had founded Corpus Christi College, Oxford, as a humanist college encouraging Greek. This led to bitter quarrels between 'Trojans' and

---

13. For the progress of the embassy see *State Papers Henry VIII,* 1; Letters 19, 21, 24, 25, 27, 29, 39, 44, 50.

'Greeks,' but after More's letter of 1519 and Wolsey's foundation of a Greek chair in 1520, Greek was studied without further opposition.

Skelton has these events in mind when, remembering the faction fights, he talks of 'our Grekis,' while the lines (167-8)

> *In Academia* Parrot dare no problem kepe;
> For *Graece fari* so occupyeth the chayre

imply that Greek had now an official position, and the *chayre* is very probably Wolsey's lectureship of 1520.   The poem is unquestionably later than 1517-18, and the end of 1521 is clearly implied in its contemporary references.[14]

Having now established that *Speke Parrot* was written at the end of 1521, we are in a much better position to understand the meaning of this hitherto very obscure poem.   It is an extremely clever piece of work and its abrupt transitions and cryptic allusions ally it closely with the more allusive poems of our own day—but with Skelton we lack the explanatory bibliography appended to *The Waste Land*.   The Parrot, like the modern poet, is a learned bird.   He can cite Latin, Greek, Spanish, French, German, and gibberish for his own purpose, and glance at a topic by the merest skimming of its surface to pass swiftly on to another hinted accusation before one is quite sure whether or not the victim has been touched.

The first section describes Parrot in fanciful language.   Parrot is the master of all languages and prays for the King and

> Kateryne incomparable, our ryall quene also.

The policy of Wolsey is hinted at—'wylfulness is vycar generall,' but he immediately drops the topic of 'Vitulus in Oreb' (i.e., Wolsey) because it is 'besynes again.'   Skelton pleads:

> I pray you, let Parrot haue lyberte to speke,

and Wolsey is alluded to under a variety of biblical names like that of 'Og, that fat hog Basan,' but Skelton again drops the theme:

> Parrot pretendith to be a bybyll clarke,

14. cf. I. A. Gordon, *T.L.S.*, 1934, p. 74, where this evidence was first published.   Wm. Nelson's article 'Skelton's Speke Parrot' (*P.M.L.A.* 1936, 59 ff.) repeats substantially the same evidence and independently confirms my original dating.

and the section ends with the dark hint that Wolsey will betray the King's confidence:

Quod magnus est dominus Judas Scarioth.

The second section is Skelton's attack on Wolsey's educational policy. As a result of Wolsey's educational schemes (it is implied) the old education has become neglected and young scholars presume to learn Greek and read Plautus and Quintilian who can hardly construe a verse of Cato Minor:

Settynge theyr myndys so moche of eloquens
That of theyr scole maters lost is the whole sentence,

and Wolsey's foundation of a Greek chair has corrupted the old Latin learning. Skelton claims the satirist's right:

But that metaphora, allegoria with all,
Shall be his protectyon, his pauys and his wall,

and the section closes with a fine appeal, for a moment reminiscent of Dunbar's *Lament for the Makers*, to Wolsey to remember that even he is mortal:

For that pereless prynce, that Parrot dyd create,
He made you of nothynge by his magistye:
Poynt well this probleme that Parrot doth prate
And remembre amonge how Parrot and ye
Shall lepe from thys lyfe, as mery as we be;
Pompe, pryde, honour, ryches, and worldly lust
Parrot sayth playnly, shall tourne all to dust.

After an inset lyric, Skelton in three 'envoys' returns to the attack on Wolsey, who is wasting his time abroad on useless embassies:

Go, litell quayre, namyd the Popagay
Home to resorte Jerobesethe perswade.

Parrot must call Wolsey home again. There was nothing to be gained by bargaining with either Charles or Francis:

For Jericho and Jerssey shall mete togethyr as sone
As he to exployte the man owte of the mone.

After a protest:

Was neuyr suche a senatour syn Crystes incarnacion,

Henry VIII is warned in Latin verse:

Rex regeris, non ipse regis: rex inclyte, calle;
Subde tibi vitulum, ne fatuet nimium,

and Skelton adds in his *Lenvoy royall*:

> For trowthe in parabyll ye wantonlye pronounce,
> Langagys diuers, yet undyr that dothe reste
> Maters more precious than the ryche jacounce
> Diamounde or rubye, or balas of the beste.

The poem rounds again on Wolsey. The King is eclipsed by the Cardinal:

> Iupyter for Saturne dare make no royall chere.

Wolsey plays his game boldly:

> He caryeth a Kyng in hys sleve, yf all the worlde fayle;
> He facithe oute at a flusshe, with, shewe, take all!
> Of Pope Julius cardys he ys chefe cardynall,

and in the final section, spurred on by the call to

> Sette asyde all sophysms, and speke now trew and playne,

the poem closes with a general lament, closely resembling Dunbar's *A General Satire,* that forms the most effective part of the poem. Indignation and moral fervour combine to make a sombre but impressive finale expressed in language at once bitter and effective:

> So many vacabondes, so many beggars bolde;
> So myche decay of monesteries and of relygious places;
> So hote hatered agaynste the Chyrche, and cheryte so colde;
> So myche of my lordes Grace, and in hym no grace ys;
> So many holow hartes, and so dowbyll faces.

Speke Parrot is not such a puzzle after all. As an attack on Wolsey in the year 1521 after an embassy that boded no good for England, it throws a revealing light on the temper of the average man, who regarded Wolsey's schemes with distrust and whose attitude Skelton reflects in every line. The time was long past when Wolsey might be counted merely the worst offender in a corrupt church. The people complained of his arrogance and presumption, of his hopes of the Papacy for himself and of Europe for Henry. Skelton—the 'royal popagay'—was more and more inclined to come into the open with his attack, and though the satire in *Speke Parrot* is often allusive, it is none the less clear. The onslaught on Og, Jerobesethe, Syre Sydrake, and Seigneour Sadoke is all the fiercer because under these names is concealed the hated title of Cardinal Wolsey.

The form of the poem is ingenious. The garrulous Parrot, who is merely Skelton, is surprisingly modern in conception. He is bound neither by logic nor by chronology, and utters his thoughts as they emerge from his mind with the association of ideas often as their only link with each other. But the dominant mood is preserved throughout and imposes a unity on what might easily have been a collection of satirical oddments. The difficulty of *Speke Parrot* has obscured its amazing originality. Here in the first few years of the sixteenth century is Skelton writing in an idiom of the twentieth. Thought order replaces the order of logic. A unity of mood and of objective replaces unity of design. How far Skelton realized what he was creating can hardly be known. But his method of writing in *Speke Parrot* is disconcertingly close to that of T. S. Eliot and Ezra Pound, and emphasizes the allusive bias of the mind of Skelton. It is hardly to be wondered at that his contemporaries misunderstood and in some cases disliked his poetry. Occasionally it could be too original even for the Renaissance.

His final attack on Wolsey came in the following year, *Why Come Ye Nat to Court?* in the last months of 1522 and the early months of 1523. Skelton is cryptic and allusive no longer. England had become involved in a foreign war, with its inevitable companion a Scottish campaign. Wolsey was attempting to raise a new war tax towards the end of 1522. Commons, clergy and people were united against his new measures, and in *Why Come Ye Nat to Court?* Skelton fights with the gloves off against a political and foreign policy that seemed to involve the country in ruinous expense all for one man's glory.

The poem is the easiest of all the satires to date, so frequent are the references to current events. A brief survey of these references leaves no doubt that the months October 1522 to March 1523 saw the composition of the bulk of the poem. The evidence may be briefly summarized:

1. At line 638 it is sixteen years, according to Skelton, since Wolsey was a chaplain 'with a poore knyght.' The knight was Sir R. Nanfan, who died in January 1507. This brings the poem down to about January 1523.   2. Line 905 makes the mayor of

London a goldsmith.   The goldsmith, Sir John Munday, became
mayor on 28 October 1522.[15]   3. Lines 150 ff. are concerned with
Surrey's expedition to France.   Surrey was back again in Calais
after his raid on 14 October 1522.[16] 4. Lines 282 ff. Lord Rose,
Warden of the East and Middle Marches, is in the north.   He
was back south again by 24 October 1522.[17]   5. Lines 269 ff.
mention with some acrimony the truce of 11 September 1522 made
by Dacres and Albany.[78]   6. Line 1096. Wolsey has made himself
Abbot of St. Albans *in commendam.*   The bull for this was
granted by Adrian VI on 8 November 1522.[19]   7. Other minor
details all point to the end of 1522—the reference to 'Mutrell'
(l. 375), i.e., Montrieul, which was in the news at the time, and
the protest throughout against Wolsey's taxation towards the end
of the year.[20]   8. A lower date is provided by the reference
(l. 784) to 'Master Mewtis,' the King's French secretary, who, it
is darkly hinted, has been privately killed for treason.   The patent
for his successor, Brian Tuke, was issued on 15 March 1523,[21]
and between this date and the October or November of the
previous year the poem was composed.   Such a reference to earlier
events as at l. 74 to 'the countrying at Callis,' i.e. the 1521 embassy,
is naturally a cut back and is not—as has been sometimes held[22]—
of the same date as the poem.

> Haec vates ille
> De quo loquuntur mille

is Skelton's introduction to the bitterest of all his attacks.   He is
not alone, not a mere minor priest crossing swords with a powerful
Cardinal, but a satiric poet of the people with all the characteristics
of the type—the faults of railing and invective and the virtues of
vigour and *saeva indignatio.   Why Come Ye Nat to Court?* is a
fine piece of satire, unscrupulous, as satire so often is, in its
charges, but quivering with indignation and a sense of justification
that raises it above the purely personal lampoon.   Skelton's hatred
of Wolsey was a profounder emotion than the dislike behind his
moral attack in *Colin Clout.*   Truth and rumour both provide

---

15. cf. Brie, *Skelton Studien,* 86.
17. *Letters and Papers* III, 2636.
19. *Letters and Papers* III, 2658.
21. *Letters and Papers* III, 2894.

16. *Letters and Papers,* III, 2614.
18. *Letters and Papers* III, 2717, 2723.
20. *Letters and Papers* III, 2707, 2706.
22. e.g., J. M. Berdan, loc. cit., *P.M.L.A.*

material for abuse of the Cardinal. Skelton aimed his blows with a savage barbarity that indicates how he enjoyed the attack, and his language becomes even more than usually vigorous and direct. Every word hits its mark. One is tempted to ask where it all came from. Satire like this had not been written in England and would not be written for many years. It is not the mediaeval English satire of the Piers Plowman tradition, and classical satire was still to come. Here again perhaps Skelton is unwittingly in advance of his time. There is nothing mediaeval in *Why Come Ye Nat to Court?* The vigour and directness is that of the Renaissance; but the conception is Skelton's own.

Reason, complains the poet, is banished in the present age. The past few years has been a period of:

> Banketynge braynlesse,
> With ryotynge rechelesse,
> With gambaudynge thryftlesse,
> With spende and wast witlesse,
> Treatinge of trewce restlesse,
> Prating for peace peasless.

Only one man is responsible:

> For whyles he doth rule
> All is warse and warse.

We have made 'a worthy truce,' and our army returns 'and never a Scot slayne' though Surrey has conquered the French. But they have overshot us and bribed the Cardinal:

> They shote all at one marke,
> At the Cardynals hat
> They shote all at that,

for the Cardinal in the 'Chambre of Starres' rules everything—but can easily be corrupted. He breaks all the strict rules against simony and fast days and has even darker vices:

> But at the naked stewes
> I vnderstande how that
> The sygne of the Cardynall Hat
> That inne is now shut up
> With, gup, hore, gup, now gup.

Skelton turns again to the course of public events, so disappointing to a public kept in ignorance of the diplomacy behind them:

> What here ye of the Scottes
> They make vs all sottes,

and the recent moves of the Warden of the Marches seem no better:

> What here ye of the lorde Dakers
> He maketh vs Jacke Rakers.

The other Warden is no better:

> What here ye of the lorde Rose?
> Nothynge to purpose.

The barons are afraid to move 'For drede of the bochers dogge,' Wolsey, who lords over everybody:

> Thus royally he dothe deale
> Vnder the Kynges brode seale;
> And in the Checker he them cheks;
> In the Star Chamber he noddis and beks,
> And bereth him there so stowte,
> That no man dare rowte,
> Duke, erle, baron, nor lorde
> But to his sentence must accorde.

Scotland is mishandled. Surrey is checked. Foreign affairs go none too well. Skelton restrains himself no longer but launches into the attack that gave the poem its title:

> Why come ye nat to court?—
> To whyche courte?
> To the Kynges courte
> Or to Hampton court? . . .
> The Kynges courte
> Shulde have the excellence
> But Hampton court
> Hath the preemynence
> And Yorkes Place
> With my lordes grace.

All laws, legal and ecclesiastical, go there by the board:

> Strawe for lawe canon
> Or for the lawe common
> Or for the lawe cyuyll!
> It shall be as he wyll.

For those who disagree there are the Fleet and the Tower and the Marshalsea. Even the King is subverted. Yet Wolsey is of lowly origin—'his greasy genealogy' is Skelton's expressive phrase! He

is not even a doctor, but 'a poor maister of arte,' and his Latin is
suspect:

> His Latyne tonge doth hobbyll
> He doth but cloute and cobbill
> In Tullis faculte,

and but for the King's favour he would still be nothing. But now
he rails 'lyke Mahounde in a play' or puts off suitors even of the
King, who ought to realize the danger:

> It is a wonders case
> That the Kynges grace
> Is toward him so mynded,
> And so farre blynded,

and illustrative tales are told from Petrarch and Gaguin, the
French historian and friend of Erasmus:

> Christ kepe King Henry the Eyght
> From treachery and dysceyght
> And graunt him grace to know
> The faucon from the crow.

Skelton then deals in a deliberately mystifying manner with the
fate of Meautis, the King's French secretary, implying that he
had earned his fate because of his treachery and wishing that
everyone

> Of his affynte
> Were gone as well as he!

Wolsey has exhausted the country with taxation and the money has
gone abroad:

> Now nothynge but pay, pay
> With laughe and lay downe
> Borowgh, cyte, and towne.

The state of England has been brought low. 'Now all is out of
facion.' Wolsey accuses even preachers:

> He calleth the prechours dawis,
> And of holy scriptures sawis
> He counteth them for gygawis,

No preacher may speak 'Of my lordis grace nor his wife'—a grave
charge to make against a highly placed prelate, though Skelton was
reputed to have a 'wife' himself.

The attack becomes more and more specific: Wolsey eats 'pigges
in Lent'; he has made himself Abbot of St. Albans; he abuses the
Great Seal and his legatine authority, he disregards the authority

of Canterbury, he is afflicted with the pox. With this final fling
the satire closes and Skelton justifies ʃhis attack with Juvenal's
Quia difficile est satiram non scribere:

> Blame Iuuinall, and blame nat me.

After a few Latin verses equally barbed against Wolsey, Skelton
concludes where he had begun:

> Haec vates ille
> De quo loquuntur mille.

The satire is one of the bitterest and most effective in English.
There is no mediaeval allegory here—no attempt to conceal Wolsey
as Holy Church or Lady Mede, nor is he concealed in the classical
satire manner as Gracchus or even as Pontifex Maximus. Every
blow is meant and every blow tells. The very indignation and
exaggeration strengthen its value both as history and as literature.
These were the feelings of the people of London at the time—
indignant, bitter, and ready to catch at any slanderous attack to
augment their hatred of the Cardinal. *Why Come Ye Nat to Court?*
is historically important because it reflects so vividly the temper of
London, and this faithful representation gives it much of its literary
importance. As a mere personal attack, *Why Come Ye Nat to
Court?* would be on a lower satirical plane. But it catches the
popular temper and expresses it in the decisive terms that a London
public would—and did—appreciate.

The pungent terms of *Why Come Ye Nat to Court?* are Renaissance in their vernacular vigour and precision. There is a whole
world and a whole civilization between the 'sugrit termis aureat'
of the Chaucerians, English and Scottish, and the stark but purpose-
ful intensity of Skelton. The depth of his hatred gave direction to
his style and meaning to his poetic vocabulary. Skelton is the poet
of plain words rebelling against the colourful but all too often
meaningless vocabulary of his predecessors as effectively (though
not so explicitly) as Wordsworth did when he abandoned the
poetic diction of the eighteenth century. Skelton's verse, as he
himself ruefully admits, is rude. But it has life and vigour. All the
intensity of the Renaissance, that so often overshot its mark and
left later ages to achieve balance, all the boisterous abandon of
vocabulary and thought that later appealed to the Elizabethan
dramatists, go into the satires of Skelton to be credited against his

blindness and his intense partiality. These faults are, however, personal. His virtues are essentially literary. If Skelton had seen the events of the day from a more impartial point of view, if he had halted to consider the rights and wrongs of the Scots and of Albany and Wolsey, we might have had a more balanced picture of his times, but the piquancy of his satire would have been lost.

The development of the attack was as rapid as it was striking. A few years sufficed to turn a possible patron into the most dangerous and hated figure in England, and from the general satire of *Colin Clout* with its dark hints, its apologetic and hesitant references to current affairs, evolved the cryptic but direct attack of *Speke Parrot* and the uncompromising fury of *Why Come Ye Nat to Court?* None of these poems was printed in the lifetime of either Skelton or the Cardinal. But for a parish priest to circulate *Why Come Ye Nat to Court?* even in manuscript must have required courage of no mean order and a passionate belief in the justice of the accusations.

As literature, perhaps *Why Come Ye Nat to Court?* is the best of them. It has all the elements of good satire—unity of object, precision of attack, intensity, sincerity, and that clarity so characteristic of the Renaissance and so seldom present in the tangled obscurities of mediaeval allegory. Skelton hit hard because he visualized clearly. He has no subtlety and no finesse. Atticus and Sporus, Zimri and Donne's Courtier are alike beyond his range. But he could produce excellent hammer strokes, and his indignation raised his satire above the mere railing of, for example, Marston. All the time he used his language with a sense of the value of his words. One seldom feels, as one does with Hawes and Barclay, that the language is running away with the matter. Skelton's line-groups in a late poem like *Why Come Ye Nat to Court?* often run into blocks of a dozen or more riming lines; but even in the longest of these groups there is an essential element of control—they do not tail away weakly into expletives and similar mediaeval padding, but continue expressive and succinct till a fresh wave catches the verse and carries the attack a stage further forward. Classical satire always excepted, there is nothing so successful till *Hudibras*—and, compared with Butler, Skelton scores both on language and on sincerity.

CHAPTER X

POETRY AND POLITICS

SKELTON'S ASSOCIATION WITH THE COURT AND THE NOBLE family of Howards meant that he was in close touch with the politics of the day, and his ready pen leapt to the service of his monarch and his patron. His sturdy patriotism for England and his more personal regard for both Henry VIII and his father resulted in a series of political poems in which the classical scholar and the vigorous vernacular poet strangely alternate. Skelton's patriotism developed along two lines—admiration of the King and hatred of his enemies. There is in the political poems no central figure, like Wolsey in the religious satires, who could be a target for his attacks and a symbol of all he was fighting against. There is nothing of the gentler aspects of patriotism, no explicit love of the English countryside, no special delight in loyalty. But there is a fierce and sometimes irreverent attack on her enemies. Now the target is the Scots, now the French. The satire plays from James IV of Scotland to Louis, the most Christian King of France, from the Duke of Albany to the rough Scots of Galloway, and elevates by contrast the deeds of Henry himself and of his able lieutenants the Lords Surrey and Howard. The attack and the satire is mainly in English, the praise in more portly Latin. Sometimes the Latin and English poems must have been written within a few days of each other, and the contrast is made all the stronger between the unemotional praises of the Latin elegiacs and the scornful denunciations of the English poems. Skelton's political poems are destructive, inspired by hatred rather than by constructive ideas, blindly prejudiced as so many of his poems are, but made all the more vital by the intensity of his hatred. He could hate a nation as heartily as he hated an individual, and the false Scots can rouse him to the same burning indignation as the arrogance of the Cardinal.

In these political poems lies the proof, if proof is required, that Skelton's poems were often circulated while they were still warm

from the anvil. His work must have been often written at speed
in the heat of the event—sometimes before he was fully aware
of the truth—and rushed out to celebrate or comment on events
still fresh in the public mind. His first ballad on Flodden was
written and published within weeks (perhaps days) of the battle
and a second revised version produced within another week or
two, when it appeared that the details of the earlier poem were
mainly rumours. At such periods Skelton appears to have composed in a fever of political excitement and hastened to be the first
to condemn the enemy and congratulate the King.

The political poems mainly cluster round the years 1513 and
1523-4, the years in which Henry had most to fear from a Scottish
invasion. But even earlier than this Skelton showed his private
hatred of the Scots in his *Henrici Septimi Epitaphium* (which he
dates 1512) where Henry VII is the great Anchises of whom the
Scottish King is in terror:

> Nobilis Anchises, armis metuendus Atrides
> Hic erat; hunc Scottus rex timuit Jacobus,

and he goes on to praise Henry for keeping the French in awe and
increasing his treasury. After the defeat of Flodden Skelton
turned back grimly to this epitaph and added four lines on the
death of James '*Qui sua fata luit,*' well pleased that his comment
had turned out to be a prophecy. In another of his Latin poems,
the *Eulogium pro suorum temporum conditione* (1512), which is
half praise of the dead Henry VII and half a eulogy of Henry VIII,
Skelton is apprehensive now of the danger from abroad:

> Undique bella fremunt nunc, undique proelia surgunt;
> Noster honor solus, filius, ecce suus!

He looks to Henry to protect England—peacefully if possible:

> Sors tamen est versanda diu, sors ultima belli.

When the war did begin Skelton has thoughts for nothing but
victory and the domination of Henry,

> ' Dulce meum decus, et sola Britanna salus.

The story of Flodden is well known and only a brief summary
of the leading events need be given. When Henry VIII decided
on 17 November 1511 to support the Holy League, Aragon,

M

Venice, and the Pope, and to go to war against France he fully
realized the danger of a Scottish invasion, but he invaded France
in 1513 and settled down to the siege of Thérouanne, which
capitulated on August 22.   In the meantime Louis xii had been
negotiating with James iv of Scotland, inviting him to attack
England. James after some deliberation declared war and crossed
the Tweed on the very day Thérouanne fell. The campaign was
short lived. James besieged Norham Castle and captured it while
Surrey, the Lord Treasurer of England, hastened northwards to
defend the Border. On September 9 the two armies met at
Flodden, and by evening the King and most of the Scottish
nobility lay dead on the field. News of the victory spread to
England immediately, though the details were garbled or unknown.
Rumour had it that James escaped, but in a few days the truth
began to filter through, and Henry's triumph was complete.[1]

One incident in the tangle of intrigues angered Skelton above
all. While Henry was at Thérouanne he received a letter from
the King of Scots complaining of Henry's invasion of France and
desiring him 'to desiste fra further invasion and utter destruction
of our brother and Cousing the mast Christan Kyng.' Henry
replied in protest that James had been merely lying in wait for
his departure, that England was ready for him, and that he
had better remember the example of the King of Navarre 'who is
a Kyng withoute a realme, and so the Frenche Kynge peacably
suffereth hym to continue, whereunto goode regard would be
taken.'[2]

Skelton rushed into print to celebrate the victory of Flodden with
the *Ballade of the Scottyshe King,* which was printed by Richard
Fawkes in 1513. Throughout the poem the King of Scotland is
jeered at in the present tense as if he were still alive. A few
days after its publication the King's body was found, and more
details of the battle came through, especially of the parts played
by Surrey and Howard. Skelton recast the whole poem and
produced this revised version, *Skelton Laureate against the Scottes,*
towards the end of the year.

    1. cf. M. Wood, *Flodden Papers,* Scottish History Society, Edinburgh, 1933 (introduction
lxv and pp. 79-83).
    2. cf. J. Ashton, *A Ballade of the Scottyshe Kynge,* London, 1919, pp. 48-9. Nelson
(p. 133) suggests that Skelton might have crossed to the continent with Henry and might
even be the author of Henry's letter.

The earliest poem of the Flodden group is in Latin, the *Chorus de Dis super Triumphali Victoria contra Gallos,* in which Skelton celebrates the victory at Thérouanne of August 22. The sixteen lines of Latin have the air of an improvisation dashed off on the receipt of the news. Henry is hailed as victor:

> Salve festa dies, toto memorabilis aevo
> Qua rex Henricus Gallica bella premit.

The pride of the French nobles is fallen. But the British are magnanimous to the defeated. The poem closes with the praise of the banner of St. George:

> Hoc insigne bonum, divino numine gestum
> Anglica gens referat semper, ovansque canat.

The *Chorus de Dis contra Gallos* is merely a complimentary Latin ode, with the victorious Henry appearing as *Validissimus Hector.* There is nothing in it that could not be done equally well by Bernard André or any other court poet, or better by Erasmus.

The *Ballade of the Scottyshe King* is different. Here the vernacular is used with Skelton's fierce vigour, set to a swinging couplet rhythm:

> King Jamy, Jomy your Joye is all go
> Ye sommoned our Kynge, why dyde ye so!
> To you nothyng it dyde accorde
> To sommon our Kynge, your soverayne lorde,

and the King of Scots is taunted for the letter he sent to Henry VIII at Thérouanne. He ought to have honoured Henry before the King of France. The defeat of Flodden is but the vengeance for James' part in his father's death:

> Thrugh your counseyle your fader was slayne
> Wherfore I fere ye wyll suffre payne.

The Scots have proved traitors to Henry:

> Ye be bound tenauntes to his estate
> Give up your game, ye playe chekmate,

and the King of Scots is now a prisoner (so ran the earlier rumour):

> For to the castell of Norham
> I understonde to soone ye cam.
> For a prysoner there now ye be
> Either to the devyll or the trinite.
> Thanked be saynte George our ladyes knyght
> Your pryd is past, adwe good nyght!

James had attacked England in Henry's absence, but he was 'beten with his own rod.' Let him remember—and here Skelton echoes, surely consciously, the words of Henry himself—the example of the King of Navarre:

> Of the Kynge of Naverne ye may take hede
> How unfortunately he doth now spede;
> In double welles now he dooth dreme
> That is a Kynge without a realme.

But the Earl of Surrey and his son Lord Howard, the Lord High Admiral, have humbled him:

> That noble erle the whyte Lyon
> Your pompe and pryde hath layde adowne
> His sone the Lorde Admyrall is full good
> His swerde hath bathed in the Scottes blode.
> God save Kynge Henry and his lordes all
> And sende the Frensshe Kynge suche an other fall!

'Amen for saynt charyte,' concludes the four-page quarto, 'And God save noble Kynge Henry the VIII.'[3] Skelton liked neither Scotsmen nor the King of Scots.

The *Ballade of the Scottyshe King* has all the signs of a popular poem. For the court Bernard André wrote a Latin poem celebrating the victory.[4] But Skelton was not to be outdone even in court verses. He turned back to his epitaph on Henry VII of the previous year and added an envoy.

> Vel mage, si placeat, hunc timuit Jacobus,
> Scottorum dominus, qui sua fata luit;
> Quem Leo Candidior Rubeum necat ense Leonem
> Et jacet usque modo non tumulatus humo.

The Leo Candidior is Surrey. The Rubeum Leonem is the Lion Gules of the Scottish arms. The Envoy must have been written shortly after the *Ballade,* because Skelton is now aware of the death of James—but his body is not yet buried. James' attack had automatically excommunicated him under an older treaty, and it was not till the 29th November that Leo x authorized the burial.[5] This fixes the date of the envoy within fairly close limits.

A mere envoy to a year-old epitaph was obviously insufficient

---

3. *A Ballad of the Scottyshe Kynge,* printed Richard Fawkes, London, 1513. Capitals and punctuation modernized, and some misprints corrected. The text is reproduced by J. Ashton, London, 1882.
4. cf. *Letters and Papers,* I, 4443.   5. cf. *Letters and Papers,* I, 4582.

and no special compliment to the reigning monarch. Skelton, who was probably during these months in his parish at Diss, wrote for the 22nd of September the *Chorus de Dis contra Scottos* as a parallel to the chorus against the French of a month previous. He rejoices in the victory over the faithless Scots:

> Salve, festa dies, toto resonabilis aevo
> Qua Scottus Jacobus, obrutus ense, cadit.
> Barbara Scottorum gens, perfida, plena malorum
> Vincitur ad Norram, vertitur inque fugam.

A brief description of the battle follows, and Skelton glories in the death of James:

> Dic modo, Scottorum dudum male sana malorum
> Rector, nunc regeris, mortuus ecce jaces!

and he concludes with the praises of Surrey—Leo Candidus—and gives thanks to God for the victory. To Skelton the country had been freed from a long threatened danger, and the heading of the poem, *'cum omni processionali festivitate solemnisavit hoc epitoma XXII die Septembris,'* points probably to some solemn ceremonial of thanksgiving for the victory,[6] which is echoed in the concluding lines:

> Anglia, duc choreas; resonent tua tympana, psallas;
> Da laudes Domino, da pia vota Deo.

This was Skelton in moments of solemn thanksgiving and of patriotic pride in Surrey's victory. But the spirit of raillery died hard. His first instinct had been to write the mocking *Ballade of the Scottyshe King,* and now the solemnity gave way once again to spirited invective. The *Ballade* must have been already in print, but by the end of September, when he wrote the *Chorus de Dis,* it was out of date. Yet he was loth to write off such excellent poetic capital. With considerable ingenuity he revised the *Ballade,* cut out the now erroneous references to James, recast his verses in the past tense, gave fuller credit to the 'White Lion,' and enlarged the whole poem to more than double the original length to make *Skelton Laureate against the Scottes.* This is the only example of his work of which two versions are extant, and some interesting light is thrown on his workmanship. We see Skelton resolutely

---

6. Nelson (p. 129), developing his suggestion that Skelton was with Henry on the continental campaign, further suggests that he wrote the chorus for the victory celebration mentioned by Hall, *Chronicle,* 1809, p. 564.

clinging to his good lines, carefully saving them from loss by transposing them to other parts of the poem if the original place or sense were unsuitable.

Against the Scottes is even more bitter than the *Ballade,* and includes a good deal more of general satire on the whole nation. The Scots are all traitors and even yet they are so proud they will not admit defeat:

> That is as trew
> As blacke is blew
> And grene is gray
> Whateuer they say
> Jemmy is ded
> And closed in led,
> That was theyr owne Kynge;
> Fy on that wynnynge!
> At Flodden hyllys
> Our bowys, our byllys,
> Slewe all the floure
> Of thyr honoure.

The poem continues with an attack on James' 'summoning' of Henry and pours scorn on his pretensions in verses of startling vigour:

> Ye may be lorde of Locrian—
> Christ sence you with a frying pan!—
> Of Edingborrow and of Saint Ionis towne;
> Adieu, syr sumner, cast off youre crowne!

In mock-heroic mood Skelton drops back for a few lines into parody of the mediaeval manner:

> Continually I shall remember
> The mery moneth of September,
> With the ix daye of the same,
> For then began our myrth and game;
> So that now I have devysed,
> And in my mind comprysed,
> Of the prowde Scot, Kynge Jemmy,
> To write some lyttle tragedy,

and still keeping up the mock-mediaeval tone he calls for help from Melpomene to write the tragedy of the Scots, and from Thalia:

> A medley to make of myrth with sadnes,
> The hartes of England to comfort with gladnes,

and the poem passes immediately into

> Kynge Jamy, Jemmy, Jocky my jo
> Ye summond our Kynge,—why dyd ye so?

and then to the recast of the rest of the *Ballade,* from which it
differs only in details. But the details are significant. There is
a new heraldic passage:

> The Whyte Lyon, there rampaunt of moode,
> He ragyd and rent out your hart bloode;
> He the Whyte, and ye the Red,
> The Whyte there slew the Red starke ded,

which may well be a reference to the incorporation of the demi-
lion gules of the King of Scots into the arms of Surrey, granted
on February 1st of the following year (1514). James had collected
guns for the battle (including 'the Seven Sisters' from Edinburgh
Castle) which led to the following addition:

> Your welth, your joy, your sport, your play,
> Your bragynge bost, your royal aray,
> Your beard so brym as bore at bay,
> Your Seuen Systers, that gun so gay,
> All have ye lost and cast away,

and there is a reference to the Pope's excommunication. The poem
continues substantially as the *Ballade* to the end.

Even this was not the close of the Flodden group. All Skelton's
readers were not equally pleased, and some, who could read the
dignified but colourless Latin verses of the *Chorus de Dis* with
approbation, were offended by the racy abuse of *Against the
Scottes.* They remembered that James was the brother-in-law of
King Henry and protested. It was not the first time his originality
had displeased the more conservative, and Skelton promptly
repeated his tactics against the earlier critics of *Phillip Sparow,*
with an appendix addressed 'Unto Divers People that remorde
this Rymynge agaynst the Scot Jemmy.' He is compelled to reply
to his critics who say his verse is merely abuse without justification:

> —Reprehending
> And venemously stingynge
> Rebukynge and remordyng,
> And nothing according.

They plead the close relationship of the two kings, but Skelton

claims that James was merely a traitor, who died excommunicated
by the church:

> He was a recrayed knyght
> A subtyll sysmatyke,
> Ryght nere an heretyke
> Of grace out of the state
> And died excommunycate.

Skelton plays a safe card.   The excommunication of the church[7]
(though it made James neither 'schismatic' nor 'heretic') no one
could lightly criticize, and the tables are neatly turned on the critics.
Even their loyalty is made suspect:

> He skantly loueth our Kynge
> That grudgeth at that thing;
> That cast such ouerthwartes
> Percase haue hollow hartes.

The argument is lifted adroitly on to major issues.   Behind the
double bulwark of king and church Skelton darkly hints at the
capital crimes of treason and heresy and leaves his critics suspect
of the gravest intentions against the temporal and spiritual
authorities, while he solemnly reproves them for the offence of
criticizing his verses!   We can almost see his sardonic grin.

The Flodden group hardly shows Skelton's best poetry, but it
is of considerable importance in a study of his verse.   The poems
can be dated accurately often within a week, one of them to an
actual day.   They reveal him dashing off a hasty ballad for
immediate publication, then turning without effort to formal Latin
court and complimentary verses.   We can see him in the act of
revising his poetry and note the changes he made and the lines
he retained; we can even reconstruct the criticism of his opponents
and note the sturdy independence of his reply and his immediate
appeal to orthodoxy—a trait that has occurred before.   In the
verse of these months, from August to November of 1513, we can
see him commenting freely on contemporary events, almost stand
behind his shoulder as he writes.   There are not many poets of so
early a date who reveal so much of themselves so unconsciously
through their verses.

During the next ten years Skelton came more and more to deal
with contemporary affairs.   But he concentrated in his public

7. *Letters and Papers,* 1, 4694.

satires on the church and attacked Cardinal Wolsey with increasing
violence and scorn.   No sooner had he completed in 1523 the
final and most bitter of these attacks, *Why Come Ye Nat to Court?*
than the course of public affairs turned his pen once more against
the perfidious Scots.   Skelton's hatred of the Scots had grown no
less in the interval.   The purely personal satire against Dundas,
where

> Skelton Laureat
> After this rate
> Defendeth with his pen
> All Englysh men
> Agayn Dundas
> That Scottishe asse,

reveals a bitterness that is part of the national attitude towards
Scotland rather than any merely personal feeling.   When, in 1521,
there were rumours that the widow of James IV, now married to
the Earl of Angus, was suing the Pope for a divorce and simul-
taneously intriguing with the Duke of Albany, who was warmly
supported by the court of France, the whole 1513 situation seemed
to be repeated.

Events moved speedily enough. England declared war on France
in 1522, and by August Surrey (the son of the victor of Flodden)
was sacking northern France.   Albany had been made governor
of Scotland and in spite of Henry's protest was supported by
Margaret and the Estates of Scotland.   Towards the end of 1522
he invaded England and besieged Carlisle but was ingeniously
inveigled into a truce by Dacres, the Warden of the West Marches,
on 11 September 1522.   On 27 October he sailed again for France.
The campaign opened the following year with the appointment
on 26 February 1523 of Surrey as lieutenant-general, and he spent
the months from April to September in devastating the Scottish
border, burning whatever castle or abbey he could lay hands on.

Albany gave the English fleet the slip, collected an army of
Scots and French and started out on 22 October for Carlisle
but diverted his invasion to besiege Wark Castle, which was held
by Sir William Lisle and a hundred defenders.   Surrey was at
Alnwick within easy reach.   The other generals were close at hand,
Darcy at Bamburgh, Dacres at Carlisle.   Surrey concentrated the

English forces towards Wark Castle, where Sir William Lisle
was still holding out, and at his approach the Scottish forces
crumpled up. It was Albany's second chance and he had again
failed. He sailed for France in the early summer of 1524 and
the erection of James v as King of Scotland in July finished his
pretensions for ever.

England went mad with delight. Scotland had been kept at bay
once again, and the Howards had won new laurels. Here was
opportunity enough for Skelton, both for satire and for praise.
He had spent part of 1523 actually staying with the Howards, for
the *Garlande of Laurell,* written and published in that year, was
composed at Sheriff Hutton Castle (near York), the most
northerly seat of the family. But while the *Garlande of Laurell*
is largely a graceful lyrical compliment to the Howard ladies,
Skelton seized on the defeat of Albany to praise once again the
deeds of the White Lion in his poem of late 1523 or early 1524,
*How the Douty Duke of Albany, lyke a cowarde knyght, ran away
shamefully, with a Hundred Thousand Tratlande Scottes and faint
harted Frenchmen, beside the Water of Twede.*

Skelton opens in triumph:

> Reioyse, Englande
> And understande
> These tidinges newe,
> Which be as trewe
> As the gospell;
> This Duke so fell
> Of Albany
> So cowardly,
> With all his hoost
> Of the Scottyshe coost,
> For all theyr boost,
> Fledde lyke a beest,
> Wherfore to ieste
> Is my delyght.

Skelton goes on to jeer at the Scots and their defeat 'at the
Castel of Warke' and compliments the defender, Sir William Lisle:

> That valiaunt knyght
> Putte you to flyght;
> By his valyaunce
> Two thousand of Fraunce,

while the Duke of Albany ran off on the news of Surrey's arrival:

> When he herde tell
> That my lorde amrell [admiral]
> Was comyng downe.

The poem then turns to the Duke of Albany himself and accuses him of aspiring to the throne of Scotland by killing the young King:

> And set his crowne
> On your owne heed
> When he were deed
> Such trechery
> And traytory
> Is all your cast;
> Thus ye have compast
> With the Frenche Kyng,

and Skelton, as ever, goes on to praise Henry VIII, who has out-witted both Albany and Francis. The poem shifts back to a savage attack on the false Scots:

> False and false agayne,
> Neuer true nor playn,
> But flery, flatter, and fayne
> And euer to remayne
> In wretched beggary
> And maungy misery
> In lousy lothsumnesse
> And scabbed scorffynesse . . .
> Nacion moost in hate
> Proude and poore of state,
> Twyt, Scot go keep they den
> Mell nat with Englyshe men,

and after a catalogue of threats back goes the poem to the Duke of Albany, who is attacked in the manner and the language of a flyting. The Scots are a mere rabble—let them creep into their caves and never dare to attack England again. The flyting of the Duke begins again:

> Syr Duke, nay, syr ducke,
> Syr drake of the lake, sir ducke
> Of the Donghyll, for small lucke
> Ye haue in feates of warre:
> Ye make nought, but ye marre,

and to underline the contrast he draws a companion portrait of:

> My lord amrell
> Of chiualry the wele,
> Of knyghthode the floure
> In euery marciall shoure.

Albany is further blamed for his cowardice with another page of abuse:

> Nor durst nat crak a worde
> Nor durst nat drawe his swerde
> Agaynst the Lyon White
> But ran away quyte.
> He ran away by nyght,
> In the owle flyght,
> Lyke a cowarde knyght.
> Adue, cowarde, adue
> Fals knyght, and mooste untrue!
> I render the, fals rebelle,
> To the flingande fende of helle.

Skelton continues on the plot of Albany and Francis against 'most royal Harry.' But the plot has come to nothing.

> Are ye not frantyke madde,
> And wretchedly bestadde,
> To rayle agaynst his grace,
> That shall bring you full bace.

After more abuse of both Albany and Francis, the poem goes on to praise the virtues of Henry in despite of his French rival, of whom he was more than a little jealous. Henry is as strong as Hercules, as wise as Solomon, as handsome as Absalom, as loyal as Hector, and so the comparisons extend to Scipio, Ptolemy and the Maccabees. His virtues are numberless, and Skelton lists a few of them in characteristic fashion:

> His nobilyte,
> His magnanymite,
> His animosite,
> His frugalite,
> His liberalite,
> His affabilite,
> His humanyte,

and so on through a round dozen. But this rude vernacular verse is hardly the dignified Latin of the *Eulogium pro suorum temporum conditione,* and Skelton puts forward a courageous

defence for addressing the King in his direct manner and not in
the style of the average court poet:

> What though my stile be rude?
> With trouthe it is ennewde:
> Trouth ought to be rescude,
> Trouthe should nat be subdude.

Henry is a noble king; he inspires his generals by his own deeds of
arms; his subjects are loyal. How could the plotters dare to attack
such a monarch? The poet closes with an envoy in which Skelton
again defends the rudeness of his style because his attack is
grounded upon truth. There is a short envoy to the Cardinal; but
of that elsewhere.

The main theme of these political satires is the bitter attack
on England's enemies and intense loyalty to the throne. Skelton's
early relationship with Henry seems to have left him with a
considerable personal admiration for the King that cannot be
credited simply to courtly adulation. Perhaps not even a king
would have been completely safe from Skelton's satire. His praise
sounds altogether sincere. In these satires religious conviction
has given way to an intense patriotism that brings Skelton closely
in touch with the current feeling of his day. The anger of these
poems is often the anger of relief. The danger of the Scots had
twice been averted—and it was a very real danger. Skelton—and
England—regarded the diplomacy of the 'false Scots' with genuine
suspicion and their Border warfare with very real alarm. They
were an alien race plotting with a foreign king against a monarchy
which had done everything to establish England's pre-eminent
position in European politics. Boisterous jubilation over a fallen
enemy may not always be decorous, but it is very human, and
Skelton in these railing attacks on Scotland and France reveals the
real feeling of England after Flodden and the defeat of Albany.
They spelt tragedy for Scotland, but for England a period of
joyful recovery. In the vernacular satire of Skelton, rather than
in his Latin poems on the victories, can be found, clearer than in
official report or documented account, the reaction of England
to the campaign. But while his sentiments are those of the
average Englishman, his relations with the victorious leaders were
peculiarly personal. Amid all the satire and abuse of the Flodden

and Albany poems, the portraits of Henry and of the Surreys, father and son, invited admiration and praise from the contemporary reader. Not every poet was so fortunate in his patron's deeds of prowess. Skelton had no need to spin praises from nothing.

The Latin poems were probably circulated at first only in the court. All three of the Latin Flodden group, the *Henrici Septimi Epitaphium* and the *Chorus de Dis* against both Scots and French, are signed by Skelton 'regius orator.' Whatever was the official significance of this title, it is clear that Skelton regarded himself as the poet specially attached to the King, and so 'orator regius' is used appropriately of the author of these mainly court poems. The English poems are more popular and were designed for public circulation—the *Ballade of the Scottyshe King* for immediate circulation—and in these Skelton designates himself merely poet laureate, without mention of his more courtly function. The difference in tone is also due to a difference in audience, and it becomes still more certain that Skelton in these vernacular satires was expressing popular sentiments and expected the poems to become known among the rank and file of Englishmen as well as in the more educated circles of the court.

Chapter XI

SKELTON AND THE COURT

The Minor Court Poems

ON THE SUBJECT OF SKELTON'S POSITION AT COURT THE RECORDS are curiously scanty. Only one payment made to him has yet been discovered, though his contemporaries Hawes and Barclay and his fellow-tutor Bernard André occur periodically in the King's accounts. Skelton had two periods at court, in each of which he served in different capacities, and the character which he presented to the outside world altered radically in the interval between his tutorship under Henry VII and his less official but privileged position of 'orator regius' under Henry VIII. In the court of the earlier Henry he was a scholar and only occasionally a poet, accepting the conventions of his post and of the society in which he moved. *The Bowge of Courte* was the manifesto of his rebellion and the retirement to Diss the result. On the accession of Henry VIII and the return of the poet to court, the position of Skelton was that of a freelance. He was no Groom of the Chamber as Hawes had been, but a poet, to whom the King granted a title and liberty of speech.

From the previous reign he had inherited an official costume of which he was inordinately proud. The Cambridge entry of 1504-5 mentions the 'habitus' of which Skelton boasts in the Garnesche poems:

> What eylyth thé, rebawde, on me to raue?
> A kyng to me myn habyte gaue.

The colours of the habit were apparently white and green:

> Your sworde ye swere, I wene,
> So tranchaunt and so kene
> Xall kyt both wyght and grene:
> Your foly is to grett
> The kynges colours to threte.

As the Garnesche poems belong to the years 1513-14, it appears that Skelton continued to wear this official uniform during the reign of Henry VIII, who perhaps suggested the addition to it of the word *Calliope* embroidered in letters of gold. Against those who jeered at the vanity that had accepted this final decoration Skelton wrote his *Why were ye Calliope embrawdred in letters of Golde?*

> Whose name enrolde
> With silke and golde
> I dare be bolde
> Thus for to were.

Calliope is regent 'of poetes al' and he is proud to wear her token. The Calliope poem must be dated fairly late in the court career of the poet as he complains in the Latin appendix of approaching old age:

> Quamquam conficior senio marcescoque sensim.

To this dignity Henry added the title of 'orator regius,' with which Skelton proudly signs all the court poems after the accession. The position seems to have been that of an unofficial poet laureate, in the modern sense of the word and not the 'poeta laureatus' university honour that Skelton boasts of so frequently. As orator regius he was granted considerable latitude to criticise and to admonish. The major result of this freedom is *Magnyfycence,* and its outspoken assurance and critical spirit are as much a symbol of Skelton's secure position under Henry VIII as the disgust with court life of *The Bowge of Courte* is the result of his relationships with Henry VII. These two poems, however, are not his only reflections on life at court. A group of minor court poems has survived, which falls into the two well-marked types of satire on his opponents and rivals, and commendations of his royal patrons.

The commendations were all written in the reign of Henry VIII. Skelton's eulogies of Henry VII belong to the period after 1509 and are expressions of conventional patriotism rather than of personal admiration. When Henry VIII came to the throne, Skelton greeted the new monarch in *The Rose both White and Rede* (1509): Justice, which has been absent for the past hundred years, will now come down from the starry sky and Right shall drive away the wolves and foxes (like Dudley and Empson) who have brought England to woe:

>Therfor no more they shall
>The commouns ouerbace,
>That wont wer ouer all
>Bothe lorde and knight to face;
>ffor now the yeris of grace
>And welthe ar com agayne
>That maketh England faine.

The praise of Henry VIII was continued in a Latin poem written about 1512. The *Eulogium pro suorum temporum conditione* after some formal praise of:

>Septimus Henricus, Britonum memorabilis heros,

proceeds to the greater glory of:

>Noster honor solus, filius, ecce, suus!

Henry VIII becomes in turn 'omne decus nostrum,' 'Spes unica tantum,' 'sola Britanna salus'; the fortunes of the land depend upon him:

>Summa rei nostrae remanet, celeberrime princeps,
>In te praecipuo, qui modo sceptra geris.

The *Henrici Septimi Epitaphium* is in a similar strain, and was designed as verses for the tomb in Westminster Abbey:

>Septimus Henricus mole sub hac tegitur.

Henry VII is Anchises and Atrides, feared by the Scots and the French. Skelton defends him against the charge of hoarding wealth—his wealth has proved England's salvation:

>Immensas sibi divitias cumulasse quid horres?
>Ni cumulasset opes, forte, Britanne, luas.
>Urgentes casus tacita si mente volutes,
>Vix tibi sufficeret aurea ripa Tagi.

The poem closes by calling all readers to pray for the soul of the King. The *Epitaph* is a more formal piece than the *Eulogy*, and lacks the air of enthusiasm with which Skelton greeted the new reign.

This group of Latin court-pieces is completed by the *Elegia in Margaritae nuper comitissae de Derby funebre ministerium.* Margaret, Countess of Richmond and Derby, and mother of Henry VII, had died in 1509. Skelton's poem, which he dates 1516, is a companion epitaph to that on her son:

>Hac sub mole latet regis celeberrima mater.

N

Skelton compares her with the pious heroines of antiquity. She had been a patron of the arts and of Skelton himself, and with a fine disregard of her sex, he mourns her as a lost 'Maecenas':

> Plura referre piget, calamus torpore rigescit,
> Dormit Maecenas, neglegitur probitas.

He concludes the verses with a curious threat against any who dare to 'tear or snatch away' the epitaph, which suggests that a copy had been hung on the tomb:

> Qui lacerat, violatve, rapit praesens epitoma,
> Hunc laceretque voret Cerberus absque mora!

These commendations have an air of formality that is entirely lacking in Skelton's other poems written for the court. The court-satires vary in type from purely private verses tossed off under the impulse of a sudden annoyance to 'official' flytings undertaken at the bidding of the King himself. Three sets of such court-satires survive, an early satire against a court musician of Henry VII's time, a group of one-sided flytings against a gentleman-usher of Henry VIII's court, and a less definitely datable poem against some mysterious adversary who had spread slanders of Skelton and against whom he storms with just indignation and with bitter regret that his adversary is nameless. Whether they are known or unknown, Skelton attacks his opponents with the hearty vigour of one very sure of his position in the court of both monarchs, and in the flytings against Garnesche with more of a literary show of coarse satirical language than any real personal animosity.

The earliest of these court satires was purely personal. *Agaynste a Comely Coystrowne* is a defence of the poet against the criticisms of a court musician, which can be ascribed from a reference in the third verse to the reign of Henry VII:

> Curyowsly he can both counter and knak
> Of Martyn Swart and all hys mery men.
> Lord, how Perkyn is proud of hys pohen!

Martin Swart was the leader of Lambert Simnel's invasion of 1487 and Perkin Warbeck, the second of the spurious claimants to Henry's crown, appeared some years later. The 'pohen' of whom he is so proud may very well be the Lady Katherine Gordon who became his wife. This brings the poem down to 1495, to which year it probably belongs. It is a somewhat cryptic but intelligible court satire against 'a comely coystrowne, that curyowsly chawntyd, and curryshly cowntred, and madly in hys musykkys mokkyshly made agaynst the Musys of polytyke poems and poettys matryculate.' Skelton begins with an attack on 'peevishness,' the eighth deadly sin, and taunts his musical opponent with social ambition:

> But, for in his gamut carp that he can,
> Lo, Jak wold be a jentylman!

The opponent is aspiring too high. Search where he may he will find no authority to make

> An holy water clarke a ruler of lordys.

For a few verses Skelton plays confidently with satirical puns on the terms of Tudor music:

> He can not fynd it in rule nor in space:
> Hys solfyth is to haute, hys trybyll is to hy;
> He braggyth of hys byrth, that borne was full bace;
> Hys musyk withoute mesure, to sharp is hys my.

This upstart must be put in his place:

> For Jak wold be a jentylman, that late was a grome.

Musician though he be, the lords and ladies who learn from him can sing neither prick-song nor plain, and Skelton warns him not to meddle again:

> A prouerbe of old, say well or be styll
> Ye are to vnhappy occasyons to fynde
> Vppon me to clater, or els to say yll.
> Now haue I shewyd you part of your proud mynde;
> Take thys in worth, the best is behynde.

The piece is of little poetic value, but the versification is thoroughly competent even for such an early set of verses. The quarrel was closed with a Latin poem, *Contra alium cantitantem et organisantem asinum, qui impugnabat Skeltonida Pierium. Sarcasmos*—the trick of writing up an incident in both an English and a Latin version developed early in Skelton; here the Latin verses take the more dignified form of a comparison of music and poetry:

> Ergo tuum studeas animo deponere fastum,
> Et violare sacrum desine, stulte, virum.

So it is often with Skelton's Latin poems. They express in dignified conventional terms what his English expressed more forcibly and naturally. The Latin lines are insipid beside the English description of the musician:

> Comely he clappyth a payre of clauycordys;
> He whystelyth so swetely, he makyth me to swete;
> His descant is dasshed full of dyscordes;
> A red angry man, but easy to intrete.

The rude power of Skelton's vernacular is still more forcibly demonstrated in the group of poems against Christopher Garnesche. This forms a flyting with one side left out—a Dunbar without a Kennedy—and it equals Dunbar's in extravagant and reckless abuse. Christopher Garnesche was a gentleman-usher in the court of Henry VIII and several references to him are made in the *Letters and Papers* of the period, none of which bring him into any direct relationship with Skelton. But from the poems it is apparent that he replied to Skelton's attacks and incurred more torrential abuse from that indefatigable satirist. The four satires are all subscribed 'By the Kyngys most noble commandment'—Henry not only sanctioned the flyting but even initiated it. The poems belong to Skelton's period of court favour after his return from Diss and can be assigned to the years 1513-1514. Such a satirical emphasis is laid on Garnesche's knighthood—he is successively Syr Satrapas, Syr Tyrmagant, Syr Chrystyn, Syr Terry of Trace, Syr Ferumbras, Syr Duglas, and finally (a shrewd blow) Sir Thopas —that one is safe in assuming Garnesche's elevation to the knighthood in 1513 is being satirized.[1]

The first poem answers the challenge of Garnesche, who has been:

> Ruduly revilyng me in the kynges noble hall.

Skelton demands what authority Garnesche has to call him a knave, and proceeds to vigorous abuse:

> Your wynde schakyn shankkes, your long lothy legges
> Crokyd as a camoke, and as a kowe calfless,
> Bryngges yow out of fauyr with alle female teggys . . .
> I say, ye solem Sarson, alle blake ys your ble;

1. Helen Stearns, *John Skelton and Garnesche, M.L.N.*, 1928, 314-6.

As a glede glowynge, your ien glyster as glasse,
Rowlynge in yower holow hede, vgly to see;
Your tethe teintyd with tawny; your semely snowte doth
    passe,
Howkyd as in a hawkys beke, lyke Syr Topyas.
Boldly bend you to batell, and buske your selfe to saue;
Chalenge yourselfe for a fole, call me no more knaue.

Garnesche was not loth to reply. He sought for assistance in court, and Skelton's second poem is an attack on both his old and his new adversary. He addresses them in scornful language:

Ye hobble very homly before the kynges borde.

The typical physical abuse of the flyting follows:

Lusty Garnesche, lyke a lowse, ye jet full lyke a jaspe
As wytless as a wylde goos . . . .

The attack concludes with mysterious references to the new opponent:

Ye grounde yow vpon Godfrey, that grysly gargon's face,
Your stondarde, Syr Olifranke, agenst me for to splay;
Baile, baile, at yow bothe, frantyke folys! follow on the
    chase!
Cum Garnesche, cum Godfrey, with as many as ye may!

In the final stanza the two are derided:

Lytyll wit in your scrybys nolle
That scrybblyd your fond scrolle.

Garnesche, finding the task of replying in verse too difficult, must have turned for assistance to one of Skelton's rival poets, possibly a member of the Household. The whole group ot poems begins to appear as an elaborate court jest, begun by Henry and carried through by the poets on his Household staff.

The first two poems had been in a variant of rime royal, with the rime royal rime-scheme, but with four-stressed and heavily alliterated lines. The third poem is written in 'Skeltonics.' It opens with a defence:

I am laureat, I am no lorelle
Lewdely your tyme ye spende,
My lyuyng to reprehende.

Has Garnesche considered his own beginnings?

Whan ye war yonger of age,
Ye war a kechyn page,
A dyshwasher, a dryuyll
In the pott your nose dedde sneuyll.

JOHN SKELTON

Altogether he is a 'gresy knyght,' and Skelton relates a tale of his
unsavoury love affairs. The scribe 'that scrybblyd your fond
scroll' is no better—his verse has neither rime nor reason, and
though:

> Ye wolde be callyd a maker . . .
> Ye lernyd of sum py bakar.

The poem returns to the abuse of Garnesche:

> Your skyn scabbyd and scuruy
> Tawny, tannyd, and shuruy . . .
> Men say ye wyll wax lowsy,
> Drunkyn, drowpy, drowsy.

Garnesche becomes in turn the more abused members of the animal
world—scorpion, boar, goat, serpent and marmoset. The poem
concludes with a hearty curse on both assailants:

> I rekyn yow in my rowllys
> For ij dronken sowllys . . .
> God sende you wele good spede,
> With *Dominus vobiscum!*

The fourth poem is set in swinging four-beat iambics:

> Wyth, knaue, syr knaue, and knaue ageine!
> To cal me knaue thou takyst gret payne:
> The prowdest knaue yet of vs tweyne,
> Within thy skyn he xall remayne . . .
> Thou thynkest thyself Syr Pers de Brasy
> Thy catyvys carkes cours and crasy.

The current court scandal is repeated with relish—how Garnesche
betrays his friends and consorts 'with Lumbardes lemmans' in
Fenchurch Street, but even with lemans his success is small:

> Sche sware with her ye xulde nat dele
> For ye war smery, lyke a sele,
> And ye war herey, lyke a calfe;
> Sche praiid ye walke, on Goddes halfe!

Skelton defends his own character; he has been honoured by king
and university and has taught the King in his youth:

> The honor of England I lernyd to spelle
> In dygnyte roialle that doth excelle.

How dare Garnesche attack one to whom the King granted such
honour! How dare he criticize a poet laureate! If the Latin
satirists were alive, Persius, Juvenal, Horace, and Martial:

> They wolde thé wryght, all with one steuyn,
> The follest slouen ondyr heuen.

Let Garnesche beware of presumptuous pride:

> Presumptuous pride is all thyn hope
> God garde thé, Garnesche, from the rope!

The poem concludes defiantly:

> A reme of papyr wyll nat holde
> Of thi lewdnes that may be tolde.
> My study myght be better spynt
> But for to serue the kynges entent,
> Hys noble pleasure and comaundement.

The four poems against Garnesche show Skelton in one of his less serious moments. The satire has none of the fire of the Wolsey poems—whether it hit its mark or not was of little consequence. All that mattered was that the exaggerated abuse should raise a laugh when the poem was read to the court. Even the victim would not take the poem too seriously.

Only one other court-satire remains—*Against Venemous Tonges.* This was a reply to his critics after the production of *Magnyfycence* in 1516 and has already been discussed in connection with the play.

The two types of verse which Skelton produced at court are not without significance. They reveal a man who is highly favoured by his monarch but who is regarded with some suspicion by the courtiers. The continual tone of self-defence throughout these satires cannot be ignored. Skelton is ever on his guard, to defend his character and his poetry. He never wearies of referring to his titles of poet laureate and 'orator regius,' never fails to seize an opportunity of reminding his readers that he had tutored the King and that the King is now his staunch supporter, honours of which he is jealously proud. In his complimentary poems to Henry he seldom forgets that the King was once his pupil. The Latin verses to him, even when the hyperboles are reduced to their real value, show a sense of unbounded admiration, while he does not shrink from admonishing him in the warnings of *Magnyfycence* and *Speke Parrot* and *Colin Clout.*

There are in his poetry none of the supplications which his con-

temporary Dunbar addressed to James iv. Though they were
both satirists of court life, a brief comparison of their verses
reveals that Skelton was more intimate with court life and more
secure in his position. Dunbar's court poems are expostulations
from a man disappointed of preferment; Skelton's are satirical
comments from one who moved with complete confidence in the
society of the court. Skelton never had to beg for a benefice, as
Dunbar did so vainly.

> The court has done my curage cuill

is Dunbar's embittered comment on his aspiration. Skelton
remained for years in favour, in spite of the jealousy of other
courtiers. When he did at length lose the protection of the King,
it was because of the hostility of the Cardinal, then almost as
great a power as Henry himself, and even the poet would have
admitted that the hostility was not without reason.

CHAPTER XII

THE RE-DISCOVERY OF SKELTON

SKELTON'S THREE HUNDRED YEARS AS AN ODDITY BROUGHT HIM at last into Disraeli's gallery of the *Curiosities of Literature*,[1] from which inglorious scrap-heap he has been only recently rescued, not merely as an accepted poet but as a pattern and the father of a tradition. Greater poets like John Donne have emerged from obscurity after a period of neglect and misunderstanding, but the re-discovery of John Skelton must surely be a unique occurrence in the vicissitudes of English critical taste. Had he emerged as a forgotten poet considered worthy of study, the renewed interest would be as understandable as the revival of a seldom-staged Elizabethan drama. The contemporary interest in Skelton is not antiquarian. It is literary. Instead of a lawless, unmetrical, 'stuttering' writer of doggerel, contemporary criticism has re-discovered in Skelton a poet of genuine merit, a satirist of pungent force, and a metrist of considerable originality and skill.

Skelton's originality as a metrist has never been fully appreciated or examined. The value of his discovery and extensive use of the 'Skeltonic' short line was dissipated by what followers he had in the sixteenth century. The 'Skeltonic' became a byword for short-line doggerel, because the principles of its scansion were at variance with the current Chaucerian-French syllabic metre. Various attempts have been made to discover an origin for the Skeltonic short line, without any realization of its metrical characteristics. Lee derived it from French poetry, finding an analogous 'jog-trot melody of five and six-syllable lines' in contemporary French verse. 'Skelton,' he considers, 'was clearly practising a French tune.'[2] Brie derived the line from the Latin hymns and quoted some unconvincing parallels.[3] Berdan cites the French short-line of Marot, the *fatrasie*, 'analogous to the type produced by Skelton,' and the Italian *frattola*, which Florio in 1611

---

1. The index reads: Shoeing-horns; silhouette silk stockings; Silli; Skelton; Sneezing; snuff-boxes. *Curiosities of Literature*, 1, Disraeli, London, 1881.
2. Sir S. Lee, *The French Renaissance in England*, p. 107.
3. Brie, *Skelton Studien*.

defined as 'skeltonical riming.' He suggests a common origin in the accentual Latin of the Middle Ages.[4] Nelson derives the line from rimed Latin prose.[5] All of these arguments ignore the essentially English quality of Skelton's verse. Ramsay alone suggests a purely English origin and points out that many lines of *Magnyfycence* fall naturally into two halves, each one a 'Skeltonic.'[6] The attempt to find a foreign origin for an essentially English metre has produced nothing but a series of contradictory suggestions, none of which can be conclusively proved.

Most investigators have fallen into the mistake of scanning the Skeltonic in trochees and iambs, allowing free substitution where the syllabic system momentarily broke down. Such an attempt ignores the powerfully accentual character of the Skeltonic, and the alliteration which it so often affects:

> He cryeth and he creketh,
> He pryeth and he peketh,
> He chydes and he chatters,
> He prates and he patters,
> He clytters and he clatters.

These lines may be scanned as three and a half iambs:

> He crýeth ánd he crékketh.

But the stress on 'and' is negligible and the alliteration gives the clue to the real scansion:

> He crýeth and he crékketh,
> He prýeth and he pékketh.

The Skeltonic is the descendant of the Anglo-Saxon alliterative line through the alliterative revival of Middle English. The original four-stressed iine has broken down into two short two-stressed lines, bound together by rime. The Skeltonic has normally two (occasionally three) powerful stresses and a group of unstressed syllables, the whole line containing a total length of four syllables and upwards. One page of *Colin Clout* supplies all these variants:

---

4. J. M. Berdan, 'The Poetry of Skelton,' *Rom. Rev.*, 6.364 ff.
5. Nelson, *John Skelton Laureate*, pp. 83 ff.
6. R. L. Ramsay, Introduction to *Magnyfycence*, which contains an excellent analysis of the metres of the play.

(Four syllables)	Fýckell fálseness
(Five syllables)	Rúdely ráyne beaten
(Seven syllables)	For though my ríme be rágged
(Seven syllables)	For, as fárre as I can sé

The metrical unit of these lines is neither the iamb nor the trochee nor any substitution for them. It is the heavily stressed foot followed by one, two or three unstressed syllables. Skelton developed this metre neither from Latin hymn nor from French nor Italian short-line, but from the native rhythm into which English speech readily falls. The long list of English romances cited in *Phillip Sparow* is sufficient evidence of his extensive reading in accentual Middle English verse. Chaucer's contempt for the 'rum, ram, ruff' of accentual English finds no echo in Skelton's ready acceptance of its colloquial and satirical force.

In the fifteenth century Chaucer's pentameter had been misunderstood through corruption of the text and the final loss of terminal syllabic -e. In the sixteenth and subsequent centuries the strongly accentual metre of Skelton was similarly misunderstood because English poetry, after a belated revival of accentual verse in the fifteenth century, accepted once more the French system of regular syllabic stress. Not till the twentieth century were the principles of Skelton's metre recognized. The 'invention' of sprung rhythm by Gerard Manley Hopkins at the end of the nineteenth century was simply a conscious return to the principles of accentual verse and less consciously a return to the Skeltonic. Hopkins' outline of the principles of sprung rhythm might be illustrated at every point from the lines of *Colin Clout* or *Phillip Sparow*:

Sprung Rhythm, as used in this book, is measured by feet of from one to four syllables, regularly, and for particular effects any number of weak or slack syllables may be used. It has one stress, which falls on the only syllable, if there is only one, or, if there are more, then scanning as above, on the first, and so gives rise to four sorts of feet, a monosyllable and the so-called accentual Trochee, Dactyl, and the First Paeon.[7]

I had long had haunting my ear the echo of a new rhythm which now I realized on paper. To speak shortly, it consists in scanning by accents or stresses alone, without any account of the number of

7. *Poems of Gerard Manley Hopkins,* ed. Robert Bridges, author's preface, p. 4.

syllables, so that a foot may be one strong syllable or it may be many light and one strong. I do not say the idea is altogether new; there are many hints of it in music, in nursery rhymes and popular jingles, in the poets themselves ... No one has professedly used it and made it a principle throughout that I know of.[8]

In his short-lined verse Hopkins wrote pure Skeltonics.

> When Henry, heart-forsook,
> Dropped eyes and dared not look.
> Eh, how áll rúng!
> Young dog, he did give tongue!
> But Harry—in his hands he has flung
> His tear-tricked cheeks of flame
> For fond love and for shame.[9]

Hopkins does not appear to have realized that he had been forestalled by Skelton—*Piers Plowman* he acknowledges and Greene was 'the last writer who can be said to have recognized it.'[10] But more recent poets who see in Hopkins one of the founders of post-war poetry have traced sprung rhythm to its source and recognize Skelton as one of the most powerful influences on contemporary verse. It is difficult to read the poetry of Robert Graves or the choruses of Eliot's *Murder in the Cathedral* without feeling in the background the rhythm of the Skeltonic. 'In the sixteenth century,' writes Graves, 'John Skelton, in my opinion one of the three or four outstanding English poets, though reducing the alliteration, adding rhyme, and even using the lineal arrangement of rhyme-royal, wrote in the native style as often as the continental.'[11] Graves uses the Skeltonic as one of his favourite metres and has paid in the measure an appropriate tribute to the elder poet:

John Skelton

> What could be dafter
> Than John Skelton's laughter?
> What sound more tenderly
> Than his pretty poetry?
> So where to rank old Skelton?
> He was no monstrous Milton,

8. *The Correspondence of Gerard Manley Hopkins and Richard Watson Dixon*, ed. C. C. Abbot, p. 14.
9. *Poems of Gerard Manley Hopkins*, 'Brothers' No. 30. The accents are the poet's.
10. *Poems of Gerard Manley Hopkins*, ed. Robert Bridges, author's preface, p. 6.
11. Robert Graves, *Another Future for Poetry*, London, 1926.

Nor wrote no *Paradise Lost,*
So wondered at by most,
Phrased so disdainfully,
Composed so painfully.
He struck what Milton missed,
Milling an English grist
With homely turn and twist.
He was English through and through,
Not Greek, nor French, nor Jew,
Though well their tongues he knew,
The living and the dead:
Learned Erasmus said,
*Hic, unum Britannicarum
Lumen et decus literarum.*
But oh, Colin Clout!
How his pen flies about,
Twiddling and turning,
Scorching and burning,
Thrusting and thrumming!
How it hurries with humming,
Leaping and running,
At the tipsy-topsy Tunning
Of Mistress Eleanor Rumming!
How for poor Philip Sparow
Was murdered at Carow,
How our hearts he does harrow!
Jest and grief mingle
In this jangle-jingle,
For he will not stop
To sweep nor mop,
To prune nor prop,
To cut each phrase up
Like beef when we sup,
Nor sip at each line
As at brandy-wine,
Or port when we dine.
But angrily, wittily,
Tenderly, prettily,
Laughingly, learnedly,
Sadly, madly,
Helter-skelter John
Rhymes serenely on,
As English poets should.
Old John, you do me good![12]

12. Robert Graves, *Poems 1914-26*, p. 6. I am grateful to Mr. Graves for his permission to quote this poem.

Skelton's metrical virtuosity extends beyond the Skeltonic.   His precise and assured manipulation of metre in lyrical measures is well illustrated in Liberty's song from *Magnyfycence*.

> LYB. With, ye mary, syrs, thus sholde it be
> I kyst her swete, and she kyssed me;
> I garde her gaspe, I garde her gle,
> With, daunce on the le, the le!
> I bassed that baby with harte so free;
> She is the bote of all my bale.

Skelton's attraction for modern poets does not cease with his influence on their metre.   The speed and variety of his verse, and the nimble rapier stroke of his satire have been influential factors in recent verse, notably in the work of W. H. Auden.   Skelton has a power of incisive abuse that withers an opponent with a few words:

> Be ye and your hoost
> Full of bragge and boost
> And full of waste wynde.

His command of English, direct, central and sinuous, is one of the delights of his poetry.   He can write with the pith and point of a vernacular proverb:

> It is a wyly mous
> That can bylde his dwellinge-house
> Within the cattes eare,

while his command of powerful phrases—often enough abusive— is astonishing.   'Rayn betyn beggers' and Wolsey's 'gresy genealogy' and

> Was hedyd, drawen, and quartered
> And dyed stynkingly martred

are a striking contrast to the uninspired diction of his contemporaries.   Skelton was so comfortable in the English tongue that one can easily mistake for mere colloquialism the easy grace of his movement:

> He wyll drynke vs so drye,
> And suck vs so nye,
> That men shall scantly
> Haue peny or halpeny.
> God saue his noble grace
> And graunt him a place
> Endlesse to dwell
> With the deuyll of hell!

This moves so like conversational English prose that one tends to underestimate the art behind it. It is Coleridge's 'neutral style,' the simple direct mode of Chaucer and Herbert. Skelton could write the English tongue with the control and precision of Swift. His poetry has many of the athletic virtues of Swift's prose. Opinion may vary whether this is the finest language for poetry, but that Skelton could write verse of such vernacular clarity at the beginning of the sixteenth century pre-supposes a mind of unusual acumen and insight. From the 'termis aureat' of fifteenth century feudal poetry he turned to the lower linguistic strata unexplored by his contemporaries, and even to the present day he provides a pattern of individual and incisive speech.

Skelton was an innovator of insufficiently recognized but nevertheless profound originality, one of the greatest anti-Romantics in English verse, a hard-headed practical poet and a poetical realist. His limitations are easy to discover, the result of deliberately chosen restrictions rather than poetical blind spots. There is no romance in his poetry, nothing ethereal or beyond the ordinary man's range of experience. But there is much in his verse that is profoundly serious and passionately thought out. The virtues of Skelton are those of sincerity—directness of approach and a continuous contact with reality:

> What though my stile be rude?
> With trouthe it is ennewde.
> Trouth ought to be rescude,
> Trouthe should nat be subdude.

A few years after his death the flood-gates of romance were thrown open, and no one can blame late Tudor or Jacobean poetry for ignoring such a resolute anti-Romantic. At the present day, however, the decay of Romanticism has brought a re-appreciation of the virtues of Skelton. He has much in his favour, powerful verse-satire, graceful lyric measures, originality of attack and incisive diction allied to a Shavian spirit of criticism and Rabelaisian powers of wit and vocabulary. How many poets can offer such an original combination?

Probably the most reliable indication of the centuries-long decline and the recent rise in Skelton's reputation is to be found

in the list of editions of his poems printed in Appendix B. Within
a few years of his death one can count almost thirty volumes, some
containing a group of his verses, others printing a single favoured
poem like *Phillip Sparow* or *Colin Clout*. This wave of popularity
culminated in Marshe's collected edition of 1568, and after that the
rate of publication dwindled to a few volumes in each century.
The only poem that apparently found favour in the seventeenth
century was *Elynour Rummyng,* and I suspect that it was the too
exclusive association of this poem with Skelton's name that earned
him such disrepute in the eighteenth century. Marshe's complete
edition was reprinted in 1736 and it was no doubt to this reprint
that Pope alluded in the note to his notorious line in the *Epistle to
Augustus* of 1737:

<blockquote>And heads of houses beastly Skelton quote,</blockquote>

to which Pope added the note, 'Skelton, Poet laureate to Henry
VIII, a volume of whose verses has lately been reprinted, consisting
almost wholly of ribaldry, obscenity and scurrilous language.' But
he may also have had in mind a contemporary reprint of the
despised *Elynour Rummyng* which had appeared in 1718.

This 1718 reprint (apparently the only copy is in the Bodleian)
is of some importance in the history not merely of Skelton's
reputation but even of eighteenth century critical tastes. In the
Augustan noon-tide this volume appears, with a fighting preface
defending Skelton's most disliked poem that is worth quoting fully:

This, Reader, is the Editor's Reason for publishing this very
antient Sketch of a Drinking Piece; and tho' some of the Lines
seem to be a little defac'd by Time, yet the Strokes are so just and
true, that an experienc'd Painter might from hence form the most
agreeable Variety requisite in a Picture, to represent the mirth of
those Times. Here is a just and natural Description of those merry
Wassail Dayes, and of the Humours of our great Grandames,
which our Poet hath drawn with that exactness, that, as Mr.
Dryden say's of Chaucer's Characters, he thought, when he read
them himself, to have seen them as distinctly as if he had sup'd
with them at the Tabard Inn in Southwark, so I may truly say, I
see before me this Variety of Gossips, as plainly as if I had dropt
into the Alehouse at Leatherhead and sate upon the Settle to view
their Gamball's.

It may seem a Trifle to some to revive a Thing of this Nature:
The Subject, they say, is so low, and the Time so long since, that

it would be throwing away more to peruse it. What have we to do to puzle our Brains with old out-of-fashion'd Trumpery, when we have since had ingenious Poets in our own Times easily to be understood, and much more diverting too.

As for Those nice Curiosities, who can tast nothing but Deserts; whose chief Perfections is to discover the fine turn in a new Epilogue, and have so much Work upon their Hands to damn moderns, that they have none to read them; it is not to be expected, that they will either read or can understand the Antients; neither was it for such Sparks that this Piece of Antiquity was reviv'd. But Persons of an extensive Fancy and just Relish, who can discover Nature in the lowest Scene of life, and receive pleasure from the meanest Views; who prie into all the Variety of Places and Humours at present, and think nothing unworthy their Notice; and not only so, but with a contracting Eye, survey the Times past, and live over those Ages which were before their Birth; it is in Respect to them, and for a Moment's Amusement that this merry Old Tale is reviv'd. The Subject is low, it's true; and so is Chaucer's Old Widow; yet the Description of her Hovel pleases as much in it's Way, as a more lofty Theme.[13]

This defence of a 'low' subject is sufficiently unusual in the early years of the century to be of peculiar significance. But the view of Pope (and of Tony Lumpkin) prevailed. There were no more editions of Skelton in the eighteenth century.

At the beginning of the nineteenth century the 1736 reprint was reprinted again in Chalmer's great edition of the English poets of 1810 and in 1843 Alexander Dyce produced his admirable scholarly edition, an edition which has not yet been superseded. There were no further editions in England during the century, though Dyce's edition was reprinted several times in America. The present century, however, has seen a greater number of different editions than any century except Skelton's own. It is indicative of the new attitude towards Skelton that several of these have been modernized in text and frankly popular in appeal. A few years ago Skelton's victory over contemporary criticism was appropriately celebrated by the production of a sixpenny reprint. Could anyone, turning over its pages, and remembering the defences of Graves or Auden, further doubt the re-discovery of Skelton?

13. *The Tunning of Elinor Rumming. A Poem by Skelton, Laureate.* London. Printed for Isaac Dalton and sold by W. Boreham at the Angel in Paternoster Row, 1718. The edition has been missed by all Skelton editors and by the Cambridge Bibliography of English Literature.

O

Appendix A

c. 1460	Birth year.	
1483	*Edward the Fourth Elegy.*	
c. 1485	*Translations of Diodorus Siculus and of Cicero.*	Accession of Henry VII
1486		Birth of Prince Arthur.
1489	Skelton by now laureate of Oxford and of Louvaine.	Death of Earl of Northumberland.
	Poem on Arthur's 'Creation' (Latin).	Prince Arthur created Knight of the Bath.
	Two Poems on Death of Earl of Northumberland.	
1490	Caxton's reference; Skelton by now tutor to the Princes.	
	Mistress Anne group of lyrics about here.	
1493	Admitted laureate at Cambridge.	
1494	*Verses to Henry as Duke of York* (Latin).	Prince Henry created Duke of York.
1495	Entertained by the University of Cambridge.	
1495-6	*Agaynste a Comely Coystrowne.* Latin verses appended to that poem.	
1497	*Translation of the Pèlerinage* about now.	Wolsey M.A. at Oxford.
1498	Skelton takes holy orders. Ordained deacon, sub-deacon and priest. Henry VII makes offering at his Mass.	
	Bowge of Courte.	
1499	Erasmus' praise of Skelton and 'Carmen Extemporale' for him.	
1500-1	Entertained by Cambridge.	

1501	The *Speculum Principis.* Payment to 'duc of Yorks scolemaster' (April).	
1502	A. Joh. Skelton 'commissus carceribus'—the poet? (10 June).	Death of Prince Arthur, 2 April.
1503		W. Skelton in Westminster.
1504-5	Cambridge: a d m i t t e d 'eodem gradu quo stetit Oxoniis.'	
1504	First appearance in Diss records: witness to will.	
1506	*Deuout Trental for John Clarke.*	H a w e s ' *P a s t i m e o f Pleasure.*
1507	*Lamentatio Urbis Norvicen.* *Epitaph for Adam Uddersall.*	
c. 1508	*Phillip Sparow.* *Ware the Hauke.* *Elynour Rummyng.*	
1509	*The Rose both White and Rede.* Skelton 'pardoned' by the new king. Skelton in Pykerill case at Diss. The *Palinodium.*	Accession of Henry VIII. Barclay's *Ship of Fools.*
1509-10		Wolsey B.D. at Oxford.
1511	*The Complaint of Skelton.* Dines at Westminster with Prior (July). Appointed arbiter in ecclesiastical case at Norwich (November). Witnesses will at Diss.	
1512	Skelton by now back in court. Latin *Epitaph for Henry VII.* First mention of appointment as 'Orator Regius.' Latin *Eulogy for his Own Times.*	William Lily headmaster of St. Paul's.

1513	*Ballade of the Scottyshe King.*	Battle of Flodden (September).
	Chorus de Dis Contra Gallos.	Bradshaw's reference to Skelton in the *Life of St. Werburge.*
	Chorus de Dis Contra Scottos.	
	Addition to *Henry VII Epitaph.*	Faukes publishes *Ballad of the Scottish King.*
1513-14	*Against the Scottes.*	Barclay attacks Skelton in *Eclogues.*
	Against Dundas (?)	
	Poems against Garnesche.	
1515		Accession of Francis I.
		Wolsey becomes Cardinal and Chancellor.
1516	*Elegy on the Countess of Derby* (Latin).	More's *Utopia.*
	Magnyfycence.	Erasmus' *Novum Instrumentum.*
	Against Venemous Tonges.	
1517		Luther's Theses at Wittenberg.
1518	Westminster *Epitaph on Bedell.*	Battle of 'Trojans' and 'Greeks' at Oxford.
	Reference to Skelton's tenement at Westminster. Skelton probably living there at this time.	
1519		Whittington's *Eulogy on Skelton.*
		Hormann's *Vulgaria.*
1519-20	*Colin Clout*—the beginning of the Wolsey attacks.	Chair of Greek founded at Oxford by Wolsey.
1520	Skelton's (lost) poem against Lily.	Whittington's *Vulgaria.*
		Horman and Lily's *Antibossicon* against Whittington.
		Lily's *Epigram against Skelton.*
1521	*Speke Parrot*—late in year.	Wolsey's embassy to Calais and Bruges.
	Against Wolsey's embassy.	Publication of the *Life of St. Werburge.*

1522-3   *Why Come Ye Nat to Court?* — final satire against Wolsey.
Calliope about this time.

Wolsey's taxation resented; his attempt at a capital levy.

1523   *Garlande of Laurell* — with dedication to Wolsey.
Skelton attempting to regain favour with the Cardinal.

Vives at Oxford.
Faukes publishes the *Garlande of Laurell*.
(Late in year) Defeat of the Duke of Albany in the north.
Albany sails for France.

1523-4   *The Duke of Albany*—contains verses to Wolsey.

1525

Wolsey founds Cardinal's College.

1527

(Late in year — December) Barnes and Bilney abjure their heresy.

1528   The *Replycacion* against Barnes and Bilney.
Dedication contains more praise of Wolsey. The attempt to gain favour unsuccessful.

1529   Death at Westminster.

Institution of successor at Diss.

THE EDITIONS OF SKELTON'S POEMS

The editions of Skelton's poems mostly belong to the period following his death. He seems to have enjoyed a wave of popularity from c. 1550 which culminated in the collected edition of his poems published in 1568. The Short Title Catalogue records some thirty editions in the sixteenth century. After that the rate dwindles to a few per hundred years.

Hand-list of Editions

A ballade of the scottysshe kynge (Anon.). 4to. R. Fawkes. 1513.

A ryght delectable tratyse upon a goodly garlande or chapelet of laurell. 4to. R. Fawkes. 1523.

A replycacion agaynst certayne yong scolers. 4to. R. Pynson. 152–.

Here folowythe Dyuers balettys and dyties. 4to. R. Pynson. n.d.

Skelton laureate agaynst a comely coystrowne. 4to. R. Pynson. n.d.

Magnyfycence: a goody interlude etc. Fol. J. Rastell. 1533.

Here after foloweth the Boke of Phyllyp Sparowe. 8vo. R. Kele. 1545?

Another edition. J. Wyght. 1552.

Another edition. A. Kitson. 1565.

Another issue with imprint. A. Veale. Here after foloweth a litel boke etc.

Another issue with imprint. J. Walley.

Here begynneth a lytell treatyse named the Bowge of Court. (Anon.) 4to. westmynster. Wynkyn the worde. Two issues, one before and one after 1500.

Here after foloweth Certayne bokes cōpyled by mayster Skelton. 8vo. R. Lant for H. Tab. 1545?

Another edition. 8vo. J. Kynge and T. Marshe. 1554?

Another edition. 8vo. J. Day. 1565?

Here after foloweth a litel boke called Colyn Cloute. 8vo. R. Kele. 1545?

Another edition. T. Godfrey. *post* 1522.

Another edition. 8vo. J. Wyghte. 1560?

Another edition. 8vo. A. Kytson. 1565?

Another issue with imprint. A. Veale.

Another issue with imprint. J. Wallye.

Christmass Carolles. Kele. n.d. c. 1544. (Contains *Vexilla Regis*.)

Little works compiled by maister Skelton. 8vo. R. Lant for H. Tab.
1547.
Here after foloweth a lytell boke, whiche hath to name, Why come
ye nat to courte. 8vo. R. Kele. 1545?
Another edition. 8vo. R. Toy. 1552.
Another edition. 8vo. A. Kytson. 1565.
Another issue with imprint. A. Veale.
Another issue with imprint. J. Wyght.
A Myrroure for Magistrates. 1559, 1563, 1571, etc. (includes the
Edward IV Elegy with ascription to Skelton).

*   *   *

Pithy, pleasaunt and profitable workes of maister Skelton. T.
Marshe. 1568.

*   *   *

Elynor Rumming. 4to. For J. Busbie and G. Loftis. 1609.
Elynour Rummin, the famous ale-wife of England. 4to. For S.
Rand. 1624.
The Tunning of Elynour of Rumming. 4to. (n.p. 1624.)

*   *   *

The Tunning of Elinor Rumming. A Poem by Skelton Laureat.
London. Printed for Isaac Dalton, and sold by W. Boreham
at the *Angel* in *Pater Noster Row*. 1718.
Reprint of Marshe's edition. London. 1736.
The Muses' Library, London, 1737 (contained Skelton selection).
Reprint of the 1736 edition in Chalmers' English Poets, Lond.,
1810.
Magnyfycence. (Roxburghe Club.) London, 1821.
The Poetical Works of John Skelton. Ed. A. Dyce. 1843.
Reprints of Dyce's edition appeared from Cambridge (Mass.),
1855; from Boston, 1856, 1866, 1887.

*   *   *

Selections from the Poetical Works of John Skelton. Ed. W. H.
Williams. London, 1902. (Text from Dyce.)
Magnyfycence. Ed. J. S. Farmer, 1910. E.E.T.S., 1918.
John Skelton; Poems. Ed. R. Hughes. London, 1924. (Text
from Dyce.)
Elynour Rummynge. London, 1928.
Poems of John Skelton. Ed. P. Henderson. London, 1931.
(Modernized English text from Dyce.)
John Skelton. Selections. Ed. R. Graves. Augustan Books of
English Poetry. London. (Modernized English text from
Dyce.)
American edition of Henderson's edition. New York. 1932.
Elynour Rummynge. Decorations by Claire Jones. San Fran-
cisco. 1931.

Appendix C

Bale's List of Skelton's Works (cf. p. 21)

Bale's collection was first published as the *Illustrium maioris Britanniae Scriptorum Summarium* in 1548, and in an enlarged edition as the *Scriptorum illustrium maioris Britanniae Catalogus* in 1557, re-issue in 1559. The notice of Skelton is almost the same in all three and the following list of works is common to all: 'Hic edidit inter cetera,'

Lauream Coronam. (Garlande of Laurell.)

Philippum Passerculum. (Phillip Sparow) G.L. 1254ff.

Cur ad curiam non venis. (Why Come . . .) Not in G.L.

Contra Linguas venenatas. (Against Venemous Tongues) Not in G.L.

Anglie tubam. (Unidentified. Not in G.L.)

De statu honoris. (*The Boke of Honorous Astate.* G.L. 1172.)

De peccatis fugiendis. (*How Men shulde fle synne.* G.L. 1173.)

Viam adquirendi honoris. (*Royall Demenaunce worship to wynne.* G.L. 1174.)

Artem ornate loquendi. (*The Boke to speke well.* G.L. 1175).

Artem bene moriendi. ([Book] *to lerne you to dye.* G.L. 1176.)

De virtute comediam. (*The Interlude of Virtue.* G.L. 1177.)

De rosario ac principe. (The Rose both Whyte and Rede) G.L. 1178.

Creatonionem Arturij principis. (*Prince Arthur's Creation.* G.L. 1178.)

De quotidiana perfidia. (*The False Fayth that now goth.* G.L. 1179.)

Dialogos de imaginatione. (*Diologgis of Ymagynacyoun.* G.L. 1180.)

Grammaticam Anglicam. (*New Grammar in Englysshe.* G.L. 1182.)

De moribus curie. (Bowge of Court) G.L. 1183.

Transtulit ex Tullio Achademion. [An error by Bale.[1]] G.L. 1184-5.

De bona deliberatione. (*Good Aduysement.* G.L. 1186.)

Adversus Robertum Gaguinum. (*Recule against Gaguyne.* G.L. 1187.)

Psytacum loquacem. (Speak Parrot) G.L. 1188.

---

1. Bale created a new work of Cicero by reading as one work the play *Achademios* and the translation of the *Ad Familiares* in:
   His commedy, Achademios callyd by name;
   Of Tullis Familiars the translacyoun. (G.L. 1184-5.)

Schedulam superioritatis.   (*of Soueraynte a pamphlet.* G.L. 1191.)

De magnificentia comediam.   (Magnyfycence) G.L. 1192.

Sales de domina Margeria.   (Manerly Margery Milk and Ale) G.L. 1198.

Humane vite peregrinationem.   (*Deguilleville's Pèlerinage.* G.L. 1219.)

Triumphus rose rubee.   (*Triumphis of the Rede Rose.* G.L. 1223.)

Speculum principis.   (The Speculum principis) G.L. 1226.

De Alienora Rummynge.   (Elynour Rummyng) G.L. 1233.

Ioannem Iuonem (*Iohnn Iue.* G.L. 1234.)

Colinum Clout.   (Colin Clout) G.L. 1234.

Cantilenas de magistra Anna.   (Mistress Anne songs) G.L. 1240.

Epitaphium Ade nebulonis.   (Adam Uddersall) G.L. 1247.

De porcorum grunnitu.   (*The Grunting of Swyne.* G.L. 1376.)

De gemitu radicis aceralis.   (*Mourning of the Mapely Root.* G.L. 1377.)

Precationem ad Moysi cornua. (*Moses' Horn.* G.L. 1381.)

Theatrales ludos.   (*lost plays.* G.L. 1383.)

De Rosamunde thalamo.   (*Of Rosamunde's Bowre.* G.L. 1390.)

De Minerua et Oliua.   (*Minerva and the Olive Tree.* G.L. 1404.)

De molendinario et eius consorte.   (*Miller and his Wife.* G.L. 1411.)

Meditationes deuotas.   (Early Hymns, e.g. Vexilla Regis) G.L. 1418ff.

Declarationes duorum hymnorum.   (The same) G.L. 1418ff.

Nacionem stultorum.   (*Nacyoun of Folys.* G.L. 1470.)

Apollinem fatiloquum.   (*Apollo.* G.L. 1471.)

De virgine Cantiana.   (*The Mayden of Kent.* G.L. 1495.)

Testamentum amasiorum.   (*Lovers' Testaments.* G.L. 1496.)

Diodorum Siculum transtulit.   (The Diodorus) G.L. 1498.

Cantilenas consolatorias.   [An error by Bale.[2]] G.L. 1495.

Contra pseudopoetam (Garnesche poems?) Not in G.L.

Meditationem diue Anne.   (Early Mistress Anne poem?)

Accipitrem deuita.   (Ware the Hauke) Not in G.L.

Automedon meditandi amoris.   (*Automedon of Love's Meditation.* G.L. 1181.)

This list is based on Skelton's own list of his works in *The Garlande of Laurell* and so includes a number of poems or treatises which Skelton claims as his own but which have been lost since his time.   These are indicated by italics.

2. Bale seems to have made two poems out of:
   My deuisis I made in disporte;
   Of the Mayden of Kent callid Counforte. (G.L. 1494-5.)

(a) *Biographical*

Public Record Office
  Early Chancery Proceedings.
  Patent Rolls.
  Court of Requests.
  Exchequer Rolls.

Westminster Abbey
  Muniments.
  Register Book.

Somerset House
  Book Bracy.

Norwich Cathedral
  Institution Books.
  Tanner's MS. Indexes and Notes. Two volumes.

British Museum
  Add. 5880. Collections for an Athenae Cantibrigienses. W. Cole.
  Add. 23013. Copy of Blomefield's Topographical History of Norfolk.

(b) *Manuscripts containing copies of Skelton's poems*

British Museum
  Eg. 2642 (Verses on Time.)
  29,729. ⎫
  Harl. 4011. ⎭ (Edward IV Elegy.)
  Harl. 2252 (Group of poems including Colin Clout and Speke Parrot.)
  Reg. 18. D. II. 5. (Northumberland Elegy.)
  Cott. Vit. E,x. (Garlande of Laurell.)
  Lands. 762. ('The Prophecy of Skelton.')
  Harl. 367. (Garnesche poems.)
  Fairfax Book—Add. 5465. (Manerly Margery and Wofully Araid.)
  Harl. 4012 (Wofully Araid.)
  Add. 4787. (Latin Verses beginning *Salve plus decies*.)
  Add. 26,787. (The *Speculum Principis*.)
  Add. 28,504. (Attempted facsimile of a Black-Letter edition of Elynour Rummyng; dated 1693.)
  Add. 38,899. (Description of a copy of Colin Clowte.)
  Add. 20,059. (To the Trinity.)

Bodleian
  Bodl. Rawlinson. C. 813. (Fragment of Colin Clout cf. Archiv. 85. 429-36.)

Cambridge Libraries
  C.C.C. 357. (Diodorus Siculus.)
  C.C.C. 432. (Latin verses *I, liber et propera*.)
  Trin. Coll. R.3.17. (Claimed by Brie as verses 'To Mistress Anne.')

211

Trin. Coll. O.2.53. (Claimed by Brie as 'Recule against Gaguin.' cf. Eng. Stud. 37.31-2.)

Camb. Univ. Library. Ee. v. 18. f. 52. (*Qui trahis ex domiti ramum pede dive leonis.*) cf. Brie, *Eng. Stud.* 37.28.

Public Record Office

Books of the Treasury of the Receipts of the Exchequer B.2.8. (The Rose both White and Rede.)

BIBLIOGRAPHY: PRINTED BOOKS (Short Title List)

No attempt is made to list general books on the early Renaissance period. Only books and articles directly concerned with Skelton are mentioned here. Other works used are mentioned in the footnotes as they occur.

H. J. D. Astley. *Memorials of Old Norfolk.* London, 1908.

W. H. Auden. 'John Skelton' in *The Great Tudors.* London, 1935.

Jo. Bale. *Scriptorum illustrium maioris Brittaniae Catalogus.* Basel, 1557.

Alexander Barclay. *The Ship of Fools.* Edited Jamieson. Edinburgh, 1874.

Eclogues. Edited B. White (E.E.T.S., 1928).

Mary Bateson. *Grace Book B,* containing the Proctors' Accounts and the records of the University of Cambridge, 1488-1511. Cambridge, 1903.

J. M. Berdan. *Early Tudor Poetry.* New York, 1920.

'The Poetry of Skelton.' *Romanic Review,* 6.364.

'The Dating of Skelton's Satires.' *P.M.L.A.,* 29.499-516.

'Speke Parrot.' *M.L.N.,* 30.140-44.

E. Bischoffberger. *Der Einfluss John Skeltons auf die englische Literatur.* Freiburg im Breisgau, 1914.

Francis Blomefield. *Topographical History of Norfolk.* London, 1805.

J. R. Bloxam. *Register of the University of Oxford* (Ed. Boase).

G. E. Se Boyar. 'Skelton's Replycacion.' M.L.N., Dec., 1913.

H. Bradley. 'Two Puzzles in Skelton.' The Academy, 1 Aug., 1896.

H. Bradshaw. *Life of St. Werburge.* Ed. C. Horstmann. (E.E.T.S., 1887.)

J. S. Brewer. *Letters and Papers of the Reign of Henry VIII,* London, 1867 ff.

F. Brie. Skelton Studien; *Englische Studien,* 37.

'Zwei verlorene Dichtungen von John Skelton.' *Archiv.,* 38.226-8.

F. Tucker Brook. *Tudor Drama.* London, 1912.

W. Bullein. *Dialogue against the Feuer Pestilence.* Ed. Bullen. (E.E.T.S., 1888.)

A. M. Burke. *Index to the ancient Testamentary Records of Westminster.* London, 1913.

Cambridge History of English Literature, vol. 3. Cambridge, 1918.

Calendar of Patent Rolls (Record Publication). London, 1901 ff.

Calendar of State Papers, Venice (Record Publication). London, 1864 ff.

W. Campbell. *Materials for History, Henry VII.* Rolls Series, 1873.

W. W. Capes. *History of the English Church in the Fourteenth and Fifteenth Centuries.* London, 1920.

G. Cavendish. *The Life of Cardinal Wolsey.* London, 1885.

Caxton's *Prologues and Epilogues.* Ed. Crotch (E.E.T.S., 1928).

R. W. Chambers. *Sir Thomas More;* London, 1935.

J. P. Collier. *Household Books of the Duke of Norfolk.*

C. H. Cooper. *Athenae Cantabrigienses.* Cambridge, 1897.

A. S. Cook. 'Skelton's Garlande of Laurell and Chaucer's Hous of Fame.' *M.L.R.,* 11.9.

W. Courthope. *History of English Poetry,* vol. 1. London, 1895.

R. L. Dunbabin. 'Notes on Skelton' (The name 'Skelton' and Skelton's Classical knowledge). *M.L.R.,* 12.129 and 257.

H. L. R. Edwards. 'John Skelton.' A Genealogical Study, *R.E.S.,* 1935.
'Pereles Pomegarnet.' *T.L.S.,* 1934, 921.
'Syr Capten of Catywade.' *T.L.S.,* 1934, 553.
'Pleris cum musco.' *T.L.S.,* 1936, 729.
'Hermoniake.' *T.L.S.,* 1936, 863.
'A Skelton Emendation.' *T.L.S.,* 1936, 19 Dec.
'Skelton at Diss.' *T.L.S.,* 1937, 396.
'The Dating of Skelton's later Poems.' *P.M.L.A.,* 1938, pp. 601 ff.

Thos. Evans. *Old Ballads.* London, 1810.

T. Fuller. *History of the Worthies of England.* Ed. J. Nichols. London, 1811.

J. Gairdner. *Letters and Papers. Richard III and Henry VII.* (Rolls Series, 1861-63.)
Memorials of Henry the Seventh. (Rolls Series, 1858.)

I. A. Gordon. 'Skelton's Philip Sparow and the Roman Service Book.' *M.L.R.,* October, 1934.
'A Skelton Query.' *T.L.S.,* 1934, 795.
'New Light on Skelton.' *T.L.S.,* 1934, 636.
'Speke Parrot.' *T.L.S.,* 1934, 76.

Edward Hall. *Chronicle* (Ed. C. Whibley, 1904). ('The Triumphant Reign of Henry VIII.')

H. Hallam. *Introduction to the Literature of Europe in the Fifteenth, Sixteenth and Seventeenth Centuries*. London, 1860.

E. P. Hammond. *English Verse Between Chaucer and Surrey*. Duke University Press, North Carolina, 1927.

Stephen Hawes. *The Pastime of Pleasure*. Ed. Mead. (E.E.T.S., 1928.)

C. H. Herford. *Studies in the Literary Relations of England and Germany in the Sixteenth Century*. Cambridge, 1886.

E. S. Hooper. 'Skelton's Magnyfycence and Wolsey.' *M.L.N.*, 16.213.

A. Jessop. *The Visitations of the Diocese of Norwich*. Camden Society, 1888.

W. Kerr. 'Note on Philip Sparow and Politian's De Angeli Puella.' *T.L.S.*, 1934, 909.

A. Koelbing. *Zur Charakteristik John Skelton's*. Stuttgart, 1904.

E. Law. *History of Hampton Court Palace in Tudor Times*. London, 1885.
New Guide to Hampton Court. London.

Sidney Lee. *The French Renaissance in England*. Oxford, 1910.

H. Levin. 'Note on possible mention of Skelton in the Paston Letters.' *T.L.S.*, 1936, 400.

L. J. Lloyd. 'John Skelton and the New Learning.' *M.L.R.*, 1929, 445-6.
'A Note on Skelton.' *R.E.S.*, 1929, 302-6.
'Note on "New Light on Skelton".' *T.L.S.*, 1934, 655.
John Skelton. Oxford, 1938.

H. C. M. Lyte. *History of the University of Oxford*. London, 1886.

J. B. Mullinger. *History of the University of Cambridge*. Cambridge, 1873.

W. Nelson. 'Skelton's Speke Parrot.' *P.M.L.A.*, 1936, 59 ff.
'Skelton's Quarrel with Wolsey.' *P.M.L.A.*, 1936, 377 ff.
'The Dating of Skelton's Later Poems.' *P.M.L.A.*, 1938, 601 ff.
John Skelton, Laureate. New York, 1939.

The Paston Letters. Ed. J. Gairdner. London, 1904.

A. F. Pollard. *The Reign of Henry VII from Contemporary Sources*. London, 1913-14.
Wolsey. London, 1929.
Henry VIII. London, 1905.

A. W. Pollard. *English Miracle Plays, Moralities and Interludes*. Oxford, 1927.

A. Pompen. *English Versions of The Ship of Fools*. London, 1925.

Pyle, F. 'The Origins of the Skeltonic.' *N. and Q.*, 171, 362-64.

R. L. Ramsay. *Skelton's Magnyfycence.* (E.E.T.S., 1908.)
H. Rashdall. *Universities of Europe in the Middle Ages.* Oxford, 1895.
A. W. Reed. *Early Tudor Drama.* London, 1926.
A. Rey. *Skelton's Satirical Poems in their relation to Lydgate's Order of Fools, Cock Lorell's Bote, and Barclay's Ship of Fools.* Berne Dissertation, 1899.
E. F. Rimbault. *A Little Book of Songs and Ballads, gathered from Ancient Music Books.* London, 1851.
G. Saintsbury. *The Earlier Renaissance.* (Periods of European Literature.) London, 1901.
   History of English Prosody. London, 1906.
F. M. Salter. 'Skelton's Speculum Principis.' *Speculum,* Jan., 1934.
   Note on 'New Light on Skelton.' *T.L.S.,* 1935, 35.
   'Note on Skelton and the Paston Letters.' *T.L.S.,* 1936.
J. Schipper. *History of English Versification.* Oxford, 1910.
G. Schöneberg. *Die Sprache John Skeltons in seinem kleineren Werke.* Marburg Dissertation, 1888.
State Papers, *Henry VIII.* Records Commission, 1830-52.
Helen Stearns (Helen Stearns Sale). 'The Date of the Garlande of Laurell.' *M.L.N.,* 1928, 314-6.
   'John Skelton and Christopher Garnesche.' *M.L.N.,* 1928, 518-23.
   'The date of Skelton's "Bowge of Court".' *M.L.N.,* 1937, 572-4.
A. Thümmel. *Studien über John Skelton.* Leipsig, 1905.
F. Thynne's *Animadversions upon Speght's edition of Chaucer's Workes.* Ed. Kingsley and Furnivall. E.E.T.S., 1865.
Times Literary Supplement. Leading Article on Skelton, 1929, 481-2 (by E. Blunden).
S. M. Tucker. *Verse Satire in England before the Renaissance.* New York, 1908.
Ten Brink. *History of English Literature.* (Trans. Kennedy and Robinson). London, 1895-6.
Valor Ecclesiasticus temp. Henry VIII. Ed. Caley and Hunter. (Record Publication, 1825, ff.)
J. and J. A. Venn. *Alumni Cantabrigienses.* Cambridge, 1927.
F. Weitzmann. 'Note on Skelton's use of "Elegy".' *T.L.S.,* 1934, 895.
H. F. Westlake. *St. Margaret's, Westminster.* London, 1914.
   Westminster Abbey in the last Days of the Monastery. London, 1921.
   'Skelton's House at Westminster.' Note in *T.L.S.,* 1921, 699.
   Westminster Abbey. Two vols. London, 1923.

R. Whitington. *Vulgaria.* Ed. B. White. E.E.T.S., 1932.
A. à Wood. *Athenae Oxonienses.* Ed. Bliss. Oxford, 1813-20.
T. Wright. *Political Songs relating to English history from Edward III to Henry VIII.* Rolls Series, 1859-61.
T. Warton. *History of English Poetry.* London, 1774-81.

217